Praise for Irene Dalis

"She had a major, major international career, and she became a trailblazer. If you look at others who founded companies, they don't have the depth that Irene brought to San José. She has apartments for her singers, a scenic shop, a costume shop. It is unique, and she looks after the singers almost like her children. I admire her no end. She is unique."
—Lotfi Mansouri, former general director of San Francisco Opera

"The luscious timbre, with its seductive shimmer, contains its own magic. Her flexible phrasing and command of text bespeak a singer who inhabits her character to the fullest, achieving a fusion of musical and dramatic elements. Miss Dalis owns a singular combination of vocal and interpretive gifts."
—Paul Jackson, in *Start-up at the New Met*

"My very first Parsifal was with your fantastic Kundry, so I have many happy, happy memories. You have always been a beautiful lady, a beautiful artist, and now prove to be a great general director. You are a great friend and a great artist. They are very lucky to have you."
—Placido Domingo, in a video interview on the occasion of Opera San José's 25th anniversary gala

And for Opera San José

"She is the iconic San José cultural figure; there's nobody to touch her. She aspired to be among the world's greats and achieved it, then came back to set a standard for San José that had not been set before. It's a spectacular legacy."
—Andrew Bales, General Director of Symphony Silicon Valley

"Opera San José is Irene Dalis' dream and she has worked very hard for more than a quarter of a century to make it a contributing, respectable presence in the area. It is both, and makes a unique contribution."
>—Paul Lorton, in *Mission Conceived versus Mission Achieved*

"Irene Dalis should be the role model for every arts administrator, worldwide."
>—Arlene Okerlund, Dean of the College of Humanities and the Arts at San José State University (retired) and former Board Member of Opera San José

Irene Dalis
Diva, Impresaria, Legend

How a Metropolitan Opera Star Created America's Unique Opera Company
Second Edition

Irene Dalis
Diva, Impresaria, Legend

How a Metropolitan Opera Star Created America's Unique Opera Company
Second Edition

Linda Riebel

Print and Pixel Books
Lafayette, California

© Linda Riebel, 2014, 2024
All rights reserved. No part of this book may be reproduced in any form, except brief excerpts for the purposes of review or education, without written permission of the author.

Riebel, Linda. *Irene Dalis: Diva, Impresaria, Legend*
ISBN (softcover, second edition): 978-0-9833051-0-1
ISBN (ebook, second edition): 978-0-9833051-4-9

Book design by Jill Ronsley, suneditwrite.com

Published by Print and Pixel Books, Lafayette, California

Printed and bound in the United States of America

"San Jose" is spelled either with or without an accent on the "e," depending on the preference of the city, university, or organization.

All profits from the sale of this book go to Opera San José.

This book may be ordered from Amazon.com and Barnesandnoble.com.

Publisher's Cataloging-in-Publication data

Riebel, Linda.
    Irene Dalis, diva, impresaria, legend : how a Metropolitan Opera star created America's unique opera company / Linda Riebel.
    p. cm.
        ISBN : 978-0-9833051-0-1 (pbk), 978-0-9833051-4-9 (epub)
    Includes bibliographical data and index.

1. Dalis, Irene. 2. Opera --Biography. 3. Singers --Biography. 4. Metropolitan Opera (New York, N.Y.) 5. Opera --California --San Jose. 6. Opera San Jose. 7. Opera --20th century. 8. Opera producers and directors --United States --Biography. I. Title.era producers and directors --United States --Biography. I. Title.
ML102.O6 .D35 2014, 2024
782.1/092/2 --dc23

for Brad Wade
beloved husband and music lover,
who makes everything possible

Contents

A Message from Irene Dalis	i
Foreword to the Second Edition by Shawna Lucey	ii
Foreword to the First Edition by Speight Jenkins	iii
Prefaces	vi
Introduction: The Last Ten Years	ix
Prologue	xi
Chapter 1. Roots	1
Chapter 2. Success	33
Chapter 3. The International Star	71
Chapter 4. An End and a Beginning	96
Chapter 5. The Little Opera Company that Could	125
Chapter 6. We Don't Import Stars—We Export Them!	152
Chapter 7. The Impresaria	178
Chapter 8. Tragic Losses and Daunting Challenges	211
Chapter 9. The Fine Art of the Opera Business	223
Chapter 10. Juicy Tidbits and Opera Lore	250
Chapter 11. Onstage Surprises and Operatic Bloopers	261
To the Reader	267
Appendix: The Resident Company Model	270
Selected Discography and Videos	273
OSJ Productions, 1978 to 2024	276
OSJ Resident Artists, 1988 to 2024	285
Irene Dalis's Awards and Honors	289
Acknowledgments	291
Photo Credits	293
Sources	297
Index	311
About the Author	322

A Message from Irene Dalis
2014

OPERA SAN JOSÉ HAS BEEN MY dream and my purpose for the last 30 years.

In this book you'll read about my career, with its fascinating stories both backstage and onstage, the creation of Opera San José, and the ensuing careers of the many singers who at one time in their lives called OSJ their musical home.

Those of you who have attended Opera San José productions will remember some of the singers mentioned here, and you may also learn some interesting tidbits about the productions you have enjoyed over the years.

One theme I have wanted to emphasize in my life is luck. People always arrived when I needed them, as you'll see in the following chapters. Linda is the latest example of this. Just as I was announcing my retirement, she had the idea for the book, pressed it on me, and had the credentials to do it.

Note: *This lovely message was accidentally omitted from the first edition.*

Foreword to the Second Edition

by Shawna Lucey
General Director of Opera San José

At the beginning of the pandemic, I lost all my freelance stage directing work as one company after another canceled their seasons. In fact, I had just returned home to New York from directing *Lucia di Lammermoor* at Lyric Opera of Kansas City, in order to repack to fly to Hawaii in March of 2020 to direct *Salome*. I love opera and I knew that coming out of the crisis of a pandemic would take all of us, together, to revive this most arresting of art forms. To prepare, I undertook a Master of Science in Nonprofit Management at Columbia University.

A friend and admirer of Khori Dastoor's, I was thrilled when she became the General Director of Opera San José and proud when Houston Grand Opera stole her away. Having been lucky to have worked at OSJ as a stage director in 2017, I jumped at the chance to apply to succeed her. I knew the company to be incredibly warm and one in which artists can do their best work. It was an incredible honor to receive the appointment for a company I love so much.

I was never lucky enough to meet Irene, but of course had heard recordings of her performances. Her vision to put emerging artists on the mainstage to incubate opera's next great talents means the world to me. In my career as a stage director, for example, I have been proud to direct three major sopranos make role debuts as Tosca. At OSJ, it is my absolute honor to do that in an even grander scale, nurturing opera's next great singers, staff, and audience. Irene's brilliant vision and the passion of our wonderfully generous patrons, who listen with their hearts, makes great art live in San José.

Foreword to the First Edition

by Speight Jenkins
General Director of Seattle Opera

IRENE DALIS HAS HAD ONE OF the great opera careers—a quarter century as a star mezzo-soprano and thirty years building an exciting opera company, Opera San José. As an opera singer, she worked with all the great names in opera in the 1950s, 60s, and 70s; as an impresaria she has started the career of many singers and been a spectacular inspiration and advisor to many. Her career is a study in how one can move from major performance mode into administration, in both cases advancing the cause of opera.

I missed Irene Dalis's debut at the Metropolitan Opera, which became her home, by only a few months as I moved to New York in the fall of 1957. I did hear her first Amneris in *Aida* on November 30 of that year, and though she sang in a cast of giants, including Carlo Bergonzi and Robert Merrill, I can still remember the thrill of her Judgment Scene. She practically brought down the ceiling of the old Metropolitan Opera House with her concluding high A, and the ovation was tremendous. That was not all. Even from the first she knew how to convey the personality of Amneris—selfish and demanding, yes, but also truly in love with Radames. She had made her debut the previous spring as Eboli in *Don Carlo*, but I didn't get to experience this signature role of hers until the final weekend of the 1959-60 season when Franco Corelli was the title character. It was the last broadcast of that season, and Ms. Dalis sang an unforgettable "O don fatale."

In her nineteen seasons with the Metropolitan I was fortunate to experience her in sixteen of her twenty-two roles. Though her Brangäne, Fricka, and Venus were memorable, my own favorite was the Nurse in Richard Strauss's *Die Frau ohne Schatten*. The role is long, difficult, and hard to make attractive. The *Frau* is not an opera with arias that can be separated out, but it abounds in memorable sections. One of the most difficult to sing is when the Nurse tries to lure the wife of Barak into giving up her capacity for children. The piece, beginning with the words, "Abzutun Mutterschaft" (To forgo motherhood) demands easy movement from a low double B flat up two octaves to a sustained A natural, and Ms. Dalis accomplished it not only easily but with shattering meaning. That role, one of the most difficult to sing in all of opera, became a trademark role for her, and she sang it nineteen times from its Met premiere in October of 1966 until her retirement eleven years later. As with most roles interpreted by Ms. Dalis, my memory is of great singing, but even more importantly, a realization of the character. This was true of the agonized Santuzza in *Cavalleria Rusticana*, the vengeful Ortrud in *Lohengrin*, the sultry Dalila in Saint-Saëns' *Samson et Dalila*, and many others.

In this fine biography, we get a whole picture of Irene Dalis, from her beginnings in California through her years in Europe and at the Met and her success as creator and General Director of Opera San José, which was founded in 1984. One of the most fascinating portraits is of Rudolf Bing, the Metropolitan Opera's General Manager from the time of her debut until his retirement some fifteen years later. Mr. Bing, as he was universally known, has often come off in biographies of many of those associated with him as cold, unfriendly, and not at all kind to singers. The portrait painted by Ms. Dalis is quite different, that of an impresario who cared about her, was generous to her and involved with her. Indeed, after he retired in 1972, she describes her lack of enjoyment of the rest of her time at the Met because of the different atmosphere. Other portraits give the reader a lot of the personality of giants of the time—Kurt Herbert Adler, the General Director at the San Francisco Opera from 1953 until 1980, and Wieland Wagner at the Wagner Festival in Bayreuth. In describing the work with these men, one gets a sense of how opera was done in that time, different not so much in the way it was done but very different in the number of houses in which a major singer could work.

Ms. Dalis's years in creating and building Opera San José receive great notice as well—and in a novel fashion. Ms. Riebel creates her life in California by frequent and piquant quotes from those with whom she worked. Staff members, singers, board members, and many others paint the fascinating portrait of Ms. Dalis at work and in the process of instructing young singers, building their careers, and helping them to realize their talent. The book is a textbook of how to take a university opera program and turn it into a professional organization specifically for young singers. It's a very American thing, and Ms. Dalis accomplished the feat brilliantly.

This fine book tells the story of her career and then how she created an opera company. It is filled with comments by those who experienced her leadership and their reaction to what she did. It testifies to her inventiveness and professionalism and is a great tribute to a great lady, a warrior in the eternal American battle to make opera exciting and meaningful to all.

Preface to the Second Edition

For the first edition, I aimed to have books in hand for Miss Dalis's retirement day, so I had one year to conduct dozens of interviews, research archives, find photographs from family and opera companies, write, edit, get corrections, design, proofread, and print the original.

This time it was easier. I've updated OSJ's list of productions and the roster of Resident Artists, introduced our volunteer group Friends of Opera San José, shared OSJ's post-Miss Dalis story, included new images, celebrated our world premiere of young prodigy Alma Deutscher's *Cinderella*, showed how we weathered the pandemic, and added two chapters at the end to share some onstage bloopers and other juicy operatic tidbits. Our new General Director has kindly supplied a new foreword.

Confession: This edition is wrapped around the unaltered original, so in the body of the text you may find references in the present tense to events that are now past.

Preface to the First Edition

IRENE DALIS HAD INVITED US TO dinner to thank my husband Brad Wade for bringing so many people into Opera San José's subscriber fold over the years. A great raconteur, our hostess regaled us with one story after another about her career at the Met, at Bayreuth, at Covent Garden, in Berlin … What unforgettable tales we were hearing!

"Miss Dalis!" I exclaimed, leaning across the table. "When is your memoir coming out?"

She looked at me quizzically and said, "Who would want to read that?"

Everyone I told this story to said, Yep, that's Miss Dalis.

So I had to talk her into it. The turning point was the suggestion to make it not only about her experiences on the international stage, but also about Opera San José. After all, she had told us, "That's my real career. Singing just made it possible."

Everyone I told this to said, Yep, that's Miss Dalis.

Other things everyone agreed on, in varying words: She's genuine, doesn't play games, cares about the singers and their careers, doesn't seem to realize how important she is, values loyalty, and is resolute about balancing the budget. I wish I could remember how many of them called her "a force of nature."

Working with her over many months, I was struck by her unusual combination of worldly impact and unassuming presence. Her list of awards and honors is impressive, but she doesn't mention them. She's approachable, unpretentious, and generous with praise. It's no wonder that so many OSJ veterans keep in touch with her. What they say is true—she cares about her singers. She literally jumped with excitement when I suggested we contact the singers from the long-ago opera workshop years and put them in the book. She immediately remembered their names, even from thirty years ago.

I was astounded by her memory. As we talked for hours over her kitchen table, the minute an incident came to mind, no matter how long ago, she would tell the entire episode, complete with dates and names—including the names of people she hadn't seen in decades: long-ago assistant directors, volunteers who got the Opera Workshop going in the 1980s, baritones who sang minor roles with her fifty years ago. Perhaps not realizing what a feat this was, she sighed one day, "I have such a bad memory. That's why I can never run for mayor."

At 88, she not only has all her marbles, she has more marbles than I do. When confronted by a computer glitch that impeded our sending chapter drafts back and forth, she exclaimed, "I can't control this!" A few minutes later she declared, "I'm going to conquer this," and she did. It's been a privilege to spend this time with her, to meet so many people she has influenced, and to befriend the force of nature that is Irene Dalis.

Introduction: The Last Ten Years

IN THE TEN YEARS SINCE THIS book was first issued, Opera San José has gone through sad, scary, stimulating, and triumphant times.

First, we lost our founder, Irene Dalis, who passed away at the age of 89, shortly after retiring from her position as OSJ's General Director. Larry Hancock, who had been Miss Dalis's right hand since the 1970s, took over and ran the company expertly for five years before retiring to Florida.

The pandemic was obviously a major trauma for OSJ, as for every person and organization in the country. How does a nonprofit survive when it cannot rehearse or present its creation? When its most fervent admirers must stay home?

Luckily, Larry's successor as General Director was Khori Dastoor, who had been a dazzling soprano with OSJ and around the world, before deciding to bow out of the life of constant travel and to become an arts administrator. Khori fearlessly met the pandemic challenge. Consulting doctors, hospitals, and government sources, she and her staff created a handbook for employee safety that was so thorough that it was adopted by other organizations. Another brilliant contribution in her two years as General Director was to brainstorm, fund, and install a high-quality video recording studio, where operas can be performed and streamed worldwide.

Miss Dalis used to say, when people asked her why she kept a stable of young singers instead of hiring famous ones, "We don't import stars—we export them!" Well, Khori's vision and managerial success caught the attention of one of America's eminent companies, Houston Grand Opera, and they lured her away with an offer she couldn't resist. So OSJ has exported a General Director, too.

But what would happen to *us*? Who could we find that would match Khori's vision and management skills?

General Director Shawna Lucey

Enter Shawna Lucey. She was already a multi-talented opera professional, directing productions at the New York Metropolitan Opera, Santa Fe Opera, San Francisco Opera, and major companies in Spain, Russia, and Germany, making valuable contacts in the process. She has taught courses on acting, design, stage management, and directing. Those of us who have met her are enchanted by her warmth and youthful enthusiasm, and by clever initiatives she has created to attract new audiences and sustain established ones.

Prologue

THE DRESSERS ARE BUSILY ZIPPING AND pinning the singers into their elaborate costumes. Makeup artists hurry from dressing room to dressing room, skillfully applying foundation, lipstick, eye shadow, and powder. Wig experts slip nylon caps over singers' heads and carefully add and adjust the wigs. Stagehands finish arranging the set and props for the first scene, then fade away backstage.

It is March 16, 1957—the opening night of a revival at the Metropolitan Opera in New York, the pinnacle of opera in America. *Don Carlo* is the passionate story of a man, the woman he loves, and the politics and the jealous princess that come between them. The man (Prince Don Carlo) will be sung tonight by the famous Swedish tenor Jussi Björling. His father (King Philip II) will be sung by the equally renowned Italian bass Cesare Siepi. The mezzo-soprano who will sing the fiendishly difficult role of Princess Eboli has never performed in America before—or sung the role in Italian. This is her Met debut. She is naturally nervous. Just before going onstage, she says a little prayer: "God, you got me here. Get me through this."

The orchestra tunes up and plays the overture. The opera begins, and for the next three hours Verdi's music is rendered with artistry and passion. The audience is carried away and gives a tremendous ovation. The reviews are ecstatic, especially about the newcomer. One critic writes:

> Miss Dalis met the exacting demands of the part of Eboli with such vocal and dramatic authority as to make her debut one of the most exciting in recent seasons. Her expert vocalism and musicianship were immediately apparent in the Veil

Song, which Miss Dalis sang better than I have ever heard it sung. In the tricky ensemble with Carlo and Rodrigo in the Queen's gardens, she was just as impressive, and her sweeping, almost torrential handling of "O don fatale" won her a genuine ovation from the capacity audience.

To describe her debut, other reviewers are lavish in their use of words like "terrific," "glorious," "magnificent," "splendid," and "brilliant."

Who is this blazing talent? Where did she come from?

ONE

Roots

THIS IS AN AMERICAN SUCCESS STORY. It reaches from Ellis Island to the pinnacle of world opera, and from a college workshop to a respected opera company which has sent dozens of professional singers into the opera world in America and abroad.

The New Americans

In 1903, a Greek immigrant named Padaskivas Nicolas Thelyis arrived in New York. Like many newcomers, he anglicized his name and was ever after known as Peter N. Dalis. He was a short man, but when he spoke, people listened, and when he walked with his firm tread, they noticed him. Though he had never studied music, he sang enthusiastically. He had a great sense of humor, but after moving to California would become a typical strict Greek father. Meanwhile, Mamie Rose Boitano came from an Italian background. Her parents immigrated to the U.S. from Favale, Italy, a small village north of Genoa. Mamie was born in Sacramento, California, to parents who were determined to assimilate to their new country.

Peter Dalis and Mamie Boitano married in 1909 and settled in San José, 50 miles south of San Francisco. They treasured their European heritage. Peter pressed grapes and kept wine casks and olive barrels in the basement. Mamie was a wonderful cook and a loving, devoted mother. Yvonne was born in 1925, the youngest of five children, and would later be known as Irene. She had one sister, Marge, and three brothers, Chris, Nick, and Louis.

Little Yvonne grew up in a musical household, in which each child was expected to learn an instrument. Marge, 15 years older, was Yvonne's first piano teacher and taught her to read music before she could read words. Yvonne also sang and played the violin in her elementary school orchestra. A childhood friend remembers the after-dinner concerts at the Dalis home: "Sister Marge would play the piano, and brother Nick the drums and Chris the violin, and little Yvonne would come in and give a song."

In spite of the financial straits of the Great Depression, her father always managed to find money for books and music. He also taught his children the value of a dollar, instilling in them a firm determination to own their own homes, to be their own bosses, and above all, never to borrow. When Yvonne was a child, she and her friends went every Saturday to San José's California Theatre, a magnificent new movie palace.

> When I was a child, it just seemed enormous. That was when I was in love with Clark Gable and Robert Taylor. And, of course, I was a big fan of Nelson Eddy and Jeanette MacDonald. I used to go to double bills there. Every Saturday afternoon I was there. Those were Depression days. I had to ask my father for the money, and I had to plead my case.

She saw Clark Gable in *Gone with the Wind* at least ten times. One weekend she asked, "Dad, can I have 25 cents?"

He inquired, "What for?"

"Well, the movie is 10 cents and the hamburger is 15 cents."

"Here's 10 cents for the movie. You can eat at home."

California Theatre, 1927

This lesson of frugality was never forgotten.

Her mother influenced Yvonne in a quieter way. Many years later, Yvonne would write:

> She was the perfect mother and raised a family of five children during the Depression. I did not even know there was a Depression. I lacked for nothing. Since I was interested in concerts, she always purchased a ticket for me, would take me to the concert, and be there when it was over to walk home with me. She always said she had too much to do to make time for concerts. It was not until much later that I realized that she could only afford to buy one ticket.

Yvonne also absorbed the drive and competitiveness that characterized the family, expecting herself to get all A's in school.

She remembers her father as working hard at his cleaning and hat-making business, rarely home for dinner, devoted to his family but not able to show it. He could be humorous, as when he good-naturedly called cousin Geraldine "Jellybean" or when he drew out his renditions of grace long enough to let the food get cold and annoy Mamie.

As the Depression faded and the children grew up, there were eventually five cars in the family with a three-car garage (with sliding doors), so two were always parked behind another car. Her father once needed one of them to be moved out of the way so he could extract his car and get to work. He asked Yvonne to move brother Nick's car, which happened to be a new Chrysler convertible, his pride and joy.

She responded, "Dad, I don't know how to drive."

He was not deterred. He said, "It's easy. You only have to put your foot on the pedal and shift the gear to reverse."

Mother urged him, "Leave her alone."

But he insisted, and in the attempt, Yvonne, instead of putting the car in reverse, went forward and crashed the convertible through a double set of garage doors. Hearing the collision, Nick ran outside in his shorts (a violation of house rules), yelling angrily. In a nervous reaction, Yvonne laughed, which certainly didn't endear her to Nick. This incident may be the reason she didn't learn to drive until she was in her thirties.

The Notes and the Words

Yvonne diligently studied the piano through primary and secondary school, continuing these studies at San José State College (later University) for her bachelor's degree, which she received in 1946. Anyone majoring in music education there was expected to be familiar with all sections of an orchestra. She therefore took lessons in viola, cello, flute, trumpet, percussion, and clarinet, in addition to her regular piano and violin lessons. She even studied composing, and in college during World War

II, she created a piano composition inspired by the war. "Swing Shift" included sound effects that were familiar to a country bent on supplying its fighting men with the industrial equipment they needed—riveting and blowtorches. "Swing Shift" won first prize in an open musical contest, and Yvonne's later song, "Thoughts Have Wings," won second prize in another competition.

One day she asked her father to drive her to class. Though San José State College was nearby, the walk was long for someone carrying a cello. He grumbled, "Why don't you study the piccolo?" but he agreed. Yvonne asked to be dropped off a block from school. He realized that she was embarrassed about his truck, which had "Dalis Hat Works and Cleaners" emblazoned on the side. To teach her a lesson, he stopped in the middle of the block and made her get out and walk the rest of the way. Telling this story, she was sad and tearful for having hurt her father's feelings. Once she was older, she realized how much he had accomplished, and she admired him and his generation of immigrants.

San José State College Vocal Department chair Maurine Thompson, who had heard Yvonne sing for her entrance examination, suggested that she take a double major in piano and voice. So Yvonne began singing and found she enjoyed it. This introduced her to a new experience: performing without fear. As a pianist, she was nervous, even paralyzed, at the thought of playing in front of an audience. However, for some reason she wasn't intimidated to sing at the recital that the college voice students were required to give at the end of every quarter.

In all her college classes, Yvonne excelled. However, there was one embarrassing incident.

> One day in a Physics of Sound class final test, I didn't follow instructions to answer *one* question. I answered all five (correctly), but the professor gave me an F. I was stunned and went to his office to investigate. He explained why he had shocked me this way—it was for not following

instructions. He then changed my grade to an A. This lesson about following instructions would be useful later when I was writing grant applications for Opera San José.

Her sister Marge encouraged Yvonne to pursue a master's degree anywhere in the world. Yvonne chose Columbia University Teachers College in New York City, with a concentration in music education, expecting to return to California and teach music. This was a big change for the twenty-year-old. "My dad was just like the father in *My Big Fat Greek Wedding*. For him, a daughter didn't leave home unless she was getting married—to a Greek! It was my sister who convinced him to let me go to New York."

Marge and her husband Tom Dallas (her name was now Marge Dalis Dallas) paid for Yvonne's New York education; Tom had a popular sandwich shop, and they could afford it. In New York, Yvonne lived in the Parnassus Club, a women's building run by two English sisters. House rules were very strict. There was a sign-out and sign-in sheet, with curfew at 10 pm. The two adults appointed themselves honorary house-parents and insisted on knowing when each resident would get home at night.

While she was in graduate school at Columbia, Dr. Harry Wilson played a pivotal role in Yvonne's life. She was in his vocal pedagogy course, learning how to teach vocal technique in a class setting. He asked each member of the class to sing a phrase from the English ballad "Drink to Me Only with Thine Eyes." When Yvonne sang her phrase, he stopped, asked her name and said, "Everyone write down this name, for it will be famous some day. Miss Dalis, please come to my office after class."

Yvonne was a bit nervous about this, because professors normally did not make time for individual students. He asked about her plans.

She explained, "I'm planning to return to my home town for a job. I've already been hired as Assistant Supervisor of Music in the Santa Clara County School System."

Wilson was sorry to hear this, because he believed she should continue her vocal studies. "Is there someone in your family I could talk to about your future?" he asked.

Yvonne replied, "Some of them are coming for graduation. You could meet them then."

Meanwhile, at Marge's suggestion, Yvonne was studying voice with a teacher recommended by Maurine Thompson. After three months in New York, Yvonne flew home for Christmas, a gift from her three brothers as a surprise for their parents. Yvonne sang for the family, with Marge accompanying her on the piano. Afterwards, Marge took her aside and said, "You sounded better before you went to New York." This was a shock, but her loyal sister also offered the solution. Upon her departure, at the airport, Tom and Marge gave Yvonne a generous check, saying, "Study with a master or do not study at all." To drive home the point, Tom added, "I want receipts for this money from the best voice teacher in New York City."

New York

Yvonne took their advice and made appointments with three outstanding vocal coaches in New York. A *coach* concentrates on following the music as written (proper pronunciation, phrasing, dynamics, interpretation, etc.), while a voice *teacher* concentrates on vocal technique (placement of voice, breath support, proper breathing, agility, and so on). One by one, she asked the coaches for the names of the three best voice teachers in New York. One name was on all three lists, but each coach Yvonne consulted would add, "But she won't take you." Of course, after hearing that three times, Yvonne was determined to be accepted as Edyth Walker's student.

Edyth Walker, who traced her singing technique to Manuel Garcia and Maria Malibran, was born in a town called Rome, New York, but made her career primarily in Europe at the turn of the century. She started as a mezzo-soprano, but soon added dramatic soprano roles to her repertoire and was the first Elektra at Covent Garden. She had sung at the Metropolitan Opera decades earlier (including *Aida* with Caruso) and was a sought-after voice teacher. Now in her eighties, she was still full of energy and quite demanding. As a Christian Scientist, she saw no obstacles, accepted no illness, and was accustomed to getting things done. At Yvonne's audition in 1947, Walker said, "Are you good? What is your range? Let me hear your range." Yvonne was asked to sing scales, going higher and higher. At one point she stopped and said, "This is too high." Walker stood up and said dramatically, "I have finally found someone who can answer this question: 'How high is high?'"

Yvonne was mortified, and Walker told her that they would start again. This time, Yvonne was not to stop until asked to do so. If she chose to stop, the door to the apartment was open for her to leave.

> By this time, I was mesmerized by this demanding woman. The vocalizing started again. Then she took me up, up, up to an area I'd never been before—I sounded like a cat with its tail caught in the door. I sounded awful, but I didn't stop. And at that moment, she taught me the best lesson a young person can ever learn—that you should never place restrictions on yourself. It went beyond learning my range. She taught me that we sabotage ourselves by placing limitations on ourselves, that anything is possible, never to fear.

Walker required that her students take a minimum of three lessons a week and she spent most of that time on exercises, followed by German lieder (songs) and finally opera. She insisted that Yvonne study Lady Macbeth's arias, even though Verdi's *Macbeth* was not in the repertoire of any opera company at the time. Walker predicted that one day Dalis would sing Lady

Macbeth at the Met. (She never called her "Yvonne." It was always "Dalis"). She also predicted that Dalis would sing Kundry (in Wagner's *Parsifal*) in Bayreuth (Germany) and advised her to learn it, as well as Isolde (in Wagner's *Tristan and Isolde*) and other dramatic soprano roles. Yvonne later described this wonderful teacher's lesson in professionalism:

> Miss Walker was a stickler for punctuality. Her door was open for your lesson time; however, one minute past the appointed time, the door would be locked. If you were late, you will have lost your lesson and you would be expected to pay for it. This was the warning she gave me when we first started working together. You can be sure that I was ALWAYS on time for my lessons!

After Yvonne had studied for a year in New York, Marge thought it would be a good idea if the family could see how she had improved. So Marge arranged for her to give a recital at the Montgomery Theater in downtown San José. It was by invitation only—friends and family—and the theatre was packed.

This recital also served as a practice performance of sorts. At that time, one started one's opera career by giving a recital at a theatre in New York called the Town Hall. When Walker thought it was time for Dalis to have an agent to prepare her Town Hall debut, she called her good friend, Sol Hurok, who was the outstanding impresario of the day. He came to Walker's studio immediately, within an hour. Dalis sang and Hurok was impressed. He agreed to represent her.

But Walker was finally succumbing to age and illness. A few days before her death, she summoned "Dalis" to her bedside and said, "Be careful. They will want to send you out as a mezzo-soprano. You are a dramatic soprano. If you sing as a mezzo, I

Poster for Yvonne's concert at the Montgomery Theater, 1949

will haunt you." As her career attests, Yvonne really was a mezzo, though she did do some of the crossover roles such as Isolde, Kundry, and Lady Macbeth, that can be sung by sopranos or mezzos. "So for many years, I would think about her just before a performance. I could feel her presence. I would say, 'Sorry, Miss Walker.'"

After Walker's death, Yvonne was fortunate enough to find Paul Althouse, another eminent singer-turned-teacher. He was a former leading tenor at the Met and had taught Jan Peerce and Eleanor Steber. In these years, Yvonne studied soprano roles: Leonora in *Il Trovatore*, the title role in *Aida*, and a role she always thought should be in the mezzo repertoire, Tosca.

Meanwhile, a friend of Maurine Thompson's set up a recital for Yvonne at the home of a socialite friend. Every chair was filled, and as she sang Debussy's *Romance*, she noticed three men standing in the back of the room—especially the tall one, "the most handsome man I had ever seen." At the end of the evening, she gave George Loinaz her phone number.

> He became my best friend. Later, when I was in Europe, if I needed something from the States like a subscription to the *Times* or a carton of tissues, I would write to George and he would fulfill my request. Nothing more. Just a friendship. I did not think he was the marrying kind.

George Loinaz came from a distinguished Cuban family and had come to the U.S. before World War II. His relatives included a saint, a Spanish American war hero, and a Miss Cuba. A highly educated man, he had earned doctorates in three fields from the University of Havana—political science, economics, and civil law. Army service and a medical discharge gained him U.S. citizenship. In New York, he went into the publishing world and became an editor at the major publishing house McGraw Hill and then served as senior editor of bilingual publications at Dun Donnelly.

The day of the commencement ceremony for Yvonne's master's degree arrived. Her mother, sister Marge, and brother-in-law Tom traveled all the way from California to attend. George privately told Yvonne's mother, "I'm going to marry Yvonne." Then he gave strict instructions not to tell her. "I won't stand in her way," he explained. He was waiting to see where her dreams led.

After graduation, Yvonne was ready to pack and return to San José. But first, she arranged for the family to meet Harry Wilson and Edyth Walker. Wilson impressed them, for he had nothing to gain whether Yvonne stayed in New York or not. He looked her mother in the eye and said, "If she were my child, she would be encouraged to pursue a career in opera. She has a unique vocal timbre. It should be developed."

The visit with Walker was less encouraging. Tom asked her how long it takes to train a voice for opera, and Walker answered frankly, "Eight years."

Sobered by Walker's dictum, Yvonne returned home to San José and began to study elementary school music pedagogy at San Francisco State University, in preparation for the position of Assistant Supervisor of Music. A few days into the course, the professor asked Yvonne to give a demonstration lesson. The professor was impressed by her lesson and asked her to do more demonstrations and to create lesson plans for the class. This was certainly a compliment, but Yvonne was unhappy with the entire situation. She made a fateful telephone call.

"Marge, we have to talk."

Marge replied, "How long will it take for you to get here?"

It took an hour for Yvonne to get to her sister's home. As she walked up the path, Marge was standing there holding the front door open. Her first words to Yvonne were, "How long will it take you to pack to return to New York City?" Marge had already spoken to brothers Chris, Nick, and Lou, who all agreed to contribute financially to Yvonne's vocal studies. With that kind of love and support, Yvonne happily returned to New York to continue studying with Miss Walker.

She also had help from another direction. In New York, she belonged to an informal group of voice students that gathered once a week to sing and critique each other. They were talented young people. One of them was a 17-year-old pianist who played for the rest as they sang and later became a prominent conductor, Thomas Schippers. One evening, a member of the group arrived with a stack of grant applications and insisted that everyone fill one out. It was for a Fulbright scholarship to study in Europe for a year. "I'm the least talented one here," Yvonne thought, and didn't take it seriously. But her beloved teacher Edyth Walker had recently died and she was at loose ends. So she went to the same recording studio her friends used, made an audition recording, filled out an application, and sent it in.

Going Abroad

To her surprise, she won. She recalls, "But I wasn't sure a year in Europe was the right thing for me. I only applied as a joke and I was apprehensive about going abroad." At a lesson with her current teacher, Paul Althouse, she told him, "I'm not going."

He replied firmly, "You are going if I have to pack your bags myself and put you on the boat. You are not the type to be successful in America yet. You have to come back from Europe." This strong-armed encouragement worked and she went on her first big adventure. Despite her doubts, she somehow knew this was her destiny.

> I've always had an inner voice. On the Queen Mary, leaving New York to go to Italy on my Fulbright scholarship, I said to myself, "I won't come back to New York until I make my debut at the Met."

Yvonne in a studio portrait

What a bold thought! Yet on the ship, she did not reveal she was to study voice. Of the many young Fulbright scholars on the boat to Europe, she found the singers to be insufferably full of themselves. Instead, Yvonne told them she was a pianist and played for them while they sang. She recalls, "I accompanied all those egomaniacs all the way across the Atlantic."

Her Fulbright year began with a month at the Università per Stranieri in Perugia, with eight hours a day studying the Italian language. She stayed with an Italian family that didn't speak English, so she became quite proficient.

Her next stop was the Giuseppe Verdi Conservatory in Milan. Yvonne looked forward to finding teachers as solid and inspiring as Walker and Althouse. One by one, Yvonne went to meet the eminent singers who were teaching at the conservatory.

> There were nine voice teachers on the faculty, all famous singers from La Scala. I was allowed to observe a lesson in each of the nine studios to help me with my choice of teachers. I came away impressed with the performance of each teacher as a performer—but not as a teacher. It was then that I realized that just because someone has had a heralded career in opera does not mean that he or she has the gift of teaching voice.

So she used her scholarship money to learn languages, which she knew were vital to an opera singer's career. In German class one day, she started crying in frustration. The teacher, Frau Delius, asked sympathetically what was the matter. Yvonne replied sadly, "I can't find a voice teacher." Frau Delius said, "Try Dr. Otto Müller." Perhaps Frau Delius knew him as a fellow member of the small German community in Milan. With nothing to lose, Yvonne made an appointment and went to his studio, which was located in his home.

> I still remember the address (Via Maggiolini 2), which was full of beautiful apartments. Throughout the entire apartment were bookshelves full of recordings. Dr. Müller was handsome, dapper, cosmopolitan, and multilingual. He explained his vocal technique. I listened dutifully, but left the interview thinking he was even worse than the other teachers I had met. But later, in the middle of the night, I woke up and heard my inner voice telling me to give him a try.

Luckily, she listened to her inner voice and became his pupil, taking two lessons a day. She was his first student in the morning and his last in the afternoon. She stayed after her second lesson to listen to the recordings owned by Roberto Bauer, a cousin of Dr. Müller's who lived with him in that enormous apartment. He had one of the largest private collections of opera recordings in the world. After an hour or so, Roberto would knock on the studio door and say cheerily, "Time for an American cocktail!" That is, he had one, while Müller drank wine and Yvonne had juice.

During her first summer in Europe, in 1952, she went to Bayreuth, where the great composer Richard Wagner had built an opera house to his specifications and where his works were produced during the annual Bayreuth Festival. That is when she first heard Martha Mödl as Kundry in *Parsifal*. She was totally mesmerized by this superb singing actress and put her on a pedestal as the ideal artist. Then, back in Milan, Yvonne was alarmed when Dr. Müller told her that someone who was in town to perform Ortrud in *Lohengrin* at La Scala would like to come to her afternoon lesson. Her name was Martha Mödl.

Just the thought of having her idol entering the room sent Yvonne into a panic. She backed up against the wall and tore her skirt on a protruding nail. Then she made an excuse. "Oh, I forgot. I'm not able to come this afternoon."

Dr. Müller knew her well enough to ask, "Tell me the truth. Is it because of Miss Mödl?"

Nervously, Yvonne said, "Yes, it is."

He said, "Very well, I'll disinvite Miss Mödl." Relieved, Yvonne attended her lesson as usual. Yvonne never knew what Müller may or may not have said to the reigning opera star, but halfway through the lesson there was a knock on the door. Yvonne was singing "Du bist der lenz" from *Die Walküre*. Müller opened it and Mödl came in. Yvonne was dismayed, but Mödl said graciously, "Please continue. I have a lot to learn." This courteous remark smoothed the scary moment and cemented Yvonne's gratitude and admiration.

After hearing Yvonne sing, Mödl said, "You should be a dramatic mezzo. It's time for you to start auditioning." The older woman then left to go to Naples. A week later, she telephoned Müller to say, "I need a suitcase I left at the hotel in storage. Would Yvonne be able to bring it to me?"

Of course, Yvonne was delighted to do so. To her surprise, at the Naples train station Yvonne was met by not only Mödl, but also the orchestra conductor and the renowned tenor Wolfgang Windgassen. After delivering the suitcase, she got ready to take the next train back to Milan, but Mödl would have none of it.

"Come to the dress rehearsal of *Siegfried* this evening," she urged. Yvonne happily agreed. At the San Carlo Opera, she was seated beside Mödl, who, as Brünnhilde, would not appear until the third act. Mödl obviously had a plan. She asked Yvonne if she would please sing for Wieland Wagner during the intermission.

Sing for Wieland Wagner? The grandson of the great composer himself? Unprepared for such a stunning opportunity, Yvonne explained, "I don't have any music with me." Mödl solved that problem, as she had with her the music for "O don fatale" (O fatal gift) from Verdi's *Don Carlo*. How could Yvonne refuse? During intermission at the rehearsal, a piano was rolled out onto the stage and she sang. After hearing the Verdi aria, Wagner wanted to hear her sing something in German. Would she please sight-read "Weiche, weiche, Wotan" from *Das Rheingold?* She would. Yvonne stood behind the pianist and read the music over his shoulder. Wieland Wagner said he was interested, but that Yvonne would have to have some stage experience before he could engage her.

Miss Mödl put her arm around Yvonne's shoulders and told her not to worry and that she would arrange for an audition in Munich with Friedrich Paasch, a German agent. A few weeks later, Yvonne went to Herr Paasch's office in Munich to sing for him and Hans Georg Ratjen, Generalmusicdirektor of the Oldenburgisches Staatstheater. Yvonne had a cold, but didn't mention it, for fear of seeming to make excuses.

After she sang, Ratjen asked, "Is your voice always this dark?"

"My voice is naturally dark," she replied, "but I also have a cold."

He then asked her, "Can you sing for me in three days in Frankfurt?" Yvonne readily accepted and made the trip. Another door was opening. But the train ticket to Frankfurt had used up all Yvonne's money. In desperation, she called Müller. He said, "Go to my cousin in Frankfurt. She will supply the money." Once she arrived at the cousin's imposing mansion, Yvonne was grilled about what she needed. Today she speculates that the cousin must have thought she was going to ask for a lot of money. But true to her father's code, she asked for just the little she needed for this brief trip.

Yvonne arrived at the Frankfurt audition. Hearing the other singers, she was so intimidated that she wondered, "What am I doing here? They're all better than I am." She sang, and was astonished when Ratjen asked her to stay afterwards. On the spot, he offered her a *Fest* contract in Oldenburg. This meant she would be a resident artist and sing principal roles for two years. Yvonne accepted and prepared to leave Milan for Germany. She loved the little German town where her career began:

Oldenburg is a small, beautiful city in Lower Saxony with a population of about 100,000 when I was there. It was a charming, typical German village with some neoclassic buildings. The Staatstheater (State Theater), baroque in style, was the center of activity. Performances were usually sold out, since the German people were most hospitable and appreciative of performing artists.

Yvonne really was a singer now, a professional one. All the years of study, in San José, New York, and Milan, would come to fruition in Germany. But first, even before her first-ever stage performance there, she was to meet one of the most powerful people she would ever know.

From "Yvonne" to "Irene"

Rudolf Bing held one of the most important jobs in all of opera—he was the general director at the Metropolitan Opera in New York. In 1952, Bing was in Europe scouting new singers. Roberto Bauer (Müller's cousin with the big record collection) was the Met's impresario in Italy and Switzerland and arranged auditions in Rome, Milan, and Zurich. Bauer insisted that Yvonne sing for Mr. Bing, even though she had no stage experience, so that he would at least know about her voice.

In one of those awkward happenings that drive impresarios crazy, the scheduled accompanist was ill and unable to appear. Bauer called Yvonne in a panic and asked her if she could accompany the auditions on the first day. Yvonne thought, "Why not? I'm a better pianist than singer anyway." Of course she knew many of the arias the hopefuls had selected, but some scenes were unfamiliar and she had to sight-read them. On this day, she found she could fearlessly accompany other singers at the piano because she was not the center of attention and she was helping other people.

On the second day came time for her own audition. She sang "O don fatale" (Eboli in *Don Carlo*), "Entweite Götter" (Ortrud in *Lohengrin*), and "Einsam wachend" (Brangäne in *Tristan and Isolde*). Bing listened with growing interest and asked, "Do you do the judgment scene from *Aida*?"

"No, I don't," she said, for she had never studied this scene.

"Can you read it for me this afternoon?" the Met director asked.

"Sure I can," she replied and dashed home to phone Müller to ask for a special lesson right away.

"Well," said Müller, "that's going to be a bit of a problem. Mr. Bing is coming to lunch, and I don't want him to see you here. I don't want him to know that I know you. As soon as he leaves, I'll call you and we'll run through the scene." They did, and Yvonne sang for Bing that afternoon. She recalls, "I had to hold the score, but I was calm about the whole thing."

That evening, Bing returned to Müller's apartment for dinner. As Müller later reported to Yvonne, they were having soup when Bing drew out the three notebooks he carried with him on these trips: One listed the singers he never wanted to hear again; the second listed those who warranted watching; and the last was labeled Engage Immediately. "There's one singer, but she will have to change her name," said Bing, looking at Notebook No. 3. "Her name is Yvonne Dalis."

According to Müller, at that moment, this perfectly mannered teacher spilled his soup and cried, "But she is not ready." Bing wanted her to sing Adalgisa to Maria Callas's Norma. Müller explained that she had had no stage experience as yet. Bing asked, "How long must I wait?" Müller replied, "Four years."

Bing responded firmly, "I won't wait longer than four years for that voice."

Then Bing reverted to his earlier point. "A singer of this stature can't bear the name of a French coquette," he said, "and I think she should have a Greek name." The three men (Bauer, Müller, and Bing) then chose her new name: Irene, an ancient

Greek name meaning "peace." In Europe, it was pronounced Ee-RAY-Nuh.

Hello to the Stage

In 1953, at Oldenburg, Irene (as she was now called) was about to give her first ever opera performance. She was to sing the role of Princess Eboli in Verdi's *Don Carlo*. In fact, she'd never been on stage before. At first, Irene could not speak German very well, so she didn't understand the director's staging.

> All during my career I would write out the role in longhand because it was always in a foreign language that I didn't quite know. I didn't even speak German, and there I was in Germany singing Eboli in German with a German stage director when I could hardly understand what he was saying. He'd say "Verstehen Sie?" [Do you understand?] and I'd say, "Ja, ja."

Eventually the truth came out, or perhaps he just gave up trying to direct her. At any rate, instead of making the customary grand entrance as Princess Eboli, she was seated onstage when the curtain went up, and the opera proceeded from there. Her debut was a splendid success. A reviewer praised "her enormous vocal talent and the timbre of her contralto voice, which was in complete control of every nuance and inflamed the role with all the fire necessary to its projection. This beautiful voice, together with a dramatically wise personality, is indeed a fortunate discovery for our opera ensemble."

Irene remained at Oldenburg for two years (1953-1955), singing in ten productions, mostly principal roles such as Dorabella in Mozart's *Così fan Tutte*, Lady Macbeth, Gaea in Richard Strauss's *Daphne*, and Waltraute in *Götterdammerung*. She was also cast as the domineering mother Kostelnicka in Janacek's *Jenůfa*. She was eagerly preparing the role when she began to feel pain in her abdomen, which got worse and worse. She had emergency surgery for appendicitis and missed the production.

The Berlin opera company, a major house, was interested in Irene. Its general director, Herr Dr. Professor Carl Ebert (who had previously helped create England's Glyndebourne Festival Opera) called and invited her to audition. She responded, "I'm not ready for Berlin!" Oldenburg was rated as a C house (small and less important), while Berlin was an A house. Normally, a singer would perform in a B house before being considered for an A house. Ebert insisted that she audition for Berlin. Once again urged forward by someone who believed in her, she agreed and sang six arias at the Berlin audition: "O don fatale" (of course), three Lady Macbeth arias, Ortrud's "Fluch," and "Brangäne's warning."

Then Ebert sent conductor Wolfgang Martin to Oldenburg to hear her perform a full opera onstage. Verdi's tragedy *Macbeth* had been scheduled, but when the general director learned a scout was coming, he switched the schedule to the comedy *Così fan Tutte* so the visitor from the big city wouldn't hear her sing Lady Macbeth. He didn't want the visitor to lure his star mezzo away. But the town's mayor died that day. Those in charge didn't feel it proper on such a day to do a comedy, so they performed *Macbeth* after all.

The Berlin conductor was impressed by Irene's Lady Macbeth, but he still wanted to hear her sing Mozart. So the next morning, she found herself singing the light romantic role Dorabella from *Così fan Tutte* privately for him. As she was describing this scene, she laughed, for nowadays such a sequence would be impossible. Singers are advised by their teachers that they must not spread themselves too thin and must certainly be cautious about which roles they can sing and how much to rest. "Placing restrictions on themselves," said Irene, shaking her head.

The man from Berlin did indeed lure her away from Oldenburg to the Berlin Städtische Oper. In German, the word "staatsoper" refers to a state, while "städtische" refers to a city.

So Berlin's opera company is called Berlin Städtische Oper, while Oldenburg's was Oldenburgisches Staatstheater. While performing in Germany, she recalls, "They paid cash, but I would never accept it until after the performance was over." The official had to sit there backstage with his briefcase, and then hand her an envelope full of cash. Looking back on this eccentric habit, she says, "Probably I thought I should not be singing for money."

On January 7, 1956, she sang her good luck role, Princess Eboli, in Berlin under unusual circumstances. The artist who had been scheduled to sing Eboli called Irene and told her she was leaving Germany, abandoning her contracted performances. Irene said, "Don't do this! You'll be barred from performing ever again in Germany." Ignoring this well-meant advice, the singer broke her contract and went home. At noon, Irene received a phone call. "They called me and asked if I'd go on without an orchestra rehearsal or a staging rehearsal and I said, 'Of course.'" So she did and received great applause, including calls for an encore.

After her curtain call, Ebert took her aside and said, "I know it's not an original expression, but tonight a star has been born." It was her breakthrough in Berlin, and sure enough, the very next day she got a cable offering a contract to sing the same role at the Met in two years' time. (Major companies often book artists four or five years in advance). Four years had passed since the Met's Rudolf Bing had heard her in Milan. Exactly as predicted, he was offering her a contract at the Met.

Throughout Irene's time in Europe, remembering her father's watchword ("Don't buy anything you can't pay for"), she lived frugally. Even when she became the leading mezzo in Berlin, she had no car, lived in a furnished room, and traveled third class. Years later when Hans Georg Ratjen (the one who had brought her to Oldenburg) visited her in Bayreuth, he mentioned that what had impressed him was her no-nonsense attitude. She had made it clear that she did not need much money, just enough to take care of her lodging and food.

Irene as Herodias *(Elektra)* with Carl Ebert

Yet she was happy. Close friend Petie Cassilly, whose husband Richard Cassilly sang in Hamburg, recalls: "Irene was always a joyful person, generous, kind, and loving. If you're a friend, you're a friend forever." She never heard an unkind word from Irene about anyone; she was generous to a fault, loyal, and always laughing. The Cassillys, who had seven children, would leave the key in the door of their home in Hamburg, and Irene would come over to visit amid the comings and goings of what Petie called their "nuthouse." One night, they all went ice skating on Hamburg's Lake Alster. Irene didn't skate, but stood in her boots on the lake handing out glasses of brandy. The very next day, the ice cracked and people fell in.

The main reason Irene accepted the Berlin contract was the opportunity to observe the esteemed Margarete Klose, the leading mezzo-soprano at the Berlin Opera who was especially known for her portrayal of Kostelnicka in Janacek's opera *Jenůfa*. Unfortunately, Klose defected to the East Berlin Opera, the Staatsoper. Management in West Berlin took a chance on their new mezzo. Irene was called on to sing Kostelnicka—the role

Irene as Kostelnicka *(Jenůfa)*

she had been preparing at Oldenburg when she had emergency surgery. She did not immediately realize that she would not have an orchestra rehearsal or a dress rehearsal. But remembering the advice of Edyth Walker, she accepted the opportunity and gave a splendid performance that brought her to the attention of the opera world. She recalls, "The role of the Kostelnicka in Janacek's *Jenůfa* is what really catapulted me to the international class."

Irene was doing so well that her mentor Martha Mödl encouraged her to audition at Bayreuth. Irene was hesitant. She thought, "I'm not ready." Mödl heard about these doubts and made a special trip from her home in Munich to Berlin to prod her protégée. Facing Irene, she said firmly, "You will never be ready. No one is ever ready. You are going to Bayreuth." This was bracing encouragement. As she had done for Althouse and Ebert, Irene obeyed, made the trip, and sang Ortrud for Wieland Wagner. To her surprise, he said she should do Kundry in *Parsifal*. She didn't want to do this, because Mödl was the reigning Kundry and it would not feel right to do her idol's role. Hearing about this generous gesture, Mödl called Irene and said, "I want you to do Kundry. You are the one I would choose."

Recalling the series of events that led to her European success, Irene says, "I've been followed by good luck all the way. The right person arrived at the right time." Many people guided her: sister Marge, Harry Wilson, Edyth Walker, the judges who awarded her the Fulbright scholarship, Frau Delius, Otto Müller, Martha Mödl, Roberto Bauer, Rudolf Bing, Hans Georg Ratjen, and Carl Ebert. Asked when she decided to be a singer rather than a pianist, Irene responded, "I never decided. The career was served to me. I was swept along."

If You Can Make It There …

Now it was time for her American debut at the Metropolitan Opera. This thrilling opportunity brought up fond memories. While studying in New York for her master's degree in the late 1940s, Irene had often been a standee at the Met. One of her idols was Jussi Björling, the Swedish tenor who was one of the Met's principal artists. She was awed by his talent. Now, in March, 1957, she made her Met debut—singing alongside him. The little voice that had spoken to her six years before as she sailed away from New York was vindicated in the most spectacular way.

When she arrived at the Met for her first rehearsal, she was escorted to the rehearsal hall. It was on the top floor of the building, practically an attic.

> I don't believe I took more than one step into the room before I was paralyzed, for before me was my debut cast for *Don Carlo:* Cesare Siepi, Ettore

Bastianini, Delia Rigal, and Björling himself. At last I came to my senses and was led around the room for the proper introductions. I told Björling what an honor it was for me to be able to perform with him. It was one of the most thrilling days of my life. On the night of my debut, I was graced with the kindness of my idol. Jussi Björling came to my dressing room before the performance and said, "Irene, I want you to know that it is an honor for *me* to be onstage with *you* tonight." I still get tears in my eyes remembering his kindness. He and Martha Mödl taught me true humility by their bearing and thoughtfulness.

Here in New York, she would be singing Eboli in Italian for the first time, having performed it only in German in Oldenburg and Berlin. The conductor was very supportive and gave her a private run-through. Since she was technically a guest artist from Berlin, members of the orchestra thought she was not an American and tried to speak to her in German.

Irene's mother, sister Marge, Marge's husband Tom, and their young daughter Michele were staying in the same hotel as Irene, where they stayed for several weeks in anticipation of her Met debut. Her mother exclaimed, "She hasn't had my cooking for six years," and found a way to do home cooking in the tiny kitchenette in their hotel suite. She even bought a tablecloth, china, a candelabra, and flowers to make each meal special. Marge took her phone calls. One day Irene returned to the hotel from rehearsal and Marge said innocently, "Oh, Mr. Clack called. I hope you don't mind, but I told him he could call during dinner. I knew you'd be here then."

Little did Marge know that he was not Mr. Clack, but rather a representative of the Metropolitan Opera claque. A claque is an organized group of opera-goers who applaud a given singer—for a fee. This underhanded custom began in the sixteenth century when a French playwright bought and gave away tickets to a performance of his play, on the condition that recipients give generous applause. In later years the opposite audience response was also plotted. Rossini's *The Barber of Seville* was hissed and ridiculed at its 1816 premiere because admirers of composer Giovanni Paisiello's opera (based on the same play) didn't want the new one to succeed. Luckily for opera lovers, the second performance was a great success, and *Barber* has been the most loved comic opera ever since. In Paris in 1820, an actual agency for this audience activity sprang up to recruit and manage the "claqueurs." Within ten years this agency was solidly established, and even developed its own specialists:

> The manager of a theatre or opera house was able to send an order for any number of claqueurs. These were usually under a *chef de claque* (leader of applause), who judged where the efforts of the *claqueurs* were needed and to initiate the demonstration of approval. This could take several forms. There would be *commissaires* ("officers/commissioners") who learned the piece by heart and called the attention of their neighbors to its good points between the acts. *Rieurs* (laughers) laughed loudly at the jokes. *Pleureurs* (criers), generally women, feigned tears, by holding their handkerchiefs to their eyes. *Chatouilleurs* (ticklers) kept the audience in a good humor, while *bisseurs* (encore-ers) simply clapped and cried "Bis! Bis!" to request encores. The practice spread to Italy (famously at La Scala in Milan), Vienna, London (Covent Garden), and New York (the Metropolitan). Claques were also used as a form of extortion, as singers were commonly contacted by the *chef de claque* before their debut and forced to pay a fee, in order not to get booed.

Not knowing any of this, Irene answered the phone and heard a voice at the other end of the line. He said, "I'm the head of the Met Opera claque. We can make you or break you."

Irene didn't understand. "What are you talking about?"

He responded, "Am I really talking to Irene Dalis, the one who, according to *Time* magazine, has only to be announced to sell out the house?"

"Yes, this is Irene Dalis," she said.

"And you have never paid a claque?"

She said, "No. I will never pay for applause," and hung up the phone. She sat alone for long while as dusk fell. Finally Marge came to the room and asked, "What's the matter?" Sadly Irene said, "I can't sing in America." Then she called the Met's rehearsal department to say she would not be coming and that they should bring in the cover (understudy).

Meanwhile, Marge was exerting her own creative brand of influence. When Irene said, "I can't do this," Marge said, "That's fine with me. The family wants to see you anyway. You don't have to do it if you don't want to. Let's go home to San José." Irene calls this maneuver "reverse psychology," and it worked. She decided to perform.

Within five minutes Bing called and reassured her. In fact, he was elated that one of his stars would stand up to the extortionists. Some other famous singers of that era did pay for applause, but Irene would rather leave the country. Bing said gleefully, "Finally, we have an artist strong enough to refuse them!"

Who says all the drama has to happen onstage?

On opening night, March 16, 1957, came all the final preparations for the big event: costume, makeup, warming up her voice.

> How can I describe the night of my debut at the Met? As was usual for me throughout my career,

Irene as Princess Eboli *(Don Carlo)* at the Metropolitan Opera

> I was very nervous and apprehensive until I was onstage. My debut cast members were all giants in the operatic world. When you are surrounded by giants, you become one yourself. There was no way I could fail. The support from my colleagues and conductor, Fritz Stiedry, carried me through a most successful evening. Having my mother, sister, and brother-in-law in the audience gave me extra strength. I looked over my shoulder and apologized to the spirit of Edyth Walker for singing mezzo instead of dramatic soprano roles. I felt she was with me, too.

After the tumultuous applause died down and the family reached her to offer their congratulations, Marge beamed and said, "I knew you'd be good, but I didn't know you'd be *this* good." The next morning, the reviews were published. In a mis-spelling that would not recur after this undeniable triumph, the eminent music professor and critic Paul Henry Lang wrote in the *New York Herald Tribune*,

> Irene Valis, who took the part of the Princess of Eboli, was put in double jeopardy. In the first place, this was her debut—all of us know what this means. In the second, her role is a little pale in the first act. The young mezzo from California used her head—a very commendable thing for a singer, and not too often encountered—and moved with caution until warmed up and secure. Then in her great scenes she unleashed a flaming temperament and a large and well-shaped voice that did full justice to the vibrant character whom Verdi created from unpromising beginnings. Apparently we have in Miss Valis a winner.

In the *New Yorker*, violinist-turned-critic Winthrop Sargeant was equally sympathetic to the newbie in the house:

> Miss Dalis has a warm, expressive voice with a fine lower register that suggests the timbre of a contralto, and she handles it with notable assurance and with a cultivated command of musical style. She is also, obviously, a theatrical personality of some stature, and, in addition, is quite pretty.... [In] her great aria, "O don fatale" at the close of the first scene of Act III, she sang with such dramatic conviction and authority that the ensuing curtain calls mounted into a frenzied ovation.... Miss Dalis will, I think, turn out to be a major addition to the Met's roster.

Howard Taubman was the chief music critic at *The New York Times,* and was unstinting in his praise.

> For the part of Eboli the Met has found Irene Dalis, a mezzo-soprano from San José, California, whose debut was one of the most exciting of the season.... In the third act "O don fatale," one of Verdi's greatest dramatic arias, she was like a veteran. Her voice, which has range, security and brilliant top notes, was now under full control. She sang and moved with a total absorption in the emotion of the character. Her singing had color and fire.

The publication *Musical America* was equally impressed, and had this to say in its April edition:

Miss Dalis, young mezzo-soprano of San José, California, who has been singing for the past three years with the Berlin Municipal Opera, met the exacting demands of the part of Eboli with such vocal and dramatic authority as to make her debut one of the most exciting in recent seasons.... Her expert vocalism and musicianship were immediately apparent in the Veil Song, which Miss Dalis sang better than I have ever heard it sung ... and her sweeping, almost torrential handling of "O don fatale" won her a genuine ovation from the capacity audience.

"Frenzied ovation!" "A winner!" "One of the most exciting debuts in recent seasons!" "A major addition to the Met's roster!"

It was a wildly successful debut. Her performance also earned praise in the *Christian Science Monitor*, *The Musical Courier*, *Boston Daily Globe*, and the *New York Journal American*.

Celebrated now on two continents, Irene had arrived.

TWO

Success

IRENE WAS NOW SINGING AT THE Met and ready to introduce new roles. On November 30, 1957, eight months after her debut, she was about to sing her very first Amneris, the jealous princess in *Aida*. Rudolf Bing trusted her so much that he scheduled her in a performance that would be broadcast nationwide on the radio. The opera world's foremost publication, *Opera News*, recognized the double challenge: "The Amneris she sings this Saturday afternoon is her first at the Met, which means that Miss Dalis will enjoy the unsettling distinction of combining her first appearance [in this role] at the opera house, in one of opera's most challenging roles, with her first hearing by an unseen audience numbering in millions."

Put yourself in her shoes: Imagine that after a lifetime of preparation, you have rehearsed a difficult and important role and are about to sing it in public for the first time. At the Met. Now imagine that this performance is also being broadcast on the radio to a nationwide audience. Along with millions of other Americans, your family back in California will be listening. Announcer Milton Cross asked how Irene would like to be introduced, and she said that the audience must know that she was from San José. So for that day and for the next twenty years, he announced, "Irene Dalis, mezzo-soprano from San José, California."

The event was just about to become even more dramatic. Arriving at the theatre at noon, Irene learned that the famed soprano who was supposed to sing the title role—Renata Tebaldi—had suddenly withdrawn because her mother had just died. A singer she had not rehearsed with (Mary Curtis-Verna) would sing the title role of Aida. Irene remained composed. She recalls, "There was no time to be nervous."

The performance went beautifully. Irene said later, "Mary Curtis-Verna was marvelous. Though she never became a household name, she was one of the best artists with whom I performed. She was an indispensable cover [understudy] at the Met, worth her weight in gold."

Her ever-supportive family rejoiced that she had reached the pinnacle of opera in America. Once one of even them meddled a bit. Her fee at the Met was $350 a performance, while the highest fee for a singer was $1,000 a performance. Her brother-in-law Tom thought she wasn't being paid enough. He urged her to speak to Rudolf Bing about it, so she did.

Bing said, "Did you know you would be such a success? Neither did I. I'm sitting here being very smug about our arrangement. If it would make you feel any better, I can show you the contract for one of our leading tenors. His debut year fee was $250 per performance." He added, "I thought you wanted an international career."

Irene nodded, "Yes, I do."

"Well, you can't have one without the Metropolitan Opera in your resume." He was right. That was true at the time. Irene was ashamed at having brought up the subject and resolved not to discuss money with him again. But in a few years, Rudolf Bing would take a very different approach to paying her.

Love and Marriage

When she was living in Europe, Irene became engaged to an Italian cellist. But one day she was shocked to receive a letter from her friend George Loinaz, saying it was time for him to think about getting married. She became very upset, and her fiancé asked her why. This was hard to explain. Later she understood. "I was in love with George and didn't know it!" She returned to America in 1957 for her sensational Met debut, and George hosted the post-performance reception at a friend's place on Park Avenue. Thanking him for his hospitality at the end of the evening, Irene said, "I'll call you." Five days later a mutual friend phoned her, saying, "You have to call George. He's expecting your call and won't leave his apartment." So now they were in touch again, only this time the friendship blossomed into romance—like the name of the song she was singing the day they had first met so many years before.

George Loinaz

That very month, March, 1957, George proposed. Irene was speechless. She thought, "But I'm still engaged to Giampiero." So she made up her mind, sent the Italian cellist a cable calling it off, and married George in July at the Carmel Mission in California.

The night before their wedding, George sat her down and told her his opinion of the prospect of being married to a famous woman. One point he made was firm: "I will never be Mr. Dalis."

Unfazed, Irene replied, "I wouldn't marry you if you would!"

And they were happy together for the next 33 years. He was a stabilizing influence and very wise. Once a reviewer wrote after a performance at Covent Garden that *Tristan and Isolde* should really be called *Brangäne and Kurwenal*, after its two supporting

George and Irene backstage in a photograph
with her handwritten message to him

characters. He told her, "You must promise me not to believe the reviews, even the positive ones." He wanted their marriage to succeed and not have her drawn into emotional roller coasters by other people's opinions.

George was also supportive of young singers. Mary Elizabeth Enmann, who sang in the opera workshop that Irene would later direct, recalls George as very courtly, sweet, gentle, and supportive of singers. Once Mary Elizabeth received great applause, and when she returned backstage, he said, "Did you hear that applause? The audience always knows." Friend Petie Cassilly remembers George as "the epitome of a gracious Spanish gentleman, elegant, kind, and gracious. They were very much in love." Irene recalled, "The first year George and I were married, whenever I had an opening night he was there, and my dressing room was filled with white orchids. The second year he'd be there, but with red roses." His memory makes Irene smile, and she says, "The best thing I ever did was to marry George."

But he couldn't protect her from all the hazards of the high-stakes opera world. At a broadcast performance of *Aida*, it was almost curtain time at the old Met on 39th Street. Irene was called to the telephone at the end of the hallway. A voice said ominously, "Miss Dalis, you will be booed today."

It was Mr. Clack.

She said, "Thank you for calling," and hung up. Walking back to her dressing room, she told herself that she would not allow this to upset her. But it did, and she asked her dresser to call Mr. Bing.

When he arrived, Bing said reassuringly, "This is really a good sign. They only threaten my superstars. Welcome to the superstar class. Do not worry. You will not be booed."

And he was right. She was received graciously. Later she learned that Bing had placed 120 plainclothesmen around the house ready to stifle any disruptions. This story seemed too good to be true, so this author asked Irene, "How did he know in advance that he would need plainclothes claque squelchers that day?" She replied, "I haven't the slightest idea. I suspect that he always had them for broadcasts, just in case."

And you thought *your* job was fraught with pitfalls!

Claques have played a disgraceful role in operatic history. They had ruined the premiere of Rossini's *The Barber of Seville* and generations later did the same to Puccini's classic, *Madama Butterfly*. After the opening night performance, the chagrined composer called it "a lynching. Those cannibals didn't listen to one single note—what a terrible orgy of madmen drunk with hate! … I am still shocked by all that happened—not so much for what they did to my poor *Butterfly*, but for all the poison that they spat at me as an artist and as a man." Fortunately for the fate of the most beloved of operas, Puccini made some important changes and three months later the revised opera was a huge success.

Today there is another kind of claque: people who write glowing or derogatory online reviews of products and services—for a fee.

Irene, however, received admiring reviews based on her talent. The jealous princess Amneris remained one of Irene's signature roles, and drew rave reviews for years. Here are a few of them:

> Singing honors went hands down to Irene Dalis, whose Amneris was electrifying, particularly in the exacting first scene of the final act, when she tries to save Radames, then calls forth the wrath of the gods on him.

> Another first-rate performance, particularly on the dramatic side, was the first Amneris sung by another young American, Irene Dalis, who brought down the house with her "Anatema su voi!"

> Irene Dalis sang her first Amneris of the season superbly. It is a meaty role and Miss Dalis missed

not one ounce of its potentiality. She raved, she ranted, she seduced, she spat fire—all with the glorious control and with that velvety sheen that is the marvel of her voice.

... You'll Make It Anywhere

By now, Irene was married and a principal artist at the Metropolitan Opera, had made her San Francisco Opera debut in 1958 as Eboli, and was singing frequently at Covent Garden and the Bayreuth Festival. Other European and West Coast invitations would come, but New York would remain her primary opera home for the rest of her career.

Irene was already famous enough in America by 1958 to hold a two-singer concert at the Hollywood Bowl, an outdoor venue that can seat over ten thousand people. The Los Angeles Philharmonic supplied the orchestral accompaniment and the other singer was Leontyne Price. Irene challenged her audience. She did not schedule safe comfortable music that they already knew, but performed difficult arias like Lady Macbeth's sleepwalking scene and her trademark "O don fatale," as well as obscure ones like "Divinites du Styx" from Gluck's *Alceste* and "Un bel raggio" from Rossini's *Semiramide*. She and Price sang a scene from *Aida*, an opera they would perform together in several cities in the following years.

Reviews of her performances for the next few years constitute a lesson in ecstatic praise. For *Don Carlo* in San Francisco (1958), one reviewer wrote:

> From her compelling entrance in the first act ... to the curtain after her excitingly dramatic aria "O don fatale," the spontaneous and prolonged applause attested to the fact that this was, above everyone else, Miss Dalis's evening.... As Princess Eboli, the prodigiously endowed mezzo-soprano

displayed a voice of sumptuous beauty, secure and confident throughout its wide range, brilliant one moment, subtle the next ... at the close of this celebrated aria ["O don fatale"] there were thunderous shouts of "bravo" from all parts of the opera house.

In 1959, her rendition of the villainness in Strauss's *Die Frau ohne Schatten* (The Woman without a Shadow) garnered these remarks:

> Irene Dalis, as the malevolent nurse, achieved a veritable tour de force of sinister characterization and dramatic singing.
>
> Irene Dalis as the Nurse received ovation after ovation for her terrific performance in this splendid part.
>
> Irene Dalis was the very embodiment of passionate, sinister malevolence. Hers was the kind of interpretation that defies conventional discussion in terms of singing, vocal color, and acting. All were unified into a single conception, and one of the most memorable in the opera company's annals.

Irene did not need an agent to receive offers of roles from major houses, but there was one other kind of performance she wanted to explore: concert tours, where she could sing German lieder and French art songs. She signed with Columbia Artists management, which arranged concerts for three seasons: 1959-1960 (in Monrovia, Merced, Paradise, Reedley), 1960-1961 (Hayward, Pacific Grove, San José, Bellflower, Crescent City, Flint, Michigan; South Bend, Indiana; Marshalltown, Iowa; Allentown, Pennsylvania), and 1962-1963 (Honolulu, Santa

Ana, Stockton, Turlock, Eureka, and Cheyenne). She enjoyed concertizing, but her opera schedule was becoming more and more demanding. She already had too little time for her family, so she stopped doing concerts and accepting summer engagements, and ended her contractual arrangement with Berlin.

Adding to her roster of evil characters and fulfilling Miss Walker's prediction, Irene sang Lady Macbeth at the Met in February, 1960, and again received high praise.

> Miss Dalis's voice, for the most part, had a ringing brilliance one might not have expected, and it soared clearly in the great ensemble numbers that end the first and second acts. Her singing, too, was flexible, pure and beautifully inflected as she pursued the long flowing lines of melody. Nearly always, too, it was infused with feeling, and she was a truly poignant figure as she wrung her hands so piteously in the sleepwalking scene.

For a broadcast of *Tristan and Isolde* at the Met in 1960, again Irene couldn't participate in staging rehearsals or the first performance, because she was singing in San Francisco. When it was time for her to sing Brangäne's warning, the assistant stage manager took her backstage and showed her a long ladder two stories high. She was expected to climb it, stand at the top, and sing through a high window. But Brangäne's warning requires long, sustained, calm breaths. To stage it so that she had to climb a two-story glorified ladder and then sing from such a high elevation was not musically wise.

"Oh no," she said. "I'm not climbing that."

The assistant stage manager did the only possible thing when an emergency arose during a performance: He called the boss. Bing duly appeared and said, "I'll go up with you," and he did, climbing up the ladder right behind her and remaining until the aria was over. The two of them then retreated gingerly down the ladder. Afterwards, she told him, "If I'd been here for staging rehearsals this would not have happened."

He replied urbanely, "I know."

Thinking back to that nerve-wracking scene, Irene says, "I've said that my pet peeve concerns voice teachers. Stage directors belong in that category also. I wish they were more cognizant of singers' needs."

Now it was time for another historic moment in the opera world. On January 27, 1961, two artists were about to make their Met debuts in Verdi's *Il Trovatore,* and Irene was onstage that night singing Azucena, with Franco Corelli and Leontyne Price. *Opera News* described it this way:

> The opening-night ovation lasted more than forty minutes, and the reviews for Price and her costars—Robert Merrill, Irene Dalis and Franco Corelli, who also made his company debut that night—were ecstatic.

But the conductor wasn't ecstatic—far from it. Fausto Cleva was a great conductor, one of Irene's favorites. Tremendous applause and great reviews followed the performance. What did Cleva do? Instead of congratulating his stars, he called a special rehearsal on Monday. Probably he was miffed that all the attention was given to the singers and not enough to the score. He was a stickler for adhering exactly to the tempi and dynamics that the composer had given. Glaring at the assembled artists, he said firmly, "Now we will do it the way it was written."

Three months later, in April, 1961, Irene sang Kundry in *Parsifal* at the Met. Judge for yourself whether she was a success:

> The Metropolitan can now boast of another memorable Kundry in the person of Irene Dalis, who was heard for the first time in the role at the season's last performance of *Parsifal.* This role, which Wagner himself considered to be his most

difficult, requires not only a musician of the highest rank, but a subtle and powerful actress. And all this Miss Dalis proved to be, in a performance that held the audience breathless and won her a stormy ovation at the end of Act II.

A few months later, she was the first American mezzo to sing this same role of Kundry at the Bayreuth Festival. Though conductor Hans Knappertsbusch had a reputation for being difficult, Irene liked working with him. Her first meeting with the great conductor was the day before the first orchestra rehearsal. It was a run-through with piano for the entire cast. After the rehearsal, the maestro beckoned Irene to stay. He said, "Please do not worry about singing full voice at the orchestra rehearsals. I know the score and, obviously, you do, too." Irene started to leave. He called her back and said, "Remember, this is the most difficult role Wagner ever wrote."

This remark was a surprise. She had never considered Kundry any more difficult than her other roles, but she returned to her hotel and went through the score page by page and found herself thinking, "Oh yes, this could be a problem and yes, this could, too." This startled her, because she didn't think of it (or any role) as difficult; she just did them. The training from Edyth Walker came back to mind: Do not sabotage yourself by setting up obstacles. She realized the role was considered so challenging partly because the character expresses the full gamut of vocal styles and emotions, all in the space of 45 minutes.

If New York loved her Kundry, German reviewers were over the moon. The first review is very long and detailed and well worth a read for its deeply felt response to the performance.

> What applause otherwise would express, this time was certainly proven by the several minutes of reverent silence in which the public remained when the final curtain fell. Any different reaction

to such a deeply moving performance of the art of Wagner would be unthinkable. But, after the second act, it took every ounce of self-control not to applaud to hail an artist whose interpretation sent chill after chill up and down one's spine. She stood on the stage of Bayreuth for the first time. She sang Kundry and her name is Irene Dalis.

Her voice commands overall phenomenal possibilities of expression. She has the profound depth of a contralto and reaches heights of glittering, alluring splendor. Freely and easily, she deftly succeeds in attaining a smooth transition as she moves from a brilliant forte to a pianissimo of silver clarity, which—even at the end of the second act—is still so absolutely true. From the sweetest-sounding melody into the hollow groan of anguished torture, from the hellish laughter and from the shattering depths in a siren song of unbelievable beauty … her interpretation surpasses even that of Martha Mödl, whom she resembles very much in timbre. Her interpretation fills the dimensions of the myth; the measurements of sin and penitence; of the seductress to the ignominious; of inordinate passion and desire finally restrained and subjugated. Extraordinary!

Young Irene Dalis was a complete revelation.… Few dramatic sopranos exist who possess such a brilliant top register with such a noble middle, coupled with the sonorous and full contralto quality, and still know that singing is more than just pouring out voice, and acting is more than giving gestures required by the stage director. Bayreuth will be wise to keep her for years to come.

> The American Irene Dalis as Kundry developed vocally the register of a dramatic soprano with surprising alto colour—a big resounding voice, the piano of which, even in the high register, was intoned without any effort. As though having attended a church service, the audience left the *Parsifal* performance silently without applause.

Irene's portrayal of this role was recorded in a live performance in 1962 with Jess Thomas as Parsifal, George London as Amfortas, Hans Hotter as Gurnemanz, and Hans Knappertsbusch conducting the Bayreuth Festival orchestra. Knappertsbusch had become Irene's favorite conductor. "When he gave a cue, it was more like an invitation. It was as if he were saying, 'Any time you are ready, I am.'" This recording was so superlative that in 1964 it won the Grand Prix du Disc, France's most prestigious award for musical recordings.

This *Parsifal* recording was reissued after 25 years ("Not because of me," Irene hastens to add). And yet another quarter century after the re-issue, this recording was *still* making news. In 2013, Irene got a phone call from an old friend, Ernesto Alorda, who is now working at the Seattle Opera. He excitedly announced that her *Parsifal* was one of the new Pope Francis's favorite recordings.

How to Make a Wagner Angry, and Other Tales

Every opera house had its own customs. In some places such as the Met, audiences gave "entrance applause" when a loved singer first appeared onstage, whether or not he or she was singing at that exact moment. (This is not entirely welcome to the singers, if the noise makes it hard for them to hear the orchestra give them their cue). At Bayreuth, where Wagner built an opera house to showcase his own operas, it is forbidden to applaud during performances and allowed only at curtain calls. But in 1962 Irene sang the aria "Entweite, Gotter" ("Ortrud's curse") from *Lohengrin* with such spectacular artistry that the audience broke the well-known rule and burst into prolonged applause.

Irene was surprised and a bit embarrassed by this, because she knew it would be awkward afterwards. Sure enough, conductor Wolfgang Sawallisch was not happy, since he had to stop the orchestra and then restart it when the applause finally died down. General director Wieland Wagner, grandson of the composer, was furious and told his public relations department never to mention it.

George was backstage, so he couldn't possibly have started the applause, as some cynical person suggested—but he did bypass the Wagner news blockade and send a cable to the American newspapers. The secret was out. This rare case of audience defiance was reported in *The New York Times,* the *New York Herald Tribune,* and (before they merged) the *San Jose Mercury* and the *San Jose News.*

Irene backstage with Wolfgang Sawallisch, 1962

Despite her great success, Irene (who was 5'4") didn't feel sufficiently imposing onstage. So she ordered 3-inch platform shoes from Berlin, in several colors, to give her a bit of height. After all, she was usually playing the villainess—and shouldn't the villainess be menacing? But people who saw her perform say she didn't need height to be imposing. Over and over, they said, "You couldn't take your eyes off her." Even four decades after the end of her stage career, her performances live vividly in the memories of admirers.

Cordell Shewell, a voice coach from Seattle, said of Irene, "You couldn't keep your eyes off of her. Even when she wasn't singing. She was a consummate performer, and completely enveloped by her characters. It was like method acting for opera." Michael Barclay, opera historian of Opera Education International, wrote:

> Dalis was my favorite mezzo during her San Francisco Opera, Bayreuth, and Met career. Irene's art was not one of refinement but of unbridled passion—she would allow herself the most potent expression, sometimes excessive. She didn't go "over the top"—she was the top. She was thrilling. She unabashedly sailed in and out of registers, using her voice with canny dramatic skill. She was flamboyantly, joyously venomous. She was a major force, both vocally and dramatically.

Still, she wishes she could have been more relaxed during her singing career and enjoyed it more. She envied colleagues like Cesare Siepi and Robert Merrill, who could joke backstage, but such levity was beyond her and they gave up trying to chat with her backstage during a performance. Her testy mood sometimes lasted even after it was over. Irene's first outing as the vengeful gypsy Azucena in *Il Trovatore* (co-starring her idol, Jussi Björling) took place in Philadelphia, when the Met was on tour. The other principals had done *Trovatore* before and didn't want to rehearse, so Irene made her role debut without having had a staging rehearsal or an orchestra rehearsal. After the final curtain fell, Rudolf Bing was waiting backstage to congratulate her, but she snapped, "If you think that was good, you have no idea what Azucena is about."

Irene may have been irritable at times, but not arrogant. One reason she isn't egotistical is her firm belief that a great voice is a gift from God. A second reason is that there are many people behind every career and every performance. Early in her tenure at the Met, the singers did not take solo bows. Irene was glad of this. "I was embarrassed at bows, because I knew I had an army of people behind me and that I never accomplished anything all on my own." When solo bows were finally adopted there, she found it difficult to accept all the acclaim and would duck out behind the curtain as soon as decently possible. Her brother told her that she should stand there amid the applause and count to 50 before disappearing.

Remembering the co-stars she calls "giants," Irene says that the very best singers are humble, regular people; they feel responsible to make each performance as good as the last one, and they don't exploit their fame. "They know their worth, but they're not impressed by it."

Family Life on the Road

In 1958, Irene became pregnant. She continued to sing in Europe for several months, and the only contract she had to cancel in the 1958-1959 season was at the Met. (That's why you may see inconsistencies in accounts of her career—she performed during 19 seasons over a 20-year period). Daughter Alida was born in 1959. This joyful arrival brought new complications to life—a nanny, for one, to take care of the baby during Irene's working hours. And at long last Irene learned to drive. For her first summer in Bayreuth (1961), George said she should rent a car, now

Success

Practicing makeup with daughter Alida

that she had received her driver's license. While dining with her host family, she told them about this plan. As it happened, the host was the owner of the local Opel car dealership and explained that in her situation, buying a car would be cheaper than renting. She ordered an Opel Rekord for $2,500, but forgot to mention that she had never used a standard transmission. When the car arrived, she was dismayed to discover she would have to learn how to use a stick shift. Her early driving adventures were idiosyncratic, to say the least. Fans would gather at the opera house to watch her try to park the car.

As an infant, Alida and her nanny always traveled with Irene. Her first birthday was celebrated in Berlin, and her father flew from New York to celebrate. There were many long plane flights. But the time came when Alida had to go to school and the extended separations began. Even though she was used to being away from loved ones for long periods, Irene now had a little daughter and missed her so much she sometimes cried. But strangely enough, before she had to leave for months, she would behave badly to her family so they'd be glad to see her go. Considering this, and the weddings and funerals she missed over the years in order to fulfill singing commitments, she says, "I hated my career at times."

Rosemarie Armenat was a photographer in Berlin. "She wrote me my first fan letter and went to all my performances." They met and became friends. When Alida was born, Rosemarie became her nanny. Later Irene stopped doing overseas tours because once she came home from a four-week trip to find that Alida was calling the nanny "Mommy." Some years later, Alida still wished she had more of her mother's time.

> One day, when my daughter was about 10, we were in the kitchen of the New Jersey house and she said, "I don't know why you can't do lunch room duty like other mothers." I asked her, "Are any of the other mothers opera singers?" She put her hands on her hips and said, "So you sing once a week. Big deal."

The rest of Irene's family was wholeheartedly supportive—except for her father. "He never understood my career and did not enjoy having to wear a tuxedo." Though Irene was now an international star, he remained unimpressed by her fame, even when he was sitting in the audience hearing the applause. On one of his rare phone calls, he said, "You're mixed up. You should have more children." It's amazing that her sister Marge had ever convinced this man to let Irene to go to New York alone at age 20.

Trouble at the Top

Most top opera singers have agents, whose job is to solicit and receive offers of opera engagements. For a short period, Irene had an agent. It was a bad experience. This agent double booked her at Berlin and San Francisco—performing at almost the same time on two continents. Berlin would not release her from her contract to sing at their Festival Week. When he found this out, Kurt Herbert Adler of San Francisco called, threatening to sue if Irene would not honor her contract. Marge, who had picked up the phone, told him calmly, "Do what you have to do." Then Adler called George, whose response was, "Go ahead and sue. That will be good publicity." Later Adler told Irene, "Your family sure protects you!"

Still, Irene was in a quandary. It would be terrible to no-show with one company or the other, so with extra endurance, she did both productions. She arrived in San Francisco to do Klytemnestra in *Elektra* too late to participate in rehearsals. Irene had studied the part in Berlin, but recalls, "I really learned it on the plane." After this, she had no agent (except for the time she did concerts) and handled all opera engagements herself, discussing her Met contracts directly with general director Rudolf Bing.

Even though she was at the top of the opera world, Irene did not rest on her fame or relax her artistic standards. Performers always look for ways to improve. "That's the great thing about opera," Irene says. "There is always room for improvement." However, striving for perfection can have a dark side if it leads to unappeasable dissatisfaction and self-criticism. Irene was being courted by the top opera companies in the world, singing leading mezzo roles at the Met, and receiving applause and adulatory reviews. One would think she'd be pleased with herself. But in fact, during this time she felt like an impostor, certain that soon everyone would discover she was a fraud. When friends wished to listen to recordings of her radio broadcasts, she would ceaselessly find fault with her performance. George finally said, "No more playing your broadcasts when friends are over. You criticize yourself so much that it spoils it for them and makes them feel stupid."

One New York reviewer never liked Irene, and despite George's long-ago warning about this very danger, she found this upsetting. Bing soothed her, saying, "I am the one who signs your contract, and for me, you are the best mezzo in the world. Forget bad reviews. After three days, everyone forgets bad reviews unless you keep talking about them." Thinking of moments like this, Irene says, "I know that Rudolf Bing has been criticized as being cold and heartless. That was never the case with me. I thought he was wonderful."

Still, the self-criticism persisted. After calming her innumerable times, George enlisted the aid of a psychologist. Within six months of weekly sessions, Dr. Wilford Beecher relieved Irene's painful affliction. He wrote notes for her to take home, with messages like "Don't expect everyone to love you" and "Allow yourself to make a mistake." Once when she was worrying, Beecher asked point blank, "Do you think Rudolf Bing runs a charity? Are you aware he can hire anyone he wants?" She hadn't thought about that. He continued, "Some of the most successful people come to me with the same problem." Irene was relieved to know that her difficulty was a known human failing.

In fact, some other people in the music world are talented artists beset by detrimental self-doubt. Connie (not her real name) wanted an orchestra job but feared the audition, saying she hadn't been practicing enough. She vacillated between extremes of hope and doubt, unsure whether to even attend the audition. One day, halfway through a session with her psychotherapist, she said, oh, by the way, she got the job.

"Congratulations!" the therapist exclaimed.

Connie shrugged. "They probably gave it to me out of pity."

The therapist replied, "Why would they do that? You're thinking they're going to fill the first violinist chair in a professional orchestra, someone they'll have to play with in public—for pity?"

"Well, they probably knew it was me." This was really baffling.

"How could they *not* know it was you?"

"Oh, you can tell sometimes." This was getting curiouser and curiouser.

She added, "Maybe they could see behind the screen."

"There's a screen?"

"Oh, yeah. Auditions are supposed to be anonymous."

"I see. They have a list of the candidates—"

"Not exactly. The day before, I told them I wasn't coming. I just went on the spur of the moment."

"Let me get this straight. You believe that people who can't see you, who don't even know you are there, who are putting their own reputations on the line, hired you out of pity?"

So, like this therapy client, Irene was now experiencing the anxiety that had hindered her as a pianist. Fortunately, it did not occur during performances, but only beforehand. It manifested itself in an unpleasant way.

> Marge traveled with me on my concert tours and assisted me as secretary and dresser. Marge told me that I was two people. The Irene before a performance was absolutely impossible and rude. Marge said, "If you weren't my sister, and I didn't know you better, I would tell you to go to h***." This was my sister whom I adored and without whom I would never have had the life I have. So you can tell I must have been churning inside to act this way to her.

Irene says, "I'm two people. Yvonne is inhibited, simple, unassuming, an average person, a good pianist but terrified to perform. Irene, on the other hand, is aggressive, risk-taking, and usually confident."

Friends and Colleagues

Tenor Jess Thomas became a close friend. He was her Parsifal in Bayreuth. They were alike in some ways: Both were Americans at Bayreuth, hardworking, faithful to their spouses, and able to communicate the depths of music and drama to the audience. "He was intellectual, and a spiritual man," she said, looking fondly at a photo of him on the wall of her office.

They met in Bayreuth when Irene was sitting at a table in an outdoor café when a tall man stopped by and began speaking to her in German. She asked him his name. "Jess Thomas," he replied. Recognizing the name, she said, "Well, why don't you speak to me in English, then?" This was the start of their friendship. Once, while they were working together in Bayreuth, Jess acquired new contact lenses. When he came to Irene's home for dinner, he found that the lights were too bright for his new lenses and made him squint. So Irene turned the lights way down and they proceeded with their collegial evening. There was a humorous sequel.

> Next day, the temporary housekeeper I hired for the summer quit, saying she wouldn't have anything to do with married people who behaved that way. And all we did was talk! I was worried that she might start a gossiping campaign in Bayreuth, but Jess laughed. He thought a little scandal would only make us more popular.

Actually, this was not a laughing matter. Jess's wife was jealous of his career, which is not unusual in the opera world, since singers often sacrifice family time to keep their professional commitments. Jess's wife would fuss before opening night, sometimes to the point of histrionics. Once he called Irene from Vienna for help, saying urgently, "She says she's going to throw herself out the window." Perhaps remembering Marge's adroit

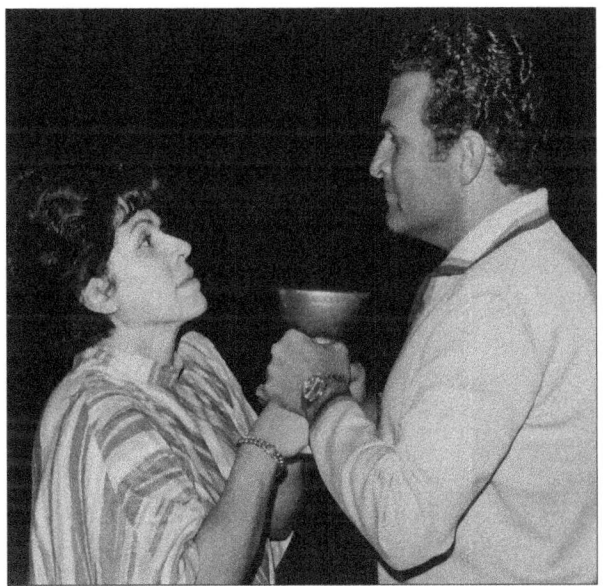

Rehearsing *Tristan and Isolde* with Jess Thomas, 1967

use of "reverse psychology," Irene said, "Open the window and tell her to jump." The next day, Jess called and greeted Irene as "Dr. Dalis," saying her advice had worked. His wife had calmed down, at least for the moment. Ultimately, though, that marriage ended in divorce.

Thomas came visiting so often that Alida called him "Uncle Jess." Irene loved performing with her friend and stoutly defended him. One time Bing was angry at him and said irritably, "Who the hell does Jess Thomas think he is, Franco Corelli?" Irene retorted, "Well, no. He's better."

Photos of other cherished colleagues have a place on Irene's wall. Leonie Rysanek was a frequent collaborator and Alida called her "Aunt Leonie." Irene says of her, "She was so dedicated and down-to-earth. Such a great actress—she *became* the role she was singing." This is high praise from Irene, who was often complimented on this same trait. Tatiana Troyanos, another friend, was much younger and would stay with Irene and George whenever she was in New York. Looking back, Irene says, "Our friendship started in Hamburg, when she was singing small roles. Tatiana was the first young talent that I could help." For sheer musical magic, Irene names Leontyne Price.

Then there were the warm-hearted men she sang with. Irene remembers Bob Merrill as jovial and friendly, "so you couldn't help but love him. He was an entertainer's entertainer" and a bit of a prankster. Sherrill Milnes was another likable man who was everyone's friend as well as a superb artist.

Fans and Admirers

A wonderful window into Irene's early career is preserved in the collection of memorabilia from an adoring young fan. Sharon Breden from Redondo Beach, California, was fifteen years old. She didn't like opera and thought it was probably boring. However, she was induced to go to one performance, in a year when the San Francisco Opera went on tour before Los Angeles had its own opera company. Breden was in for a surprise. As she wrote later,

> On October 30, 1960, my piano teacher [Ellen Dukes], my mother and I went to the Shrine Auditorium, a virtual barn of a performing theatre, for the San Francisco Opera production of *Lohengrin*. As the action of the first act unfolded, I found myself riveted to a singer seated on a trunk, stage right. She had not sung a note, but her face was working from the moment she took the stage. I was fascinated. *Then she sang*. That was it—I was hooked.

Breden was so awestruck that she wrote Irene a fan letter. Some time later she received a signed photograph. Then, in one of those eerie coincidences, she happened upon a live radio performance. "One Saturday morning I was flipping through the stations, and all of a sudden I heard the voice. 'That's that lady singing!' The voice was unmistakable." From then on, Breden followed Irene's career, collecting programs, cutting reviews out of newspapers, and corresponding. "When I was a junior in high school, Irene wrote me on numerous occasions—a short note, a post card, a birthday card." Breden had still not actually met Irene. Bravely, she decided to do so the next time Irene was performing in Los Angeles.

> My senior year arrived. I had decided to enter the Sisters of St. Joseph of Carondelet the fall after graduation. I wrote to Irene and invited her to visit my high school glee club and maybe even come out to our home.... Much to my surprise, Irene said yes, she would come out to the high school and then to our home! ... The performance [of *Don Carlo*] was wonderful. Dalis was Eboli for those few hours. But when it was all over she was Irene Dalis, real person, coming out of that stage door saying, "Where's Sharon? Where is Sharon?" Sharon was rooted to the pavement! But when she hugged me, it was as if we had known each other for years.

And they would know each other for years—decades, in fact. But the best encounter occurred just before Breden entered the convent. It was a story that would be reported around the world.

> Ellen Dukes and I traveled in Europe that summer of '63 and arrived in Bayreuth with no tickets—but a lot of hope. We both got in for the performance—a spiritual experience that cannot be put into words for someone who has not been a part of that musical

masterpiece.... When Irene welcomed me to her dressing room between acts she said in Italian "My little one" as I towered over her with my six feet of height. The photo that was taken at that moment was in BRAVO magazine the next musical season with the caption: "Breden and Friend." But the best caption was the headline for the article about my visit to Bayreuth in the United Press International release: "Opera Singer Fulfills Girl's Last Wish Before Entering the Convent"!

"Girl's last wish?" That's dramatic headline material. Here is the story as it was reported in the newspapers and opera trade press. Of course, this was decades before inexpensive long-distance telephone services and the internet made it possible to secure a ticket well in advance. A story for a music trade publication mentioned Breden and then said:

> Wagner's *Parsifal* was her favorite opera, and mezzo-soprano Irene Dalis was her favorite singer. When 18-year-old Californian Sharon Breden told her parents that this very special combination of singer and opera was taking place at last summer's Bayreuth Festival, they flew her there, for Sharon was entering a convent and it seemed like the perfect gift. She arrived ticketless on opening night, but at the last moment a ticket was procured—though the opening had been sold out a year in advance. Sharon got her wish, plus a backstage welcome from Miss Dalis.

The regular press took notice as well, and treated the general public to the story of the disconsolate fan and her lucky break.

> After traveling more than 6,500 miles to Bayreuth, Sharon's dream came within a split-hair of ending in disappointment. When the tall

slim teenager arrived in Bayreuth, she found that the performance had been sold out for months and an extra ticket was harder to come by than a dinosaur egg. Learning of her plight, everyone from idol (Irene Dalis) to Wieland Wagner, the composer's grandson, went to work on her behalf. But to no avail.... Then a Scotswoman who had heard of Sharon's problem took pity on her and gave her a ticket. That evening, Sharon discovered she had not one, but two tickets. Mme Dalis had also managed to get her a ticket, and Sharon attended the performance with the singer's husband, George Loinaz.

Breden was not the only person to idolize Irene. A young woman named Madeline Lorton became an unexpectedly close admirer—unexpected, because she had to be dragged kicking and screaming to the stage door. As she wrote later,

> An English friend of mine (who has since gone home) liked to go to the stage door to see the artists leave and collect their autographs, and begged me to go with her.... Finally, my friend prevailed upon me to write her a letter. I even balked at this, since I've never written a fan letter and didn't want to start. Well, I wrote on a Wednesday. Mailed it and went to a Dalis performance the next night. After the performance, we trekked back to the stage door and my English friend asked the doorman if my name was on Miss Dalis's guest list—and it was!!! Sharon, I was petrified, but what a beautiful, beautiful experience. I knew she would be nice, but I couldn't in my wildest dreams imagine that she could ever be *that* wonderful. About the only way I can describe her is "genuine" and simply beautiful and beautifully simple.

> She couldn't have been nicer if I had been a dear friend for years.

That did it. Madeline Lorton started a fan club. Quite a few young people joined, sharing their enthusiasm about their favorite singer. Breden became a devoted member. The members didn't hesitate to let Irene know they were behind her all the way. One day in late October, 1961, she sent them a handwritten note.

> Dearest Friends,
>
> On the night of my first appearance at the Met this season, I found my dressing room filled with flowers and telegrams. Not since my debut in 1957 have I ever received such tangible expressions of encouragement, and I felt, as I was called on stage for the opening curtain, an inner calm and strength which I had never before experienced. After the performance, Madeline added to my joy by telling me that I have friends in eighteen states and four countries. This has come as a great, wonderful surprise to me, and I thank each and every one of you most sincerely, Irene Dalis-Loinaz.

Lorton was a faithful correspondent as well as the newsletter editor. She wrote a letter to Breden, telling the story of a bizarre premonition.

> I'm sure you heard the December 23rd broadcast in which our mezzo sang Fricka in *Die Walküre*. Well, after the performance I drove her and George Loinaz (her husband) home and when she asked if I was going to "come upstairs for a while," I told her "No" because she would have to rest for her *Aida* performance that night. She was the first cover for Rosalind Elias, who was to sing

Amneris. I told her that I had a feeling she would have to sing. She told me to bite my tongue. So, before I rushed off for home, I asked her to call me or have George call me if she got a call from Rudolf Bing that night.

That night, sitting at home, the phone rang at 9:45 pm and George's voice on the other end said "Madeline." That was enough. I knew. Well, to make it a short story, Bing sent a limousine to pick her up and rush her to the Met. He said he would hold the Judgment Scene curtain if necessary. However, La Dalis arrived at the stage entrance just as the third act curtain came down. He asked how long she would need to get into costume and makeup, and good ole Dalis replied, "Just give me ten minutes." The audience was delighted that she was to sing, and as soon as her name was announced, gave her quite an ovation. So, without any vocalizing whatsoever, your gal was ready within the ten minutes and all set to make her entrance at the fourth act curtain. Sharon, she received ovation after ovation for what many call the greatest Judgment scene at the Met.

Here is this story from Irene's viewpoint. She had sung Fricka for the matinee broadcast of *Die Walküre*. Rosalind Elias was scheduled to sing Amneris for that night's performance of *Aida* and Jean Madeira was scheduled to cover the role. But Jean lived in Newport, Rhode Island—quite a distance from New York City. Irene generously offered to cover the role, saying, "I live right here in Manhattan. Go on home for the holidays." Irene called the Met office to say she would be covering and thought no more about it.

That afternoon, for the first and only time in her career, she went home from performing without removing her makeup. Hors d'oeuvres and dinner were already being served, so she didn't have time to take off the makeup.

The telephone rang. It was Rudolf Bing. He said, "I'm not so sure Roz is going to get through this tonight. I've heard you've offered to cover. Is that correct?"

"Yes."

"Good, I'll keep in touch."

An hour later the phone rang again. Irene immediately said to Bing, "You know, I think I'd rather be downtown just in case you need me."

Bing said, "That's good, because I've had a limo waiting in front of your apartment building for an hour."

So with no more ado, Irene got in the limo and was driven down Broadway through heavy snow at a snail's pace, arriving at the Met just in time for the last act. The makeup man was delighted she still had her stage makeup on, saying, "I just have to do your eyes."

Conductor George Schick didn't know there would be a change and, apparently, did not hear the announcement made by Rudolf Bing before the curtain. He was totally surprised when he heard her first notes, looked up, and realized he had a new mezzo for the last act. Later he told her that her appearance reenergized the performance. Perhaps there was an extra reason. Irene had had wine with dinner and cognac with dessert. "I was feeling no pain. When I went onstage, I just had a ball."

Other admirers contributed to the growing cache of Lorton's newsletters. Lloyd Free was an American music student and journalist studying abroad. By coincidence, he met Irene and George in Bayreuth.

> I was immediately struck with their lack of phony artiness or turgid, frigid successful egos. There was

such a spark of naturalness and friendliness in each of their natures that, despite the chasm separating my student world from their lofty world of the theatre, I was immediately put at ease. Their warm-heartedness was not limited to mere verbal phrases, but it was demonstrated countless times in spontaneous little kind acts. I was not the only one to find Irene Dalis a wonderfully kind and generous person. There were others—people like myself—possessing no theatre names and able to give nothing in return except sincere, profound gratitude.

Now that Irene was a Met regular, she was now the kindly established singer who supported others, as Mödl had supported her so many years before. She welcomed new talents on the night of their debuts, as she had with Franco Corelli and Leontyne Price. Irene was onstage performing Princess of Bouillon for Placido Domingo's Met debut in *Adriana Lecouvreur* in 1963 and sang Brangäne when Birgit Nilsson sang her first Met *Tristan and Isolde* in 1960. In her autobiography, the eminent Birgit Nilsson said of her,

> Irene Dalis was wonderful to interact with: active, alert, but at the same time solicitous, as Isolde's servant must be. I have had colleagues who ceaselessly tried to convince the audience that they should be the one singing Isolde. Then everything goes wrong and nothing in the relationship works. But here, everything ran perfectly.

Nilsson's appreciation of Irene went beyond this one production. Rudolf Bing told Irene that, like some other artists, Nilsson would specifically ask him to cast Irene to sing alongside her.

As Brangäne in *Tristan and Isolde* with Birgit Nilsson, 1962

Irene loved working with Birgit Nilsson, who was an absolute professional, always prepared and cooperative, and never made negative remarks about anyone or anything. Even when one young conductor in Berlin gave her an incorrect musical cue, she didn't complain but took the cue and kept on singing, so he would find out his mistake and learn. Still, Nilsson came to Irene to commiserate privately over young conductors so narcissistic that even to correct them was difficult. They both preferred an older conductor with experience to a young supposed genius.

Conductor Georg Solti typically made his orchestras play too loud and sometimes drowned out the singers. Once Nilsson told Irene, "Tonight we won't sing *fortissimo* [extremely loud], we'll

Success

Irene with cherished colleague Birgit Nilsson

sing *Soltissimo*." This coming from Nilsson was surprising, for she had the most powerful voice imaginable and certainly did not have to worry about an orchestra overpowering her.

Irene had a wonderful career, was steadily employed at top opera houses in Europe and America, and singing major roles. In a letter to an admirer who became a friend (more about him later), Irene wrote in 1964,

> This has been, perhaps, my most successful season at the Metropolitan, and I have had a dream repertoire for a mezzo-soprano. So far, I have sung Amneris, Azucena, Eboli, Waltraute, and Ortrud,

with Santuzza and Lady Macbeth coming up soon. Where in the world, outside of the Met, could I have such a variety of roles in one season?

I am looking forward to next season. It, too, will have an interesting repertoire for me. In San Francisco: Amme in *Die Frau ohne Schatten* and Kundry in *Parsifal* (two of my favorite roles) and Amneris. In New York: Dalila, Amneris, Fricka, and Herodias (in the new production of *Salome* starring Birgit Nilsson). Then I will be off to the Deutsche Oper in Berlin. It will be my return there after five years of absence.

A Daughter's Viewpoint

Irene's opera career meant many sacrifices. She was away when her mother, father, and brother died. She missed weddings, birthdays, and important events in her daughter's early years. This did not make for a harmonious relationship. When small, Alida would say after a performance, "Everyone was good except you." But this friction didn't last. Irene was later delighted when Alida brought four of her high school friends to see her sing. "That was the biggest compliment."

Alida sometimes went to the opera when her mother was performing. One time, when she was about five years old, she performed a feat of backstage mollification.

> For some reason, Franco Corelli was being antisocial, not allowing anyone into his dressing room and telling people he was not sure he would sing that night. I was trained to go to every principal artist's dressing room to wish him or her "Toi, toi, toi" before the performance. Despite throwing everyone out of his dressing room, when I knocked he welcomed me in. We chatted. Apparently,

being with a small child was therapeutic. His attitude changed and all was well.

Mother never would leave the house without make-up and would run around the house like crazy so as to leave it in perfect order. She was confident in her ability to learn whatever she had to learn, had high standards, and wanted to be appreciated on her merits without having to sell herself. How did she achieve her high standards? A lot of methodical preparation, with a system, such as using red and blue pencils to mark lines in a score.

She had to be fastidious about her vocal health, which meant making sure she stayed healthy, had enough sleep, and ate healthy food. She visited her ENT (voice) doctor and trusted him completely. He recommended inhaling some kind of tincture. It would be boiled on the stove, and she would cover her head with a towel as she inhaled the steam. It stank throughout the house.

My mother used to send *lots* of letters to me when I was younger. She would address them to Angel, Doll Baby, and Monkey Face, always special endearments. She wanted me to learn to cook, so she would have me work beside her. Eventually, the familiar tasks were mine to do. It was a good process. My mother was a natural teacher.

I was the center of attention at many adult gatherings. Our house was filled on Christmas Eve. She made sure I had all the toys I wanted. Christmas was insane. I loved dolls and she kept me supplied. She always had treats for me. Any time she returned home from a singing contract, she would bring me gifts. She brought me Hummels from Germany. I loved them.

I traveled with my mother until I was 7. I had a governess from age 2 months to age 10: Rosemarie Armenat ("Rosi") was a photographer, a fan of my mother's in Berlin. She traveled with us.

My mom has always liked order, and she is fastidious about some details. She has always liked the precision of both math and music. She is an instinctive mathematician—an intuitive sense of numbers is almost part of her make-up. She kept a little red notebook—very small—in her purse. It was a precious item. In it she recorded in perfect, tiny print all of her most important information. I am sure it included contact information for people she loved as well as those essential numbers, but what I remember is that it listed every performance she had ever done of every operatic role. It was how she knew when she was singing her 100th Amneris.

My mother could do anything. She had summers off and was home most of the time during summers. One year I wanted a dollhouse, a huge dollhouse. She asked me to design it and she built a wing of it—she did all the carpentry and it had working electricity. She did that at a time when none of the dads I knew did anything like that for their daughters. The workshop in the basement was hers, not my dad's.

I was proud that my mother had skills and was successful. My friends' parents were impressed by her career. Sometimes I took advantage of the fascination my teachers had with my mother's fame: getting on their good sides by asking my mother to get them tickets to the opera or using "going to the opera last night" as an excuse to not do homework.

Backstage with daughter Alida in *Don Carlo*, 1964

All the institutions we were involved with, from casual carpools to the schools expecting parental involvement, cut my mother a lot of slack. Dads were exonerated in those days. The other working moms were expected to juggle their commitments, but not my mother. It was as though the whole world understood that being an opera singer meant that the singer did not have time for family commitments.

I loved being with my handsome father at the opera. My governess, mother, father, and others all tried to help me understand the story. When I was little, I had difficulty understanding the difference between stage and real life. I knew the singers were playing roles on stage, but if I knew them as people, too, I was confused. One day I was watching my mother and Jess Thomas in *Samson and Dalila*. When he was Samson, I was fine, but suddenly I realized that he was Uncle Jess … and here my father was watching him getting *way* too close to my mother. I cried, "Daddy, Uncle Jess is kissing Mommy."

Daddy explained that Mommy and Uncle Jess were only pretending. After the performance, family members and invited guests were relaxing at a restaurant. Jess arrived after everyone else was seated. Little Alida had not forgotten his onstage advances to her mother and greeted him sternly. "Hello, Jess Thomas." To her, he was never Uncle Jess again.

Just a few weeks before this book went to press, the author received a request from a reporter in Oldenburg, Germany, asking for information about Miss Dalis. Recall that this is the place where Irene began her career in the 1950s, and where she first encountered the "fest contract" idea that inspired her to create Opera San José. Even today, she is still remembered in Oldenburg, 70 years after she left.

THREE

The International Star

AFTER PLAYING NUMEROUS PRINCESSES ONSTAGE, IRENE was finally introduced to a genuine royal, Queen Elizabeth II. She was in London in 1958 for a new production of *Tristan and Isolde*, and Queen Elizabeth wanted a command performance. Since she was not really a Wagner-lover who would happily sit through three and a half hours of his music, at her request four scenes from different operas were presented, concluding with the triumphal scene from *Aida*.

Immediately after the performance, the leading artists and other dignitaries were presented to the queen onstage, including Maria Callas, Blanche Thebom, and Irene (who was still in her Amneris costume). It was very formal. The royal couple arrived and faced the singers. Reporters and cameramen appeared. An emcee with a microphone made the introductions. Irene became apprehensive about the entire affair, suddenly realizing that she was totally unprepared for this grand occasion. She turned anxiously to the small lady beside her and asked how to curtsy. The small lady said, "You sing Eboli. Curtsy the way you do in the opera."

Then the emcee announced in a booming voice, "IRENE DALIS FROM THE METROPOLITAN OPERA." Irene almost turned around to see who this Irene Dalis might be. Then she recovered her senses, and the curtsy went well. Prince Philip shook her hand and said, "I fear I will not recognize you in your regular attire." Irene's response to this cordial bit of small talk was, "Please don't talk to me. I'm so nervous I can hardly think." Then she heard the presentation of the "small lady" who stood beside her in the line: famed ballerina Dame Margot Fonteyn.

When George asked afterwards what she had said to the prince, she said, "You do not want to know!"

As Amneris *(Aida)* with Leontyne Price, 1964

Friends in High Places: Conductors and Impresarios

This incident of stage fright was highly unusual. After all, Irene had faced down a claque and wowed sophisticated audiences. As an established and reliable star with a mastery of Italian and German repertoires, Irene was on good terms with the powerful men who were in charge of important opera houses. Before each performance Bing told her that he considered her presence "luxury casting" and said to her, "Please don't agree to any engagements until you talk to me." She had a good relationship with him. Though others found fault, "I never found any reason to criticize him. If he had a problem with you, he'd tell you himself."

One day in Bayreuth in 1961, Irene was in the audience waiting for *Das Rheingold* to begin and noticed Wieland Wagner's secretary searching the faces in the crowd. Finding Irene, the secretary sighed in relief and beckoned. Irene, assuming that the woman scheduled to sing Fricka was indisposed, was reviewing the role in her head as she entered Wieland Wagner's office. But to her surprise, he asked her to sing in a new production of *Tristan and Isolde* with Jess Thomas. Wieland Wagner said, "I want you to do Isolde." She laughed out loud at the very thought and declined. He was disappointed, but he made her promise to take a serious look at the role and call him when she was ready. That never came to pass, for Wieland Wagner died within two years of this conversation. But when she recounted this story to her mentor, Martha Mödl said, aghast, "You laughed at *Wieland Wagner?*"

General directors could sometimes wheedle her into doing roles she was dubious about singing. For example, the mezzo role in Richard Strauss's *Die Frau ohne Schatten* (The Woman without a Shadow) is a series of complicated vocal gymnastics and she hesitated to take it on, even though it was the kind of evil character that was her specialty. But San Francisco Opera's general director Kurt Herbert Adler urged her to do it, saying, "This role is perfect for you." She finally agreed. The conductor was Leopold Ludwig, music director of the Hamburg Staatsoper, and the production was excellent. As a result of the success of *Die Frau ohne Schatten* in San Francisco, Ludwig engaged her immediately to sing the role in Hamburg, and it became one of her signature roles. Later Adler asked her to sing Isolde.

> Kurt Herbert Adler I considered a genius and I had a love-hate relationship with him. He could charm you. Wieland Wagner wanted me and Jess to do *Tristan and Isolde* right after we did the *Parsifal*. When Kurt Herbert Adler called and asked me to do Isolde, I said, "Why would I refuse it in Bayreuth and then do it in San Francisco?" [In Bayreuth] I would have had those hour-long intermissions, and the orchestra's under the stage. It's so easy to sing Wagner in Bayreuth. You can sing pianississisissimo and it's heard.

Undeterred, Adler somehow got her private phone number in Connecticut and asked her to look at the role. Sighing, she sent her family out of the house and proceeded to sing along with a Kirsten Flagstad recording. She called Adler the next day and told him that she had sung the entire role along with Flagstad and had come to one conclusion: "I can't do it." He persisted, sending flowers and calling her on a daily basis.

> With his charm, Adler finally talked me into it.... I called [Bing] and I said, "I want to tell you something, so if you're going to laugh, I want to be the one you hear this from. I just agreed to do Isolde at the San Francisco Opera." Bing said, "Wait a minute, wait a minute. Is this a news report or are you calling me for advice?" and I said, "No, I'm telling you that I've agreed." And he said,

"Why on earth would you agree to do an Isolde when you have people like Birgit Nilsson out there? Why would you want to be the second of anything, when to me you're the greatest mezzo soprano? ... Irene, I'm disappointed in you."

Still, at the end of the conversation, Bing said, "Why didn't you ever let me know that you would consider doing Isolde? I would have had you do it at the Met."

This was a nice compliment. But her Isolde was not an easy experience. The conductor for this run of *Tristan and Isolde* at San Francisco Opera was Horst Stein, who was later music director at the Vienna Staatsoper. The rehearsal period was painful. He was so unpleasant and difficult that Irene wanted out. He demanded that she sing louder when she was already at full voice. He said, "Why are you doing Isolde? You'll ruin your voice." He was against her doing the role. Since she had been reluctant to do it in the first place, she tried her best to convince Adler to use another singer, but he refused. And then the unthinkable happened—on the day of the final dress rehearsal, her father died. Irene was naturally distraught and rushed the fifty miles to San José. Her mother bravely said, "Now we will see the stuff you are made of"—an implicit command to do her professional duty. So Irene returned to San Francisco and sang the role, but she made a pact with God: "If you get me through these four performances, I'll never do Isolde again." And she never did. Yet she had sung it very successfully. Here's one review:

> Irene Dalis exhibited a wide-ranging voice that achieved great moments of penetration and insight. Her work in Act I was full of bitterness and murderous contempt, but in the final two acts, she revealed a voice of tenderness, introspection, and quiet concentration. In the Liebestod music, there was a lovely floating quality and emotional richness in her voice.

With Jess Thomas *(Tristan and Isolde)*, 1967

Adler was important to Irene's career. He was very demanding but usually right, and he could be very charming if he wanted something. Irene made many role debuts under him: Ortrud, Isolde, Santuzza, Amme (in *Die Frau ohne Schatten*), Klytemnestra in Strauss's *Elektra* (the one she did without an orchestra rehearsal because she had been double booked). Long after his retirement, when Irene, too, had retired from the stage and was living in San José, they were guests at a dinner hosted by the Italian Consulate General in San Francisco. They were able to have a lengthy conversation about Irene's dream of starting an opera company in her home town. She remembers vividly the advice he gave her. His last words on the topic that night were, "Remember, an opera company is not a democracy."

She almost had an opportunity to sing *Tosca*. One season when she was in San Francisco for her first Ortrud, Robert Herman, the Metropolitan Opera artistic administrator, called with an urgent request for her to sing Abigaille in Verdi's *Nabucco*. He was willing to send a substitute to San Francisco to replace her as Ortrud. She said she would take a look at the role, on one condition: *If* she would undertake the role, the Met would have to cast her also as Tosca. He agreed to that. As it happened, Irene found Abigaille not to be suitable for her voice and the deal fell through.

This story illustrates the care Irene took in selecting roles. Rather than accept all offers, Irene would carefully evaluate whether a role was right for her. For instance, she simply couldn't imagine herself as Carmen and never sang that role, though early in her career she recorded some selections in German. Likewise, she couldn't see herself as that other temptress, Dalila. But once she was persuaded to accept an engagement to sing Dalila at the Met, she lost 80 pounds in the months leading up to the run. To her surprise, Rudolf Bing was not pleased with her svelte figure, fearing that the change in her body might affect her voice. He telephoned her and said sharply, "Who asked you to lose weight? Please put that weight back on."

But usually Bing defended her. Conductor Karl Böhm didn't want her to sing the nurse in *Die Frau ohne Schatten*, though he hadn't even heard her in the role. Irene told Bing,

> "You decide, because I'm going to be on the Merv Griffin Show and if I'm not doing *Die Frau ohne Schatten* there's no reason for my staying at the Met and I'd like to announce [on the show] that I'm leaving."… And I meant it. It was not an act on my

> part. I said, "I don't think it's correct for any conductor to refuse a singer before they've heard that person in the role. At least in a [rehearsal] room." I thought that was just plain unfair and I thought, I don't need the Met Opera. I had been there at least 10 years. Apparently Bing went and told Böhm, because I did the role, and with great success.

This story shows that not all the important opera people were collegial or easy to work with. One confident young conductor was perhaps too full of himself. At their first music rehearsal together at the Met, he told Irene to sing the cadenza in the veil song in *Don Carlo* in one breath.

> Apparently, he had done it with a mezzo who did it in one breath. But for a voice my size, it is not advisable. Normally, I would try anything requested by a conductor, but his attitude was unacceptable. Besides, this was not a new role for me. Then, further into the music rehearsal, he kept interrupting and criticizing. Just before the aria, "O don fatale," I told him that as far as I was concerned, the rehearsal was over.

So she left. By the time she got home, her housekeeper said that Bing had already called seven times. Finally he got her on the phone and said,

> "I have an irate conductor waiting to talk to me to complain about you. What on earth happened?"
>
> I told him exactly what had happened.
>
> He responded, "But he is a young genius."
>
> I responded, "Frankly, I would prefer an older, experienced conductor." I told Bing that obviously, this genius would prefer another mezzo and that was fine with me. I would be happy to be released

from that assignment. Bing did not accept that option. He even made the impudent conductor apologize to me. That was a big mistake. After that, the conductor *really* hated me.

Their working relationship did not improve. At the final dress rehearsal, because of the negative attitude of the conductor, she sent for Mr. Bing after the first act, for she had decided she would definitely withdraw from the cast. She was told that Bing was not available. In fact, however, he was behind the curtain waiting to escort her to her dressing room after her bow. When they got there, he refused to allow her to cancel, saying, "I won't let you. I want you on that stage. You're the best Eboli in the world. Do it any way you want."

Unlike this conductor, top singers appreciated Irene's artistry; Bing told her that several of them would ask him to put her in the cast when they were drawing up the schedules. Once she was doing *Don Carlo* in Berlin with famed baritone Dietrich Fischer-Dieskau. The conductor said, "Everyone else can go home now. I want to rehearse with Miss Dalis." Fischer-Dieskau snorted and said, "She can show *you* how to do 'O don fatale.'"

Life Among the Stars

One season Irene was in Bayreuth singing in *Parsifal* when she got a call from Robert Herman at the Met to invite her to sing in *Norma* with Joan Sutherland in two years' time. Irene replied, "Let me think about it. I'll get back to you tomorrow." She decided she didn't want the engagement. But how do you decline such an offer without offending management and perhaps losing future offers? Her friend, tenor Jess Thomas, who was in Bayreuth with her singing the title role, came up with a clever solution. He advised her to propose a crazy contract that was sure to be declined. He even helped her write it, putting in high fees and a guaranteed number of performances.

As Princess de Bouillon with Renata Tebaldi
(*Adriana Lecouvreur*), 1963

To their astonishment, the proposal was accepted. Later Robert Herman told her why: "Rudolf Bing said to give her anything she wants." That high praise was a mixed blessing. The offer was tempting, yet Irene still had reservations. Two weeks later she received a letter from Bing saying that no matter how hard he tried, he could not convince Madame Sutherland that Irene's voice was not "too big for the role." Chagrined, Bing had to retract the offer. Irene was relieved, with only one regret. "What really bothered me about this is that I had always heard from everyone how wonderful a person Joan Sutherland was. I regret that I never met her or sang with her."

However, the sequel to this imbroglio was gratifying. Upon her return to New York after the Bayreuth engagement, Bing summoned her. Expressing regret about the *Norma* incident, he said he would agree to those outrageous contract terms for as long as she sang at the Met. He said, "We've been taking advantage of you long enough. I want you to know that we'll honor the terms of your contract." Today she says with some satisfaction, "Because of Joan Sutherland turning me down, I became one of the highest paid singers at the Met."

In May, 1971, Irene joined some esteemed colleagues in a little prank. Tenor Franco Corelli was known for a bit of artistic cheating: during duets and ensembles, he would often stop singing a bit before the end of his part, saving his breath to hold a high note longer than the others to win extra admiration and applause.

> We were on the plane to Dallas to do *Aida*. I was sitting next to Birgit Nilsson. Halfway through the flight, Bob Merrill came down the aisle and perched on the armrest with a wicked gleam in his eye. Referring to Corelli, he said, "Why don't we prove to Corelli that anything he can hold, we can hold longer?" We laughed and agreed. So that night, every chance we got, we too left out a few notes so that we could hold the high notes as long as Corelli—if not longer.

Of course, this was contrary to the rehearsed version, and the orchestra had to hurriedly adjust. Conductor Fausto Cleva was furious. During the long applause after the triumphal scene and unseen by the audience behind him, he glared at the three of them and gave them a rude Neapolitan gesture.

Irene's choice of roles fascinated reporters, who always seemed to ask about it. In response, Irene would say:

I was a female Boris Karloff; I did all the heavies. Whenever I walked onstage, I went out to kill somebody or to see that they'd be killed. I always went out to make trouble.

I am destined to play villainous women. You name the mean, frustrated, vindictive, jealous, egotistical females in opera, and I've done them. But I wouldn't give up Kundry, Klytemnestra, Azucena for all the sweet soprano roles. I can really get inside these characters.

I like characters with strong personalities—the nastier the better. Once my favorite role was Dorabella, but now I can't imagine putting on a pretty dress and being sweet all evening. I think I sing a dream repertoire. My roles provide fascinating contrast, and include every facet of human personality, though I like any role which affords me a chance to act and provides excitement, drama and challenge.

Maybe my true self comes out. Or maybe just the opposite—that I enjoy hiding behind what I am not. But I only like problem personalities, the nastier the merrier. This morning I was practicing Klytemnestra at the Opera House—no stage, no orchestra—and I had a marvelous time, like playing Hallowe'en.

Whatever the reason, Irene was such a good villainness that at least one co-star was intimidated by her onstage. The great soprano Lucine Amara remarked, "She was always so impressive onstage! Whenever we did the confrontation scene in *Aida*, I

As Lady Macbeth *(Macbeth)*, 1962

couldn't help but keep my head lowered as she'd turn her venom on me. It was truly scary! She made me *believe* I was the terrified slave I was playing."

Being in high demand sometimes had its down side. Famed conductor Herbert von Karajan asked her to do the Mozart Requiem, but she was already booked. "He held it against me. I was also unavailable to do *Don Carlo* with Solti, and he resented it, though I worked with him on other occasions. The pity of refusing him that time was that it would have included a recording."

As Azucena *(Il Trovatore)* with Richard Tucker, 1963

Medea: The Role Written for Irene

In 1972, she had an unusual opportunity: to perform in the world premiere of an opera in a role that was written explicitly for her. Alva Henderson, a young composer, had been in the San Francisco Opera chorus when Irene sang the harsh stepmother in *Jenůfa*. He was awed by her performance and knew at once that she should sing the title role in *Medea*, the opera he was then working on.

Once Henderson got approval for his new opera from the San Diego Opera board, he had to convince Irene. She was not interested. "I am planning to sing Adalgisa in *Norma* opposite Montserrat Caballé. How could I consider anything else?"

Henderson sent her the score and some roses. Irene took the score to two voice coaches in New York for their opinions. Both said it was interesting, but incredibly demanding. "They told me what I already knew—that if I decided to sing *Medea* I would need to block at least six months out of my schedule." Still, she decided to do it. "It's such a marvelous piece of music and a great opportunity. I've rarely believed in anything as much as I do in Alva and this new contribution to the repertoire." A reporter asked why she took this unnecessary risk, and wrote:

> When you talk to Miss Dalis, she is natural, unassuming and radiates a considerable emotional warmth. You tend to believe her when she tells you, "I feel I'm at a time in my career when I can afford the luxury of helping a young composer. I believe in his talent and I believe in *Medea*. Doing this gives me a larger reason for being a singer than just singing."

Working with a composer was an entirely new experience for Irene, so she invited him to be her guest in her New Jersey home in July of 1972 so they could work on the score together. Irene laughs now when she thinks about the ordeal it was for two such strong-minded people to be in the same room. She discovered that to ask a composer to change or omit something he has written is like asking someone to kill his or her own child. He stayed a month and they hammered it out—with hammer and tongs, one might say, since each had firm opinions. Henderson commented on that strained collaboration: "The tension between Irene and me got so intense in New Jersey that I moved out of the house and stayed the rest of my time with friends in New York. I was young and full of myself. How impertinent I was!" Recently he said with a smile, "We almost killed each other."

The artistic differences were ultimately worked out and the production went on as planned. "When we actually met again for rehearsals in San Diego, she was full of warm friendship. We got on very well during rehearsals. She gave herself over to the rehearsals with all of her intelligence, instincts, experience, and talent. I'm grateful to Irene for having the faith to bring her star power to my first opera." They ended as friends and have remained so to this day. Henderson continues:

> The title role had been written as a virtuoso piece for mezzo-soprano, and ever since I heard Irene Dalis as Kostelnicka in Janacek's *Jenůfa* in San Francisco (1969), she was the one I had in mind. Her great, dark voice, intensity and stage presence provided a model of the voice and temperament for which I had been composing. I was impressed with her attitude. At a point in her career when she no longer needed to take risks, having been at the top for nearly twenty years, she was willing to gamble on a new opera by an unknown composer.
>
> Miss Dalis was growing more exciting in the part. Through her strong, broad-painted style, I saw the part coming to life with a wealth of theatrical craft and musical nuance.

In case you've forgotten your Greek classics, Medea was a princess who was abandoned by her husband; enraged, she killed their children in revenge. Irene told a reporter,

> This role is a tour de force, almost a one-woman show, following the Robinson Jeffers play, and with very little relief for the mezzo singing Medea. I spoke with Dame Judith Anderson about the difficulty I was having with the final scene. I had seen her fabulous and justly famed [theatre performance of] *Medea* in New York years before, so any words of advice were more than welcome. She maintained that she had the

same trouble with the play. But she said not to worry about it because "it works without too much fuss." She gave me a sandal she wore as Medea, and I must admit I had it hidden under my costume for opening night.

All the rehearsals (musical, staging, technical, orchestra/dress rehearsals) went well, but because there is very little opportunity for the Medea to rest, Irene planned not to sing at full voice for the final dress rehearsal, especially since she felt a cold coming on. Then she realized that Kurt Herbert Adler was in attendance. So she gave a complete performance, but it was a strain. Henderson wrote afterwards,

> From the moment she started her lines behind the great bronze doors—"Hear me, God! Let me die!"—I knew what Miss Dalis was going to do: give an all-stops-out performance. The voice from behind the doors was terrifying in its molten intensity. She was summoning every ounce of her energy, technique, experience and spirit. To a dark auditorium with a maximum of fifteen people in it she sang her heart out. I felt drained by her performance, overwhelmed with the realization that what I had dreamed about was coming to pass.

On opening night, November 29, 1972, Irene sang the premiere, though she was beginning to feel ill. After the performance, Henderson recalls,

> Barrages of flashbulbs kept firing. I was pleased that so many of the general public had come backstage. Above the hubbub Miss Dalis, not pleased with her final high A, could be heard in her dressing room repeating her last line over and over, singing high A after high A: "Scorn! Scorn! Scorn!" After nearly two hours of steady singing.

But her voice was suffering and she had to step down, from a role literally written for her. She had laryngitis. There was no way to sing around it and the cover took over for the remaining performances. Irene never told Henderson she had canceled many other opportunities in order to do his *Medea*.

Illness Cuts Both Ways

For performers, illness creates both losses and opportunities. Sometimes they are the ailing singers who must cancel, and sometimes they are the ones who step in to save a performance. Seasoned opera-goers have a sinking feeling when the general director steps out in front of the curtain to announce that a long-awaited artist is ill and will not be singing tonight.

During a performance of *Parsifal* in Bayreuth on August 10, 1962, Irene began to feel ill and knew she should not continue. Luckily, American singer Astrid Varnay was in the audience and completed the performance. Asked how anyone knew Varnay was there, Irene replied with a knowing smile, "Management always knows who's in the audience!" She added that leaving in the middle of a performance made this "one of the saddest nights of my life."

It could also have been one of the most frightening. The German doctor she consulted diagnosed pre-cancerous lesions in her throat. Naturally alarmed, she consulted her own doctor when she returned to New York. He assured her this was not the case, and indeed she sang successfully for fifteen more years.

Two of Irene's 29 Met broadcasts were last-minute replacements for indisposed singers: Eileen Farrell in *Cavalleria Rusticana* and Birgit Nilsson in *Macbeth*. The first of these was especially noteworthy as an example of sheer endurance. In the 1962-1963 season, Irene's Met contract began on December 10, and her first scheduled performance was *Aida* on December 26, 1962. It would climax a hectic season. Since September, she had

The International Star

sung two performances of *Don Carlo* in San Francisco, two concerts in Honolulu, her first Santuzza (*Cavalleria Rusticana*) in San Francisco, *Aida* in New York, *Don Carlo* in Los Angeles with the San Francisco Opera, a concert with San José Symphony, *Cavalleria Rusticana* in San Diego and Los Angeles with the San Francisco Opera, followed by five community concerts (Santa Ana, Stockton, Turlock, Eureka, and Cheyenne). She arrived in New York Friday, December 7, allowing herself three days of much-needed rest before starting rehearsals for *Aida*. Saturday morning she received a call from Mr. Bing.

Bing: Irene, welcome back to New York. How would you like another broadcast this season?

Irene: Like when, for instance?

Bing: Like today, for instance.

Irene: Today? Which opera?

Bing: *Cavalleria Rusticana.*

Irene: *Cavalleria!* Today! I haven't even seen the production here!!

Bing: That doesn't bother me.

Irene: But, Mr. Bing, I am not even on contract yet.

Bing: We will take care of that.

Irene: But I know you have a cover. Why don't you call her?

Bing: Of course I have a cover, but I want *you* on that stage.

Of course, I said, "Okay, I will do it" and was very soon on my way to the Met. The conductor was the great Fausta Cleva and my Turiddu was Barry Morell, who turned out to be the best Turiddu I ever had. Barry and I conferred for about 15 minutes. Cleva insisted I sing through the entire role with him, which we did in my dressing room. After going through the role, I saw he was frowning. I asked if there was a problem. He said, "Yes. You didn't make one mistake." I said I did not make musical mistakes.

With Rudolf Bing, 1959

This isn't strictly true. Irene remembers that once she entered on the wrong beat in Hamburg and once muffed a word in *Lohengrin* in San Francisco, singing "lebwohl" instead of "fahr heim." As it happened, for technical reasons that word suited her voice better than the original one, so she kept using that word in future performances. No one ever objected. At any rate, here's one review of this last-minute performance in *Cavelleria:*

The International Star

Singing Santuzza for the first time at the Met, Miss Dalis thrilled her audience with an appealing, powerful, utterly secure top register, and low organ-like tones that give the overall impression of a black, velvety orchid or a jet-black diamond. The voice is the epitome of oneness with the same depth and richness of her lower range in the top register and the top brilliance and alluring splendor on the bottom tones.

Then there was the *Macbeth*, when again Irene stepped in for a radio broadcast. In the Bing era, when a role was double-cast, one artist would sing the opening night performance and the other would have the radio broadcast.

For the 1963-1964 season, I was to share the role of Lady Macbeth with Birgit Nilsson. In the negotiations for my contract, Bing explained that there would be five performances of *Macbeth* and that he really couldn't divide the number of performances evenly and thought Nilsson should have both the opening night and the broadcast. I agreed without hesitation. After all, Birgit was a vocal phenomenon. When we left that meeting, my husband said, "You did not have to agree to that." I answered serenely, "If God wants, it will happen."

Birgit had a reputation of never canceling, so I was amazed when I received a phone call early on the morning of the broadcast, telling me she would not be able to sing that day. So I got ready, arrived at the theatre, put on my costume and makeup, and went on. At my entrance as the ruthless Lady Macbeth, I was greeted by a shout of "Viva Callas" from someone in the audience.

This rude behavior didn't throw me, because I had already entered the character and had no self-doubt.

For a production of *Aida* in Hamburg in 1968, Irene was ill, but management insisted, "You must perform." So she did, feeling strained the entire evening. She took her curtain call with more trepidation than usual, dreading the whistling that Europeans give instead of booing to indicate their displeasure. To her surprise, "It was the longest ovation I ever received." Still, it came at a price: She couldn't talk at all the next day.

A few years later, Irene was the healthy last-minute replacement when the scheduled singer was unable to perform. In a San Francisco production of *Elektra* in 1973, the Klytemnestra fell ill. One reviewer wrote:

> After the first performance, Miss [Claramae] Turner became indisposed and Miss Dalis graciously stepped into the role at the proverbial last minute, without any rehearsal at all and wearing Miss Turner's gown, which did not fit. But this reviewer still remembers Miss Dalis's shrewd characterization of this terribly difficult role, and the splendor of her voice.

Unforgettable

Among those who were fortunate enough to hear Irene perform was Ernesto Alorda, who is the current Community and Artist Relations Manager at Seattle Opera. He came to America from his native Cuba in 1960, gravitating to New York for its opera and symphony riches. Alorda remembers Irene vividly.

> On December 18, 1960, I attended my first opera at the Metropolitan Opera, a matinee performance of Wagner's *Tannhauser*, which also marked the

The International Star

exciting debut of conductor Georg Solti. Leonie Rysanek, Hans Hopf, Hermann Prey, and Jerome Hines were in top form. However, it was Irene Dalis, unknown to me at the time, who blew me away as Venus. There was something special about Irene on stage—unbelievable, bigger than life, with such magnetism. Not a beautiful voice but dramatic. You couldn't take your eyes off her, even when she wasn't singing.

A few weeks later, I saw her Brangäne in *Tristan and Isolde* with Birgit Nilsson and Ramón Vinay. After this performance I was hooked. I wrote a note to her asking to meet her after one of the performances, and she very graciously invited me backstage to her dressing room. There I found out that her husband George Loinaz was also from Cuba. I was very fortunate to see her perform several times at the Met from 1961 through 1964, singing Ortrud, Brangäne, Fricka and Waltraute in the Ring, Kundry, Azucena, Eboli, Amneris, Santuzza, Princess di Bouillon, Lady Macbeth, and Dalila.

In the winter of 1964, I was drafted into the U.S. Army, but was very lucky to be assigned to Heidelberg/Mannheim in Germany. I managed to see Irene in a couple of performances of an excellent production of *Die Frau ohne Schatten* in Hamburg in April, 1966. I did not see her again until 1971 in a new production of *Tristan and Isolde* at the new Met with Birgit Nilsson and Jess Thomas.

In 1973 in San Francisco, I saw her again in *Elektra*. She was an incredible Klytemnestra, a performance that I remember to this day. Irene also graciously helped singers in the beginning of their careers. I remember mezzo-soprano Tatiana Troyanos, who came to Hamburg in the 1960s, and a young soprano from Salt Lake City named Linda Kelm. Linda arrived in New York in the late 1970's, totally unknown and with very little money and no connections. I arranged for Irene to hear her, and she very graciously agreed. She recommended her to an excellent teacher in New York, Judith Oas, who took Linda as her student immediately at no charge, thanks to Irene's recommendation.

Her years at the Met brought many opportunities to work with the giants of her generation—including one she had known when he was a teenager. Thomas Schippers, a member of that student group in New York that filled out the Fulbright applications, was now a renowned conductor. In 1965, he was on the podium when Irene sang her signature role of Princess Eboli, in a dream cast that included Richard Tucker, Robert Merrill, and Nicolai Ghiaurov.

Reflecting on the 25 years of her performing career, Irene says, "I sang every role I wanted to." She had overcome her impostor feelings, was in demand, and was able to request and get good working conditions. It was a rewarding and satisfying life.

But on Christmas Eve, 1974, the high personal price of her career was felt again. Irene received a conference call from brother Chris and sister Marge, saying that their mother was in the hospital for a gall bladder operation. How soon could Irene fly to California?

She replied, "I have a broadcast of *Il Trittico* on Saturday and can fly out on Sunday."

On the morning of the broadcast, she called Marge to see how their mother was doing. The housekeeper answered and said, "Mrs. Dallas is not here. She is at the mortician's, making arrangements for the funeral." That is how Irene learned that her mother had passed away. Irene sang that day, but asked that no one come backstage to greet her. Fifteen-year-old Alida guarded her dressing room door. For the second time, she gathered her professionalism and artistry to sing through the pain of a parent's death.

Irene had special experiences a handful of times during her singing career. These were moments of extraordinary magic, when she seemed to melt into the music. She was always deeply immersed in the roles she sang, as those who saw her attest, but these moments were different. There was no way to predict when they would happen. It was as if the music was making itself. "It just happened. I didn't do it. I felt I was 'being sung.' I felt cleansed after. I never told my peers. I was in the role, not worrying about singing." Such moments have occurred to all kinds of people. Athletes call it "being in the zone" and psychologists call it "flow," meaning complete absorption and spontaneous enjoyment, and "peak experience," meaning a euphoric, other-worldly state. It's almost supernatural, in that one's sense of self seems to dissolve into the experience. These magic moments cannot be commanded, but those who have them never forget.

Still ahead for Irene was Opera San José, which she calls "my true destiny and most important career."

FOUR

An End and a Beginning

Rudolf Bing headed the Met for twenty-two years and was an invaluable ally for Irene. Now he was ready to retire. A huge gala was organized to celebrate his unmatched artistic and fiscal contributions to the company. On April 22, 1972, dozens of stars performed at the event, including Martina Arroyo, Carlo Bergonzi, Montserrat Caballé, Franco Corelli, Placido Domingo, Tito Gobbi, Robert Merrill, Sherrill Milnes, Luciano Pavarotti, Birgit Nilsson, Leontyne Price, Regina Resnik, Cesare Siepi, Teresa Stratas, Joan Sutherland, Renata Tebaldi, Giorgio Tozzi, Richard Tucker, and Jon Vickers. Of course, Irene was one of them. With Gabriella Tucci, she sang the duet "Fu la sorte" from *Aida*.

Goodbye to the Stage

After the gala, the Met didn't feel like home to Irene any more. In an interview, she disclosed how she was feeling by 1975:

> I feel my career at the Met ended when Mr. Bing left. I didn't belong there after that. I lingered, but I no longer had Mr. Bing. I barely knew the man,

An End and a Beginning

Jon Vickers, Irene, and George backstage at the farewell gala for Rudolf Bing, 1972

> but he believed in me, and I'm the kind of singer that needs that. I never had to call to ask, "What are you thinking about me doing?" They called me. I always knew it would be worked out, that I'd do the right repertoire, the right number of times.

Another factor that contributed to her decision to conclude her performing career was the gradual change in her voice.

> What happens to the voice [as you age] is that you start losing confidence. That part is true. The last time I sang Eboli—whatever season was that, 1969?—that was the season I thought I better kiss goodbye to that role. I felt the top was not as easy as it used to be, and not as good as it should be.

Having decided to retire from the professional opera stage, within a year Irene also made the decision to end her singing career altogether.

> In 1977 or 1978, I was asked to sing at the old St. Joseph's Cathedral for a San José State University scholarship concert. As we were driving to the concert, I told my husband that this would be my farewell appearance. At the end of the concert, I silently said good-bye.

Star of Stage, Radio, and Corner Office

What does an opera star do after being on the world stage for 25 years? If she is Irene Dalis, she immediately begins another line of business. Much to her surprise, the new career awaited and she didn't have to go looking for it—or even possess the usual credentials. Irene had once planned to be a music educator at the elementary level. She now received an invitation that led her to a very different type of school.

> Having heard that I was considering retiring from the stage, Dr. Jack Bunzel, the president of San José State University, called me in New York and offered me a full professorship if I would come back to San José and join the faculty. I said, "No, I'm a performer, not a teacher," but he persisted. "Come out for three days. Let *us* decide if you're suitable to be on the faculty." I thought, "Hmm, I could visit my family," which was a real inducement. I checked my performing schedule. At that time, after the regular Met season in New York, the company visited seven major cities on tour, and I happened to have a free week.
>
> For those who aren't old enough to remember, the Met tour was discontinued many years ago

An End and a Beginning

when the cities developed their own companies. This was really a sign of the success of opera in America, that more and more cities had their own companies and wished to support them. In June, 1962, at the Seattle World's Fair, I was in the cast that sang three performances of *Aida,* the first opera production in a city that would later develop its own world-class opera company.

So I accepted Dr. Bunzel's invitation and flew from New York to San José. I reminded Dr. Bunzel that I didn't have a Ph.D., and he responded soothingly, "Anyone with a career like yours has the equivalent of two Ph.D.s." Dr. Bunzel and Dr. Gibson Walters, chair of the Music Department, the person who had recommended my appointment to Dr. Bunzel, convinced

Irene at work in her new career

me to join the music department faculty at my alma mater. So I agreed. Unfortunately, by the time I joined the faculty, Dr. Walters had retired, so I did not have his support during the early years of my new career.

It's not unusual for a singer to move into the academic world. Every retiring Met star gets these invitations. I could have gone to one of the more established music departments in a prestigious university, but I wanted to help SJSU students. These people were working their way through school and really wanted an education.

SJSU organized a big fanfare when I arrived—newspaper articles, press conference, and so on. This did not endear me to faculty members who had worked for decades in the music world with much less recognition. I can imagine them thinking, "I've been here ten years or more and I'm still an associate professor, and here comes someone who has never taught a day in her life named full professor."

Luckily, someone who was at SJSU at that time, Arlene Okerlund, defended her. She writes:

> I first met Irene Dalis in the mid-1970s when I was Associate Dean for Curriculum in the College of Humanities and the Arts at SJSU. Everyone in the Office of the Dean (from student assistants to the Dean himself) anticipated her first visit with some anxiety and considerable excitement, since we were expecting a "diva from the Met." Instead, we encountered a down-to-earth, hard-working faculty member intent on developing the opera program at SJSU.

An End and a Beginning

> Irene's early tenure as a faculty member at SJSU was not always easy. The problem originated in the fact that Irene had been hired outside of the normal faculty review process and had not been evaluated by faculty committees. Some professors objected to her joining the faculty as a full professor, while they had spent years working their way up the promotion ladder. Others resented the prestige and fame that she enjoyed. After I became Dean of the College, I had to deal with the increasing resentment. In a meeting with members of the Music faculty, I pointed out that Irene's years of training and performance—at Bayreuth, at the Met—equaled their own struggles as faculty members.

Irene continues the story of her early years as a professor. Entering a career she hadn't expected, she began the transition from international opera star to professor, artistic director, visionary, businesswoman, mentor, raconteur, and magnet for talent.

> The new music department chair didn't know what to do with me, for I was adamantly against teaching voice. I was in Milan as a Fulbright student with full tuition paid at the Giuseppe Verdi Conservatory of Music and had the choice of any of the nine voice teachers, all former famous La Scala stars. They were charming and could give a good show, but they were not *teaching*. That is when I realized that just because someone has had a great career does not necessarily mean that they can teach voice. That is a very special talent … and this has become one of my pet peeves: too many people are teaching voice who should not

be doing so. I have heard too many remarkable voices ruined by "teachers."

In spite of this, I agreed to take a few voice students the first year. One was Helen Centner, who joined the workshop, then had a singing career in Germany, then became an arts administrator there.

During that first year, 1977-1978, whenever I had a problem, I called Jack Bunzel. You see, I was such a neophyte in academia that I didn't know you don't just pick up the phone and call the president of the university. I quit three times, but every time Jack Bunzel talked me into staying and promised that I would not have voice students the next year. My first year on campus was my last year at the Met, so I did a lot of flying between the two coasts.

Starting from Scratch: The Opera Workshop

I can imagine what happened while I was in New York when the new chair of the music department was scheduling classes for the next year and thinking, "What on earth can I do with Irene Dalis? She will not teach voice. I know—I'll put her in charge of opera workshop." Upon my return to San José, I received my assignments for the next year (1978-1979) and immediately went to the chairman's office and asked, "What is an opera workshop?" I found it consisted of a performance of opera scenes at the end of each semester presented by the more advanced voice majors.

"Where do you keep the sets?"

"We don't have any."
"Do you have costumes?"
"No."
"What's the budget?"
"Budget?"

So the opera workshop had no resources at all and was actually dormant. I took it over and revived it, and then went out and got the money myself. I wasn't intimidated by the magnitude of the task, because I thought to myself, "Anything I can do will be an improvement."

A good omen was that at precisely that time, Dr. David Rohrbaugh joined the faculty to replace a professor who was on sabbatical. David Rohrbaugh had received his Doctorate of Musical Arts from the University of Michigan in 1971. He apprenticed as a singer for two years at Santa Fe Opera, performing secondary roles (such as Bartolo, Sharpless, Colline, and Basilio) and covering major roles. He taught at Oberlin College and then served as artist-in-residence at the University of Akron for six years, where he regularly performed in recitals, oratorios, and opera throughout the Midwest. At Akron, in addition to singing and teaching, he developed an opera workshop, for which he conducted, coached the singers, produced, and built the sets. This juggling act made it clear to him that he did not want to continue to be in charge of the workshop but was most interested in being its music director.

Rohrbaugh was well aware of who Irene was and, indeed, had heard her sing. While in graduate school at the New England Conservatory of Music, he had met Irene in Boston, when she was touring with the Met in *Lohengrin*. His job was to hold back the curtain as she went out for her curtain call. When Rohrbaugh moved from Ohio to the West Coast in order to pursue his singing career, their paths crossed again.

David Rohrbaugh in the early years

Irene felt very fortunate to have him as a colleague who understood what she was trying to do.

> When he started teaching at SJSU in 1977, we shared office and studio space, and became well acquainted. I observed him putting together the initial opera scenes programs, conducting, and teaching voice and I realized he was a very good voice teacher and conductor. He emphasized clear enunciation—he specialized in pure vowels. Even better, he didn't force students to change their

natural technique. I recognized his skill by seeing his students improve and could easily pick out his students at juried competitions.

While helping Irene develop the opera workshop, he continued to sing secondary roles at the San Francisco Opera. However, Rohrbaugh says, "After three seasons with San Francisco Opera, I decided that my duties with the budding opera company in San José required too many time conflicts to continue in San Francisco. So my focus became the opera workshop at San José State University, teaching voice, and later helping develop Opera San José." Irene wrote,

> Fortunately for the university and for me, Dr. Rohrbaugh was later hired on a permanent basis. Because of his experience as a singer, professor of voice, and music director of an opera workshop, he brought the perfect set of talents to this nascent project. We became co-directors of the San José State University Opera Workshop and have remained colleagues ever since.
>
> He was in charge of music preparation and conducting, and I was in charge of the production. This was the beginning of an ideal working relationship which eventually led to the founding and development of Opera San José. David was an excellent singer, a great addition to the voice faculty, and had experience in directing the opera workshop in Michigan. I consider him to be one of the best voice teachers on the West Coast.

So now Irene had a solid artistic partner and was ready to take the next step—opening the doors of the workshop to see who would show up.

> When the university announced that we were taking over the opera program, the enrollment was amazing. Half of the students came to us through Open University (which was a vehicle for taking classes without matriculating) so they were older and more advanced than regular college students. We had so many students we triple cast the scenes to give everyone a chance to perform. Triple casts means triple the number of music rehearsals, triple staging rehearsals, and triple costumes! In short, triple the cost and the time.
>
> We started with one-act operas but gradually began offering full-length classics like *Madama Butterfly*, *La Traviata*, and *La Bohème*. I found that I really enjoyed stage directing, something I had never done before. The scenes programs were accompanied by piano, but the full productions required an orchestra. The university did not have one at the time, so I hired a faculty member to hire musicians and I insisted that they be paid. So even as a university workshop, we had a union orchestra.

Violinist Virginia Smedberg was one of those orchestra members and has been with OSJ ever since. She says Irene always respected the orchestra, knowing its value and coming to them in the green room before opening night to offer her appreciation and good wishes.

So now Irene had a highly qualified co-director and a professional orchestra. It was time to take the next step.

> It was very clear to me that to make the opera workshop more than a perfunctory class recital, I would need to pay for sets, costumes, and the other things needed for a proper production. I would have to raise money. I opened a bank

account and raised money by holding fundraisers, asking friends and family for donations, and calling everyone I knew. My husband George encouraged me to create a budget, so I started thinking about money in a systematic way.

Here's another piece of luck: someone coming along just at the right time. One day I was at the San Jose Museum of Art admiring the collections when a woman came up to me and offered to help with the Opera Workshop. That was Stephanie Drozdiak. In 1978 we created Friends of Opera, a 501 (c) 3 nonprofit organization. Evelyn McGrath (an educator who taught student teachers) took it over in the second year and organized the volunteers. Through Friends of Opera, we could hold fundraisers and submit grant requests.

From ovations and requests to sing in the major opera houses in Europe and America, Irene had shifted gears completely and was now engaged in the largest and the humblest tasks of getting tiny productions off the ground.

I found myself doing whatever had to be done: write grant applications, shop for lumber, shop for costume material, shop for props and, most importantly, stage the scenes, none of which had I ever done before. I discovered I just loved staging. Soon 75 students were signing up for the Opera Workshop. The first year we performed in a little studio theatre in the Theatre Arts Department. The "stage" was merely a platform at one end of the room, 18 inches off the floor. The room was filled with folding chairs. Tickets were $1.50. Despite this rudimentary setup, we sold out. Even Dr. Bunzel, who was not an opera lover, attended.

Of the earliest beginnings of what was to become Opera San José, David Rohrbaugh recalls:

> At the end of our first season, Irene mentioned that she did not know the one-act opera repertoire, crucial for an opera workshop with young singers. So I loaded my copies into the trunk of my car, drove to San José, and went to a wonderful barbecue at Irene's sister Marge's house. I spent most of the evening and well into the wee hours of the night discussing these operas and listening to recordings from Irene's private library. I left the scores with Irene, and she returned them after a few months, having studied them thoroughly. As a pianist, she had played through the scores and learned them well. These scores formed the repertoire for many of our first productions.

For the first five years, fundraisers were called Jubilees and held in private homes. Irene's family, ever supportive of her dreams, helped out. Some of them were in the restaurant business and supplied food and a bartender. But a lot of money and materials had to be obtained by sheer determination and audacity. Asked how she steeled herself to ask for money, going hat in hand to merchants to request in-kind donations, Irene replied,

> When I would see what we needed, I'd have to go out and get it. We had no staff. "I'm there with my tin cup" is not a comedown. The world doesn't end if the person says no. Just take the rejection and move on. On the other hand, some prospects would use the opportunity to ask about the workshop, and some friendships were started that way.
>
> I would get lumber and fabric donated. One year I needed a wrought-iron chandelier for *Gianni Schicchi*. I drove to the store, and before

An End and a Beginning

going in I sat in the car rehearsing the answers to 20 questions. What exactly do we need? Why do we need it? Why should it be donated? I realized I was worthy of their help, but I had to convince myself first. It was a bit embarrassing in the beginning to ask people for favors, but I really wanted to help emerging talent.

Of course if someone gave once, I would ask them again. I'd say, "Thanks for answering the phone, since you know I'm going to ask you for something."

The workshop students would pitch in, sewing costumes and building sets. I sat there with the workshop students sewing little pillows for *Chanticleer*, a one-act opera we performed at outreach events.

It took a while to realize I needed help—a staff. That was a good lesson. It's not my nature to ask for help. At the university, I had graduate students for my "staff." Years later, when Opera San José started, my first hire was a bookkeeper, and the second was my former graduate assistant, Larry Hancock. I depended on volunteers, who were mostly my students. I could only offer minimum wage, so hiring experienced personnel was not an option. One of the first administrative assistants was so inexperienced that I would write out my letters in longhand for her to type. The first time I did this, I drew a square in the upper left corner and printed "OSJ logo here." When the letter arrived on my desk to sign, I discovered that my new hire had drawn a square and typed in "OSJ logo here."

I did have some actual professional assistance. Two people were my anchors: an elementary school teacher, Barbara Barrett, and the university piano accompanist, Kim Plowman. Barbara helped in so many ways that it is difficult to name them all. Wherever I needed help, she could do it brilliantly, for she had been a theatre arts major at Stanford. She still is one of my favorite costume designers, and she was also my assistant stage director as well as our stage manager for years. Then there was Kim. She was the official accompanist for our opera workshop. Not only was she an outstanding musician, but she became one of the most enthusiastic members of Friends of Opera and was a major influence in our fundraisers and publicity.

This budding organization began to get attention from the media. To a reporter, Irene said,

> This company was really built by the singers. Back then, and for many years, our singers did all the work in staging an opera. They constructed and painted sets in their garages. They hauled them to the theatre, hunted for props, helped make costumes—they did everything. And during our earlier fundraisers, the 60 singers carried the tables and chairs, sold drinks, emptied the garbage—whatever needed to be done.

Where Shall We Put on the Show?

Things were moving along. Students and members of the community were pitching in. The next step would be a big one.

> Obviously, we needed a real theatre to perform in. I had heard about a spectacular campus, Independence High School, being built on the East

An End and a Beginning

Side with a 500-seat theatre, under the auspices of the East Side School District Superintendent, Dr. Frank Fiscalini. I told Jack Bunzel about this. He arranged for me to meet Dr. Fiscalini, who became one of the most important supporters of my dream to build a professional company. This was another stroke of good luck. Jack drove me to the high school to meet Dr. Fiscalini. It was awesome to observe these two executives negotiate an agreement which allowed the SJSU Opera Workshop to rehearse and perform in a beautiful new theatre at no cost to us in our second year. It was a great lesson in diplomacy.

We used the beautiful new theatre for a scenes program (several singers performing various scenes from opera) and then a full production with orchestra, a double bill which we repeated the next year.

I wrote my first grant application to the City of San José in 1977 and we received our first $10,000 grant. This was a lot of money for us, but I still had to raise more. I contacted the Musicians' Union in New York and received another $5,000, which was matched by Joseph Ritter, uncle of Tony Ritter, publisher of the *San Jose Mercury News*.

This enabled us to present our next production (in 1979) at the Center for Performing Arts in downtown San José. This venue has a seating capacity of 2,677. I concentrated on raising the money to make this happen: I called everyone I knew, asking them to make a donation. The set and costume shops of the Theatre Arts Department helped enormously.

Workshop production of *Gianni Schicchi*, 1979

There we were at the CPA, and quite frankly, we were good. We did two one-act operas, *Gianni Schicchi* by Puccini and *The Mother*, a one-act opera composed by Stanley Hollingsworth, who had been a fellow student of mine in the 1940's. We did this double bill four times a day during Arts Education Week for schools, plus one public performance. It was then that I had an epiphany. To develop into a seasoned artist, a young singer must have repeated performing experiences. As I sat in this large theatre, I said to myself, "This is crazy. I need to find a smaller theatre so we can do more performances." I started to think about having an actual opera company.

My original hope was to develop a company on the campus of SJSU, but there was no interest from the university community, and the theatre department had announced that we could no longer even use their theatre for a performance once every two years.

Then I remembered that upon my graduation from Columbia University (1947), I had returned home and given a recital in a small venue that was part of the Civic Auditorium, called the Montgomery Theater. Why hadn't I thought of that before? It was perfect for us, with a seating capacity of 529. At that time, no one was using it regularly.

Jim Reber was in the process of founding the San José Repertory Theater at the same time and wanted to use the Montgomery, so we collaborated with them. The San José State University opera workshop and the Rep started the same year in the Montgomery Theater. His was a professional company; ours was still a university program.

From Workshop to Professional Company

It's one thing to have a dream, but quite another to make it come true. Irene was now working as a professor, and while she loved putting on opera *workshop productions,* it was a different matter to establish an opera *company.* How did she make the leap?

> Workshop participants were responsible for giving me the confidence to start a company. They were very talented young singers: Helen Centner, Randy Cooper, Kathy Edgerton, Mary Elizabeth Enmann, Ron Gerard, Larry Hancock, Mary Linduska, Patrice Maginnis, and Brian Staufenbiel, to name a few. They are the ones who inspired me to establish a professional opera

company. I thought, "Just where do these singers go after they finish school? They are not ready for the professional world. They need a company where they can develop."

I thought back to the place where I had started performing. I did not start at the Metropolitan Opera, but at a small theatre in the small city of Oldenburg, in northern Germany, where I was able to hone my craft. In Germany, any city with more than a hundred thousand residents has an opera company. The Oldenburgisches Staatstheater was a beautiful baroque theatre that had survived the war undamaged. It had 900 seats, and the opera company offered eight productions a year. Symphony and operetta were also performed there.

So I had gone directly from a vocal studio in Milan to Oldenburg, where I had a two-year contract to sing leading roles. That's what we needed in San José: a place for gifted young singers to have repeated performing experience.

We went through several name changes. First, we were San José State University Opera Workshop, followed by SJSU Community Opera Theatre. Then I was called by a program officer from the California Arts Council and told that I should take SJSU out of our name if I wished to have support from the California Arts Council. By this time Jack Bunzel was no longer the president of SJSU, having joined the Hoover Institution as a senior research fellow. I went to the then-president, Dr. Gail Fullerton, who agreed wholeheartedly to the name change; thus, we became San José Community Opera Theatre and later, San José Opera Theatre. Still later, I wanted to name the company San José Opera, but there was a San José Opera Guild that supported the San Francisco Opera. To avoid confusion, we named our company Opera San José (OSJ) in 1984.

After a few productions, Irene stopped directing (though several people interviewed for this book said she was a superb director). She enjoyed working with the singers to devise dramatic scenes, but realized that lights, sets, costumes, make-up, and so on, are specialties that need knowledgeable staff. "I'm afraid I offended some people because I didn't realize that lights, sets, and so forth take so long to set up. I wish I had spent more time learning about these things when I was singing."

Building the Team

After seeing director Daniel Helfgot's student production of Lee Hoiby's one-act chamber opera *The Scarf* at Stanford University, Irene hired him as stage director and he became an integral part of developing this young company. Irene then received an unsolicited grant from the California Arts Council, for which she was to choose a student to tutor. The student would receive a small stipend. CAC assumed this would be a voice student, but Irene explained that she did not teach voice. However, there was a very gifted pianist in the opera workshop who had the potential of becoming a conductor. Irene was allowed to choose Barbara Day Turner as a student opera coach and conductor. Turner's first assignment in 1981 was to conduct Menotti's *Amahl and the Night Visitors*, and she became OSJ's associate conductor. She later became the founder and principal conductor of the San José Chamber Orchestra.

Irene was fortunate in her partners. Conductor and voice teacher David Rohrbaugh, who became known as "Doc," was the first. Larry Hancock arrived as Irene's graduate assistant and was a lead tenor in the workshop. His first meeting with Irene had been embarrassing, however. He extended his hand and said, "It's an honor to meet you, Madame Dalis"—to Jeanne Garson, a faculty member who was standing beside her. Still, after his audition he was offered a role on the spot and joined the workshop. Since he didn't foresee a vocal career for himself, he didn't bother reading the reviews that the *San Jose Mercury News* and even *Opera News* were publishing about this little West Coast enterprise. When Irene heard he wasn't reading his reviews, she asked sternly, "If you don't take your career seriously, who will?"

He responded, "But I don't want a singing career!"

This was news to Irene, who demanded, "Then what *do* you want?"

Larry acknowledged, "I want your job" (being a university professor charged with running the opera workshop). Unimpressed, Irene retorted, "And you'll be a charlatan like all the rest, telling people how to do what you've never done." That sobered Larry. Suddenly he realized there was a purpose for him to sing opera seriously, at least for a while. So he sang in the workshop for two years, doing five roles, concurrently performing in four recitals and various oratorios. He occasionally experienced Irene's unsparing comments. When asked why he was looking down while singing a particularly heartbroken aria, he said, "Leon is very sad, and I'm looking down out of instinct, really." She responded, "Don't trust your instincts. You haven't any." He got the message, making sure the audience could see his facial expressions as well as hear his voice, and later Irene would remark after rehearsals, "I never have to give Larry a note." (A note is a director's instruction to a performer to change or correct something).

After thirty years, Hancock remains at Opera San José, serving as its second general director as of July, 2014. If ever a general director was well prepared to understand all parts of an opera company, Hancock is. He has held most of the jobs one can have in opera administration: media relations director, artistic administrator, director of marketing, director of development, director of production, and general manager.

Workshop production of *Dido and Aeneas*, 1980

Barbara Barrett, who has college degrees in theatre arts, has also worn a wardrobe full of OSJ hats. In over 30 years, she has been a costume designer, stage manager, and artistic administrator, in addition to offering lodging for singers in her spacious home. Along the way, she has been Irene's sounding board, ally, and friend. Her latest duty is to create supertitles, the projections above the stage that translate what the singers are singing. This is not an easy job, since one has to distill long ruminations into crisp one-liners and capture complicated dialog in a few words. A three-hour opera may require up to 700 supertitle slides. Barrett recalls that the first ones, which she created while OSJ was still at the Montgomery Theater, were 35-mm slides created on a dot-matrix printer. Still, this task has its benefits. Barrett, who punctuates her conversation with interjections of "wow" and "cool," says, "The great thing about doing supertitles is that you can do it in your jammies at midnight."

Barrett is among those lucky souls who also heard Irene perform and willingly takes on whatever job needs to be done. In 1986, she was sweeping the loading dock at the Montgomery the night before the opening night of a double bill: *Suor Angelica*

(Sister Angelica) and *Gianni Schicchi*. When Irene drove up and parked her car, Barrett said, "I have to tell you. You're going to be upset. The program says SOUR Angelica." Indeed, Irene was understandably upset. But it was after business hours the night before the premiere. What could possibly be done? Irene immediately went straight to the printer's home (his print shop was in the garage) and demanded that he deliver a set of corrected programs—by the next day. With her combination of persuasion and determination, she got him to do it.

The decade of the 1980s was a time of fertile invention in the once-obscure California region that would become known as Silicon Valley. In 1981, a little shop called Silicon Graphics was founded. The following year saw the birth of Adobe, Cypress Semiconductor, Electronic Arts, and Sun Microsystems. Two years later came Cisco Systems. Irene's dream was another startup, but in the arts. The first tentative steps at directing a university opera workshop would gradually lead to one of the premier artistic entities in Silicon Valley.

Irene was a magnet for talent. During the early years of OSJ, Irene attracted a number of outstanding singers who could also act.

Patrice Maginnis had heard Irene lecture at SJSU before she retired from the Met ("She was mesmerizing"). Then she met Irene in person on a day when people were signing up to join the opera workshop. Not that she was applying for a place—Maginnis went on behalf of her voice teacher. Irene asked, "Why aren't you signing up yourself?" Maginnis explained that she had a serious eye condition and had been gradually going blind since birth. In a wry non sequitur, Irene replied, "That's okay. No one can see at the Met, either." This is such an Irene story: Instead of accepting an obstacle, she worked around it, offering solutions so that Maginnis could perform, urging her, "Just try it." Sure enough, Maginnis eventually did numerous leading roles at the Montgomery. Irene didn't worry about her vision and later told her, "You were one of my stars." Like so many others in the early years, Maginnis did whatever was needed. She went to

Irene's office one day, saying, "We need a truck to carry the sets to schools." Luckily, Evelyn McGrath, head of Friends of Opera, had a sympathetic plumber who donated his old van.

Humble beginnings—the first van

After a few years of heavy duty, this van needed to be replaced. Never one to lose an opportunity, Irene made a request at a speaking engagement at the downtown San José Rotary Club. Before giving her talk, she said, "When I appear before a prestigious group like this one, I'm allowed to make a commercial. We need a truck." Before the event was over, she received a handwritten note that had been handed forward from someone in the audience. It was from Glen George, who owned the biggest wine and spirits company in the area. The note read, "How big a truck do you need, honey?" That same day, she went to his plant and picked one. True to form, she dazzled him with her vision, and later he became chair of OSJ's steering committee.

In 1980, the workshop was staging Cimarosa's little-known opera *The Secret Marriage*. Irene wanted Maginnis to sing the leading role, Carolina. Conductor David Rohrbaugh had doubts that she, with her failing eyesight, could follow the tempo he would set with his baton. Undaunted, Irene put them in a room together and said, "You two work it out." So they did. Someone at SJSU suggested putting a Christmas light on the end of the baton. This ingenious idea was brilliant in conception but somewhat awkward in practice, since an electrical cord dangled from the illuminated baton. The technology was faulty, but it made a difficult situation workable. They ended up using the lighted baton during rehearsals until Maginnis had thoroughly mastered her moves, and then performed with a regular baton. This vignette shows Irene's attitude: rather than lamenting an obstacle, always look for a solution.

Edwin Stafford was an undergraduate music minor and business major at SJSU from 1982 to 1987. He sang in the chorus in 1984's *Die Fledermaus* and remembers to this day every show he did thereafter. He recalls that in her role as director, Irene was candid, though a bit alarming sometimes. She was strict: "One learned quickly to be professional, to be prepared." He credits her with teaching him the stage presence that has helped him in his academic and business careers. Ed Stafford came back into Irene's life years later, when he secretly plotted to solve one of her most distressing problems.

Barbara Swartz joined the workshop in 1982 and stayed for ten years, through its transition to OSJ. For her, Irene was the draw. True to Swartz's hopes, Irene expected a professional attitude on the part of the singers. Yet she was not intimidating and (amazingly) never talked about her own career. She was encouraging, knowledgeable, and never condescending. "She had this long-term vision and was always moving toward it. There was never a moment she wasn't working toward it."

Nick Lymberis joined the workshop a bit later. He was smitten by Swartz and, after outlasting her other admirers, proposed to her in front of everyone at an opera party. He recalls that some people were intimidated by Irene, perhaps because she could be tenacious if she wanted something different than what they wanted, and she could say "No" rather abruptly. "I was never intimidated by her because I understood her vision and single-minded purpose in achieving it. I also appreciated that she included me, an actor who learned to sing, in such an ambitious project of talented singers." Swartz Lymberis adds that in the early years Irene was very hands on, putting her stamp on every aspect of every production. Lymberis remembers that Irene attended rehearsals, visited the costume shop, and did myriad other things, all while handling the business side of the enterprise. Artistically, she loosened the reins a bit and let director Daniel Helfgot expand small roles, letting Lymberis do inventive bits of stage business.

All this time, Irene was here, there, and everywhere, conveying her vision. Wrote one reporter at the time, "Dalis crackles with energy. She's like a finely wrought coiled spring. Passion electrifies the air, even when she talks about house receipts, square footage, bills, and grant applications."

While they were building an opera company, Irene, her team, and San José opera lovers were also building the audience. The opera workshop had 75 talented singers, and their friends and families formed the core audience. On Sunday evenings the singers gave a recital of arias for free in the Palm Room at the St. Claire hotel. It happened this way: Steven Lin, who owned the St. Claire and the Bank of America building, called Irene one day and invited her to lunch. He said he wanted to help and would offer office space in the Bank of America building. Irene replied, "I'm not the type to accept this gift unless I can reciprocate. What can I do for you?" So he asked for the once-a-week recitals at the hotel. An added advantage was that this counted as additional performing experience for the singers.

In the late 1990s, Irene made the most of opportunities for attracting audiences and funds. To a reporter, she observed, "This area is undergoing a real renaissance, and we're part of it. These big companies are always expanding, and how would they get people to come here if we didn't have any cultural life? That is one reason OSJ gets a lot of support."

Operathon and Operafest: Fundraisers with a Twist

One year Jim Reber of San José Rep remarked to Irene, "If I had your company and those singers available, I'd hold an opera marathon as a fundraiser." Barbara Swartz Lymberis and Barbara Day Turner jumped on this madcap plan and created an opera marathon—the longest continuous display of live opera singing ever attempted. Not only could this serve as their annual fundraiser, but they might even get into the Guinness Book of World Records. They convinced Irene they could execute this quixotic proposal and feverishly made the arrangements.

In January, 1986, the first 30-hour opera marathon was held at the San Jose Museum of Art; 80 singers performed 300 arias. Irene was there the whole time. "As long as my singers were willing to be there all hours of the night and morning, I had to be there for them. I just pretended I was on a flight from Europe to San Francisco, via the North Pole." Unfortunately, one of the six videotapes made during the 30 hours was lost, so they couldn't prove their feat and didn't get into the Book of Records. But they raised money, built audience appreciation, and created some indelible memories. To this day, people tell stories about Operathon.

The second year, Operathon was held in the first floor of the old Bank of America building, and in 1988 at the Red Lion Inn. There was a definite advantage to holding a marathon in a hotel. Patrons Laurie and Mike Warner stayed the whole 30 hours. They rented a hotel room for their kids and went upstairs to the room for periodic naps and then descended for another round of arias. At 3 am, various bewildered hotel guests wandered in. History does not record whether they went on to become fans of Opera San José or whether they woke up the next morning wondering if they had drunk too much the night before.

In the 1988 Operathon, mezzo-soprano Mary Elizabeth Enmann drew the midnight-to-8 am shift. She had an ingenious idea. At her first appearance, she came onstage fully dressed. The next time she took the stage an hour later, she was wearing a bathrobe. An hour later she appeared in the bathrobe and curlers. Next time she added her faithful teddy bear (named Wotan) to her ensemble. Then, step by step she reversed the process until, at her morning appearance, she was fully dressed again.

These crazy events usually had a theme, and guests were invited to come in costume. Some attendees followed the Warners' example and rented hotel rooms so they could nap and change clothes as the evening became progressively less formal. A thermometer was used to keep track of funds raised. Singers walked around the hall to collect cash donations, singing all the while. Douglas Nagel, who would later become the first resident baritone, brought his own students to sing between 2 am and 5 am. Some of them later became resident artists themselves. One year a skit was performed at 2 am by members of Friends of Opera.

Inevitably, sanity set in, and the marathon was transformed into a more manageable two-evening fundraiser called **Operafest.** The first of these was held at the Red Lion Inn in 1992, from Friday 5:30 pm to midnight, and Saturday from 4 pm to midnight. Admission was free, but there were auctions, raffles, and prizes to raise funds to benefit the company's school outreach program. Operafest was a wonderful evening of music and a good way to befriend other audience members, those familiar people one sees at intermissions but never has time to socialize with. Unfortunately, after some years the then-board of trustees said Operafest wasn't elegant enough, and it was discontinued. But plans are afoot for new forms of revelry and ways to support OSJ. Operafest might even return!

Reflecting on the steady growth of her dream of creating an opera company, Irene is certain that the ultimate purpose of her singing career was to prepare her to create OSJ and transmit opportunities to young singers.

Fun at the fundraiser—Irene as a movie director, complete with beret and megaphone, Operafest, 2004

The reason I was allowed to have an international career in opera in past years was to help young people today. For twenty years, I was surrounded by the world's great singers. If those years were given to me only so I could look at my scrapbook in retirement, they would not have been valuable. Instead, when I see young singers develop their talent through our program, it's a greater satisfaction to me than anything I accomplished on stage. I'm ready to get on the phone again and ask for more money.

FIVE

The Little Opera Company That Could

ENTHUSIASM, AMBITION, AND SHEER TALENT FUELED the early years of rehearsing, performing, and managing the company in various locations around San José. How did this dedicated group of dreamers turn their workshop into a fully professional opera company with its own splendid performing theatre?

Working on the Art

Of course, the team focused on their shared love: the music and drama of opera.

Irene admires the composers' gifts and emphasizes the importance of understanding their intentions. Communicating to the audience is the prime goal, and it's important for singers to avoid the mistake of too much method-type acting, since opera acting is very different from stage acting.

In the 1980s, Irene occasionally invited her former colleagues to teach master classes to the singers or to have lunch with the Board of Trustees. They included luminaries Sherrill Milnes, Giorgio Tozzi, and Tatiana Troyanos from the Metropolitan Opera; Tito

Capobianco, stage director of the New York City Opera and later general director of San Diego and Philadelphia Operas; Robert Jacobson, editor of *Opera News;* and conductor Peter Mark.

In one of these master classes, a student asked Tatiana Troyanos about the fine points of doing a pants role (when a woman sings the part of a male character, usually a teenaged boy): "How do you walk when you do Octavian?" Troyanos replied, "When you put on the costume and look in the mirror, you'll know." Irene was impressed by this response. It was not an evasion, and reminded her of the time she called Otto Müller for advice on how to sing the "pianississississimo" (extremely quiet) passage required in the last measures of Mahler's "Das lied von der erde." Müller had replied, "It's an attitude, rather than a dynamic."

Rohrbaugh says of the early workshop years. "It was such a joy to watch the singers grow, to do bigger roles. Who would have guessed so-and-so could grow so much?" This can be a surprise, because auditions are still an "educated guess, with no guarantees." He and Irene would have continuous conversations about which singers to consider for roles and which ones to hire.

At the conclusion of almost all performances, after Rohrbaugh took his bow, he would walk back off stage and the first person he would see was Irene. Many times she had tears in her eyes, marveling at the level of excellence of the performance. The two of them would embrace warmly and then say, "Let's do it again tomorrow!" And they did. He adds,

> Our casting decisions have always been arrived at quickly and directly, as both of us have similar tastes and sensibilities about what quality of voice and interpretive ability we are looking for in a performer. Over the years, after hearing many auditions, we have developed our own version of verbal shorthand to evaluate someone's ability

directly and quickly. If someone picks a certain audition aria, we know that they may have picked that because it masks a limited top voice or whatever may be missing. We would either not consider them further, or we would request an aria that would reveal that potential deficiency. It was always an effective way to cast and answered a lot of questions.

It's continued to be a source of great satisfaction to work with a singer who may seem initially inexperienced. I work carefully and help them evolve as they try to figure out the process and mature into confident performers vocally, musically, and dramatically. It is a wonderful and very gratifying experience.

Of course, the philosophy was always based on Irene's firm conviction that the foundation of a singer's art is complete vocal security and knowledge of the score. In her own career, she never worried *how* she was singing, only about *what*. This includes two things: understanding the language and knowing what the other characters in the opera are feeling and singing.

Among the key players in Opera San José's early years were director Daniel Helfgot and conductor Barbara Day Turner. They worked tirelessly to put on one production after another and deserve credit for helping shepherd these productions to the stage.

By the late 1980s, knowledgeable observers were impressed by what Irene had accomplished. "To judge by this production of *La Bohème,* she and her company have already succeeded to an extent you would scarcely believe. San José ought to burst with pride over every one of these gifted young artists," wrote one reviewer in *Musical America* in 1989. Not only the singers, but also the repertoire drew praise. Wrote *Opera News:* "The OSJ repertory is eclectic and remarkably sensible. The company has produced Purcell, Cimarosa, Mozart, Donizetti, Verdi, Puccini, Johann Strauss, and Lehar. But it has also performed contemporary operas by Kirke Mechem, Bernstein, Britten, Hoiby, Pasatiere, and even a world premiere." The quality continued to grow. In 1997, OSJ put on Carlisle Floyd's *Of Mice and Men*. Among its reviews was one in the German opera publication *Opern Welt*: "The production of Floyd's *Of Mice and Men*, based only upon viewing it on a video, belongs among the most moving of all my operatic experiences."

Irene was a visionary, literally. She sometimes used a technique she called "white framing"—envisioning the solution to a problem and then surrounding it with the image of a white frame, as if making the image come true. She got this idea from Madeline Lorton, the star-struck teenage opera lover who had started the fan club newsletter. Lorton was now a close adult friend and urged Irene to take a class called "Mind Control and Dimensions." Though Irene was deeply skeptical of this New Age idea, she signed up and enrolled in the class. As attendees sat in a circle on the floor, the instructor told them to select a specific thing that they would like to see come true that very night, and then apply the white frame technique he had taught them. Snorting quietly to herself, Irene thought, "Fine. I create that Robert Herman will call me with an offer." She thought nothing more of this until, that evening, the phone rang. It was Robert Herman of the Metropolitan Opera, asking her to sing at the funeral of an important board member. Somewhat unnerved but intrigued, Irene attended the class the next day, telling herself that Herman's call was a fluke. Giving the technique one more chance, she thought, "Okay, I create a parking space right in front of the building." Since she was in New York City, this was a big wish. Sure enough, just as she arrived, a car pulled out, and she got a parking space right in front of the building on Madison Avenue.

Actually this is not some ditzy daydreaming tactic. Creative visualization is an established method that's been used by athletes, among others, to impact their own performance or the outer world by shaping their thoughts and images. Irene used white framing successfully for years and urged others to take the class. OSJ board president Laurie Warner recalls taking many walks with Irene around their neighborhood for exercise during the early years of Opera San José. One day, Irene needed $30,000 for the budget. Warner suggested white framing it, and the money showed up unsolicited within a week from the Ann and Gordon Getty Foundation.

Unique in America

As time went on, Irene's vision began to solidify. Her own experience as a young singer formed the template. "The bridge between voice lessons and major operatic performance simply didn't exist in America. This is a serious problem for new singers. You can't go from voice lessons or a university workshop to the Met." The resident company was the answer.

OSJ's resident artist program began in 1988 with two contracted singers: soprano **Eilana Lappalainen** and baritone **Douglas Nagel**, who were hired for a year at a time with guaranteed leading roles. Thereafter, when it was time to choose the following year's company, there was never a shortage of applicants. Said Irene, "When singers heard about our resident ensemble concept, they would contact us for an audition. In the past, we have had singers fly from New York to audition for us, on their own nickel." Serious aspiring opera singers realized that this would be the opportunity of a lifetime. Elsewhere, if they could find a paying engagement at all, they were considered apprentices and were lucky to get any onstage time, usually in very small roles. Tenor **Tom Truhitte** remarked about these apprentice jobs with major companies, "You're basically singing third coat-hanger from the left." Irene continues:

> A reporter once asked me why I didn't just hire established singers for our productions. It would

be much simpler merely to hire guest artists for each production, as other regional companies do. I blurted out what has become the guiding principle of Opera San José: "We don't import stars, we export them."

Opera San José is a resident company, unique in America, for a core of singers who are contracted on a yearly basis, renewable up to four years, and, in some cases, five years. It would be simpler to be a typical regional company and hire established singers for individual roles, but my desire is to help singers at the most important stage of pursuing a career in opera: the first years after they complete their formal training. Most of our singers are graduates of respected conservatories, prestigious university programs, and outstanding young artist programs. Many already have agents, so they are no longer "students." Actually, I believe a performer remains a student forever, for there is always something that can be improved. That is the exciting part about being a performer.

Artists at OSJ not only have repeated performances in leading roles, but they also have the advantage of longer rehearsal periods. This luxury allows them to develop a unique ensemble experience for the audience.

Dan Montez, who has since made an impressive career as singer, composer, and the founder and general director of his own opera company (Taconic Opera), recalls:

> Being the first tenor hired as a full-time resident was an opportunity I could never have imagined. Before Opera San José was around, singers would have to travel abroad for such a possibility. I

Dan Montez in *The Elixir of Love,* 1990

remember the weekly meetings with Irene Dalis that went on for years. I cannot tell you how much I looked forward to them.

As a resident artist, I received weekly coaching, went on television to do interviews, and worked with well-known conductors and directors. I learned more than most singers get in a career. In about ten years, I had done about fifty leading roles, thanks to both OSJ and the contacts I made through the company. I couldn't have imagined doing this without this kind of support.

Each resident artist at OSJ spends hundreds of hours in vocal study, learning opera scores, languages and history, rehearsals, mainstage performances, outreach events, coaching sessions, and career guidance. **Silas Elash** says, "The OSJ schedule is intense. You learn and perform four roles and perform at outreach events. Some people are stressed by this, especially if they are still learning vocally." But singers can make amazing progress and stretch themselves. Elash, a bass who was also given bass-baritone roles, now has performed 26 roles. This is a solid professional resume.

Layna Chianakas loved living in OSJ's apartment building, which she fondly called "an opera commune." As a recent arrival on the West Coast, she welcomed the opportunity to make friends in this built-in community. "I literally would not be where I am today without Irene. OSJ had great directors and coaches, and gave us incredible hours of stage time, where you can hone your craft in front of people. OSJ gave us every opportunity to be successful artistically." One day Irene pulled Chianakas aside and said, "Honey, you don't know how to take a bow." Chianakas was at first too modest to enjoy the applause she was getting and to acknowledge it gracefully. Having learned this lesson herself long ago, Irene continued, "You need to learn a good diva bow."

This is important. During a performance, the audience's feelings have been stirred, and they long to show their gratitude by applauding the artists and offering special acclaim to their favorites. This is what the entire company has been working for—the magic, trust, and intimacy when all the labor fuses and becomes art. A curtain call gives the audience the opportunity to show appreciation and release built-up emotions. Applause conveys an enthusiastic "Thank you." A graceful bow says, "You're welcome." Such fine points of performing are exactly the kind of thing one can learn in a year-long engagement.

OSJ orchestra violinist **Virginia Smedberg** says, "It's a joy to see young singers develop within a production, across a year, across several years." She especially appreciates this because she is a teacher herself. Like most opera companies, OSJ of necessity cycles through the most popular operas every six or seven years, but Smedberg likes this because she always discovers something new about each opera, even after seven productions of *La Bohème*. And she appreciates getting to know the singers, how they think, to know which ones tend to take a slower or faster tempo, and generally how best to create beautiful music with them.

Baritone **Daniel Cilli** mentioned that OSJ gave him four stable years. This was a selling point when he was first considering auditioning for OSJ, since he had already moved around a lot in his years of training. It also marked an inward turning point. "The conscious decision to no longer think of myself as a young artist in training but a self-reliant artist was the turning point that allowed me to take on such a substantial commitment as the OSJ residency." He adds, "It's a great opportunity for a person at the right stage." Cilli put his faith into action and recommended OSJ to two of his friends (Michael Dailey and Khori Dastoor), who joined the resident company and distinguished themselves in many excellent performances.

Tenor **John Bellemer**'s first contacts with Irene and OSJ were memorable. Upon learning from a friend late in the spring that OSJ had yet to find a resident tenor for the following season, he recorded an audition tape and sent it in, and a few days later his phone rang. When he picked it up, he could hear his own recording playing in the background! Irene invited him to come to San José for a live audition and he gladly accepted. His visit happened to occur during an OSJ run of *Rigoletto*. So he attended a performance. That evening, the tenor began to show signs of vocal trouble during the first act, and the other resident tenor could not be reached. At the first intermission, Irene turned to John and asked if he would like to finish the show, saying, "I'll put you onstage right now in costume if you know the role." As it happened, he did not know the role and so did not make his OSJ debut that night. The next day, Irene offered him a contract which would bring him to OSJ for three seasons that were very important in helping shape his career. He debuted many roles at OSJ and has done most of these roles many times since. He recalls, "OSJ gave me the tools and connections necessary to build a career. They took a chance on someone so young. It was a unique experience, with great colleagues, conductors, and

Mel Ulrich and John Bellemer in *Eugene Onegin*, 1995

directors." He is always ready to give credit to OSJ when people ask about his career path, and always encourages young singers to check it out.

Tenor **Michael Dailey** had received much encouragement as a singer but had little formal training. He chose OSJ to test himself. He certainly got what he was looking for. He fondly calls his time as a resident "Opera boot camp," and adds, "It was one of the best decisions I ever made." Not only did he get leading roles for years, he loved the way the audience gets to see performers who know each other and have developed artistic chemistry. "We all have something to prove, people on the verge of greatness giving their all." Of Irene he says, "She taught me what it was to be an artist."

Soprano **Khori Dastoor** agrees that the resident model allows performers to form relationships, chemistry, and connections. Dastoor wishes that the concept of the resident company would be established elsewhere in the U.S., for an additional reason that shows just how risky an opera career can be: In the opera world, you are paid only if you perform. Even after weeks of rehearsals, if you fall ill at the last minute and are unable to sing, you lose weeks of compensation. OSJ, by contrast, offers unheard-of financial security. If a singer is ill during a run and OSJ has to hire a substitute, the company absorbs that extra expense and pays the indisposed singer anyway.

Tenor **Michael Mendelsohn,** who is not a resident artist but sings smaller roles, has found that OSJ's reputation helps him land roles elsewhere, since casting directors see from his resume that OSJ keeps hiring him. "All OSJ productions are well realized, always high quality, with such dedicated singers. No one's along for the ride. OSJ is one of the best places I've ever worked." He especially remembers the *Madama Butterfly* of 2007. "That was not just another production. It rose to the level of art. It was truly different, beautiful, well thought out and staged. I was proud to be part of it."

For soprano **Cynthia Clayton,** OSJ filled those difficult years singers face after graduate school, while they are waiting

Cynthia Clayton in *The Marriage of Figaro,* 1996

to become seasoned and competitive in the music marketplace At OSJ, she got role debuts and gained confidence singing in a small, intimate house. She says frankly, "I learned my craft there." Now a voice teacher as well as active performer, she is especially sympathetic to her students' needs and wishes there were more companies like OSJ for them to join.

José Maria Condemi, who had recently arrived in the U.S. from his native Argentina, was hired as an assistant stage director for *The Elixir of Love* (2000). Suddenly the director left in the middle of rehearsals, and Condemi was promoted to bring the production to fruition. This was his first U.S. directing job and the beginning of his notable career—he has directed at San Francisco, Seattle, Houston, Lyric Opera of Chicago, Atlanta, and other companies, and is now artistic director of Opera Santa Barbara. Though he has work opportunities everywhere, he returns to OSJ again and again because of its sense of family, Irene's presence as "charismatic, a big mother," and the extraordinary resources OSJ provides for its artists.

Bass **Jesse Merlin** was singing in a production of Gilbert and Sullivan's *HMS Pinafore* when OSJ resident artist Joseph Wright heard him and encouraged him to check out OSJ. He auditioned and joined the chorus for a production of *Eugene Onegin*. Irene spotted him coming in for his costume fitting and flashed her million-dollar smile. As he was one of the featured dancers for the big waltz scene, she spotted him again and was impressed by his detail work on stage. After the show, she asked, "Who are you? I have my eye on you." She suggested that he audition for a resident slot. Young and largely untrained, he was unprepared for this challenge and did poorly. Recognizing his raw talent, she encouraged him to study with Rohrbaugh, which he did. A year later, after seeing him in a local production of *Faust* at another company, she asked him to audition again, saying, "I've had my eye on you. I think you're star material." The second time he sang more successfully and, at age 24, he was offered a resident slot.

Merlin performed fourteen roles at OSJ and says, "You realize what OSJ offers once you leave and enter the real world. Being a freelancer is brutal, managing yourself, your health insurance, and more. You learn the trade by doing. OSJ was invaluable and informed everything I've done since. The value is impossible to measure." After OSJ, Merlin went to Los Angeles to star in a hit musical that ran for a year. "There is no way I could have done it before OSJ."

Several former resident artists emphasized how valuable it was to have a professional home in the first years of their careers. They were thinking primarily of the exposure they got in many aspects of the art form and the priceless opportunity to perform leading roles year after year. Some also mentioned another advantage: a stable personal life. **Daniel Cilli** remembers making friends with his neighbors, planting gardens with them, designing a chicken coop for the urban garden Veggielution, and going together to San José's Friday night street fairs called South First Fridays Art Walk. **John Bellemer** had grown up in the military, living all over the country, and he appreciated the stability that the resident company program offered.

This stability can make a big difference in a singer's life. Reflecting on how hard it is for an itinerant artist to form and sustain intimate relationships, tenor **Michael Dailey** said gratefully, "I met my wife because of OSJ. It was the ability to be in one place for four years, while doing what I loved, that gave me the opportunity to meet someone special and cultivate a relationship." When they were house hunting in 2012 and found the perfect house, they included in their purchase offer a pair of tickets to an OSJ performance (and their offer was accepted). Chianakas says the same about the stability of OSJ and meeting her husband. In fact, some couples have gotten married after meeting within the OSJ family: Barbara Swartz and Nick Lymberis, John Bellemer and Sarah Blaze, Lori Decter and Joseph Wright, Sandra Rubalcava and Chris Bengochea.

Mezzo-soprano **Betany Coffland** is grateful that in her four years as a resident artist, she performed twelve leading roles, saying, "This is rare by age 34. It was the perfect situation for me. I never wanted to live out of a suitcase in a hotel." She recalls the OSJ apartment living: one could hear one's colleagues warming up their voices and practicing their roles. "They became my family. They'll always be part of my life." She gained an additional benefit: Because she and her husband were provided housing for those four years, they were able to save enough money to buy their first house. She learned many things other than the twelve roles: How to carry a show if you have the lead role, such as Carmen, and the other side of the coin, discovering you *don't* have to be the star and enjoying being part of an ensemble, as in *Così fan Tutte*. Another lesson was learning to deal with the different personalities of singers, directors, and conductors. These artistic partners also vary in speed and style of working (such as giving precise directions from the first day of rehearsals versus letting singers explore their roles).

Soprano **Lori Phillips** was not originally scheduled to be a resident artist, but came to replace a soprano who left suddenly. In her year at OSJ, she sang Rosalinda in *Fledermaus*, Cio-cio-san in *Madama Butterfly*, and the Countess in *The Marriage of Figaro*. Phillips says that her time in San José opened new possibilities; after a lifetime on the East Coast, she felt freer in California in what felt like a more open culture, realizing, "I can be whoever I want to be." She made new friends and lived with her sponsors Carole and Keith Yettick, who became like family. She made a telling remark: At OSJ, she felt there was no hidden agenda between singers, since all were there to learn and support each other.

Performing at OSJ confirmed to Phillips she could become a professional singer. Rohrbaugh cemented this conviction when he told her, "There's no doubt now. You'll have an opera career." And it came true: Immediately after her year at OSJ, she secured a contract with the San Francisco Opera and soon performed at

Lori Phillips in *Madama Butterfly*, 1996

the Kennedy Center and in Leeds (England), where she made her European debut in 1998. Since then, she has performed leading roles at the Met, Portland, Atlanta, Vancouver, Boston, Nashville, and many other venues. In August, 2013, she was covering the daunting role of Brünnhilde in Seattle's production of the Ring, when the scheduled singer fell ill. Without having a staging or orchestra rehearsal, Phillips prepared to sing the most challenging role in opera before a sold-out and very sophisticated crowd. Let's share the moment with those who were there, as told by the *Seattle Times* critic.

> When Seattle Opera general director Speight Jenkins stepped on to the stage just before the last act of *Siegfried*, the grateful audience erupted in applause. How nice! He came out for a curtain call! In their enthusiasm, the listeners had forgotten that almost the only reason a general director takes the

> stage is to deliver bad news: In this case, the cancellation of Alwyn Mellor (as Brünnhilde), who had awakened with an allergy attack that morning and could not sing. (Jenkins later said he had waited until the last act of *Siegfried*, the only act in which Brünnhilde sings, for the announcement, so that the audience wouldn't be thinking about the cast change during the two preceding acts). As it happened, the replacement singer was Lori Phillips, a company regular who opened last season in the title role of *Turandot*.... She did an excellent job of both singing and acting on Wednesday evening. Her voice is powerful and resonant, her stage presence unaffected and convincing.

The San Francisco Chronicle's music critic was even more enthusiastic about the second night Mellor was ill.

> Lori Phillips stepped in once again, and that in turn meant that between her and tenor Stefan Vinke, this performance boasted the single best "Brünnfried" combo the Stephen Wadsworth production has yet witnessed. Phillips sure seems like the real deal. She's got a big, tireless voice with enough color and clarity to do more than simply ride out the assignment; she brought pathos and emotional transparency to Act 2 and her Immolation scene was a forceful and canny response to the scene's challenges.

Opera maven and OSJ subscriber Heidi Munzinger was there. After the performance, she wrote,

> As soon as the last notes faded and the curtain came down, the audience exploded in a roaring standing ovation that seemed to go on forever and measured at least 7.0 on the Richter scale.

The Little Opera Company that Could

Finding a Home

But these great successes were in the future. Back in the 1980s and early 1990s, OSJ was operating out of various widely dispersed spaces, making it problematic to organize a production.

> We had sets on Brokaw Road, costumes and shop on Kiely Avenue and the Bank of America building basement, rehearsal hall in the Children's Discovery Museum, and performances at the Montgomery Theater. "To get the department heads together, we had to leave voice-mail messages all over town," says development and marketing director Larry Hancock.

"We were like gypsies," Irene recalled. Putting into practice her father's advice ("Own your own home"), she decided to stop renting and get her opera company its own buildings. First was a rehearsal space. The company held its first capital campaign in 1989 to build a rehearsal wing at the Children's Discovery Museum, which was not far from the Montgomery Theater. The goal was $250,000 for the rehearsal hall, but they raised $450,000. OSJ signed a long-term lease at the museum and had its first stable location.

Now what about administrative headquarters? Irene started poring over the real estate ads and found a listing for a building at 2149 Paragon Drive. This building was so large it could accommodate both administration and rehearsals. At this time, Frank Fiscalini was the president of the OSJ board and also vice president of the Children's Discovery Museum. Fiscalini arranged for the city's Redevelopment Agency to buy back the remaining four years of OSJ's lease, and the proceeds went toward the purchase of 2149 Paragon Drive.

This would be a wonderful new headquarters, where department heads could work and meet easily. However, important structural changes were needed: Although offices already existed, the rest of the huge space had to be divided into the set shop, costume shop, storage, and rehearsal spaces. One day, a couple who were OSJ patrons stopped by to see Paragon when it was still empty. Irene showed them around, describing the changes she planned, mentioning that she would have to arrange for a $350,000 mortgage. In a stunning demonstration of her power to communicate her vision for OSJ, soon $350,000 arrived in their bank account, anonymously. The renovations were duly made, and OSJ moved into its new headquarters. Having one central building was a wonderful change. This building housed the box office, administration, coaching rooms, staging rehearsal space, costume shop, set shop, board room, and reception area. Irene said at the time, "Now we have control; before we had 'surprises.'"

Irene was thinking about more than her own opera company. San José was her home town and she envisioned it having a thriving art scene. Theatre director Timothy Near wrote,

> Miss Dalis believed that all the arts should flourish in San José. She cared about the city. Although she always fought for OSJ, she also saw the big picture and was a real collaborator with the other arts leaders. It was at times a rough path, as there were so few facilities for the performing arts, but she always kept her cool.

Near became the artistic director of San Jose Repertory Theatre and was there for 22 years. She vividly described the use of the Montgomery Theater:

> Until 1997, San Jose Repertory Theatre shared the city-managed Montgomery Theater with Opera San José and a number of other community theatre groups. As we all clamored for time in this "town hall" style theatre, one might have thought Miss Dalis would have done all she could to elbow me out. This was not the case *at all*. Irene welcomed

me, and we had many a lunch at Eulipia Restaurant as we figured out how to share the space.

The ceiling and walls of the Montgomery were basically white, and so it was impossible for us to get a good blackout. Light bounced all over the place. I was nowhere near the generous collaborator that Irene was, and I arranged for a company to come in and paint the theatre dark brown. I wanted it to be black, but I thought brown was a compromise.

Our designers were delighted, as we finally could light a show properly. Irene was horrified and felt I had made the theatre gloomy. We had also put heavy curtains in the multiple entrances into the theatre to cut down on noise and dampen the echo of the space. This, too, was awful for opera. Looking back on it, considering how I was plunging forward in a way that might have seemed bullheaded, Irene was amazingly patient and calm. She removed the curtains from the entrances when the opera was in there and put them back in at the end of their run. She expressed her disappointment in how I had made the theatre dark, but she never expressed anger to me. I think she is a great leader and understood my ambition for my company and honored that, because she knew that I was trying to raise the quality of our work. Irene had the big picture of the arts community in her vision, and she wasn't going to let brown paint ruin our relationship.

When San José Rep began our lobbying with the city to help us build a new theatre, there were many, many public city council meetings where I and the Rep board of trustees spoke of our theatre's needs and painted the vision of a world-class city with multiple world-class arts facilities. Miss Dalis was at every single one of those meetings. She often expressed her support for our theatre and lobbied energetically for the city to give us land and support the building of a new theatre. I am forever grateful for her collaboration on this monumental project. All along the way, I enjoyed her feisty sense of humor about the uphill battles we all faced as arts organizations.

Housing for the Artists

Now Irene thought of another real estate venture: apartment buildings where resident artists would live while they were under contract with OSJ. In 1997, she saw a likely eight-unit building on 15th Street one Wednesday and told the board about it the next day at their regular monthly meeting. One board member, who clearly did not have Irene's kind of decisiveness, said, "How can you bring up a topic that we didn't discuss in the executive meeting on Tuesday?" Her answer: "I just heard about it yesterday!" At the time, one could not view the interior of the apartment house without making a bid on it first. She was only asking the board to allow her to make a bid (which could, if necessary, be withdrawn). Ultimately, the 8-unit building was purchased. Now OSJ could make their singers' contracts even more tempting by including rent-free housing.

In 1999, a 6-unit apartment building was offered for sale, and Irene convinced the realtor to permit prospective buyers to go through the building before making a bid. She took two executive committee members with her to view the building. Happy with what they saw, the three made an offer. Because OSJ's offer was for cash, it was accepted over higher bids.

Building the Audience

Now they had the artistry, the facilities, and a modest but growing audience base. With more people buying tickets, the company could offer more performances. This was a wonderful gift to the singers, since mastery of a role increases with every performance.

Raiders of the Lost Aria. The task of building the audience was helped by an ebullient cluster of young people who called themselves the Raiders of the Lost Aria. During the 1980s, dozens of them formed an opera group, whose agenda included a lot of dating and partying. They would reserve most of the orchestra seats, share dinner before the performance, and party afterwards till the wee hours. Tony Piazza, San José's deputy district attorney, was the leader of this gang and his friends called him "Mr. Opera." He would actually chat up strangers in bars to get members for his group. Piazza acquired almost 150 subscribers for the Montgomery. Then came the Raiders fundraisers. Piazza told a reporter,

> Even the first one was a big success. We hired three bands—a Hawaiian band, a 26-member group, and a rock-and-roll band.... I think it's easier to introduce people to opera with a party. After they hear a few arias in the middle of eating good food and having fun, it isn't scary any more. When I tell them, "That's opera," they like it.

Friends of Opera. This group of volunteers was crucial to OSJ's early years as an opera workshop and fledgling company, and lasted until the late 1980s. The volunteers did mailings, made telephone calls, helped organize the fundraisers—whatever was needed to enhance public appreciation of opera and support the company itself.

Subscriptions. Subscribers are highly valued members of any performing arts organization, providing a dependable source of income as well as the foundation of the audience. In the first year season tickets were offered (in 1978-1979 when the opera workshop was doing two productions with two performances each), there were 79 subscribers. This number grew to a high of 5,566 in the year 2006-2007, before the economic downturn. The recently revitalized auxiliary, Friends of Opera San José, helps new friends discover OSJ and the turnaround in subscription numbers has already begun.

School Outreach. To inspire new generations of opera lovers, OSJ has taken opera to the schools since 1979. *Let's Make an Opera* was a charming school program OSJ ran from 1984 to 2010. It was the brainchild of Larry Hancock and Barbara Day Turner. Using existing opera music, the kids would devise their own plot and lyrics, with guidance from the resident artists, who would also serve as the producers, directors, and conductors. After an approximately six-week period of creating and rehearsing, this 20-minute show would be performed by the children once in the daytime for the school and once in the evening for parents.

One current program is the 45-minute mini-opera *Billy Goats Gruff*, based on a classic fairy tale. In the 2012-2013 year, it was given 47 times to a total of 12,837 children and school staff members. The librarian at the Cupertino Public Library wrote in appreciation, "The children loved the performance! One child commented afterwards, 'I wish there was more!' The children were quiet and attentive throughout the entire performance—we know that is a sign that it was excellent and that they enjoyed it." A short version of *Hansel and Gretel* was performed 55 times in the 2010-2011 year, to over 14,000 attendees. All told, between 1979 and 2013, over 2,850 K-12 school performances were given, reaching a total of 809,343 children.

Another program is the *Master Class*, when resident artists teach older students, focusing on breathing, technique, and diction. Wrote Maggie Schwartz of the Stratford School,

The Opera San José visit at our school was amazing. I cannot thank you enough for a truly life-changing experience for our drama students. Rebecca and Zach were natural teachers. Their feedback and validation were so positive. The students showed immediate improvement in performance and confidence. I can honestly tell you that our students will never forget the experience. So, I am sending one huge *thank you* to Opera San José for an incredible master class.

Students from middle schools and high schools are also invited to attend final dress rehearsals without charge. This gives them a chance to see a complete opera, and gives the company one last opportunity to polish the production in front of a real audience.

How to Discover an Opera Singer

All over America and overseas thousands of young people fall in love with opera and dream of making it their life's calling. They face a whole infrastructure of lessons, vocal competitions, and graduate degrees—even before auditioning for a single professional role. All this amounts to a gauntlet, or a set of opportunities, according to one's viewpoint. How do all these people find OSJ? And how does OSJ find them?

To identify a singer skilled enough to become a resident artist, one could call an agent or look through a photo book of headshots and request an audition recording. Instead, Irene and Rohrbaugh conduct live auditions and meet the applicants in person. This is especially important since OSJ offers an ongoing contract for multiple productions.

Bass **Kirk Eichelberger** came up through the traditional opera pathways, getting his bachelor's and master's degrees in vocal performance and entering prestigious competitions. He won the 1999 MacAllister Awards for Opera Singers and in 1999 was a national finalist in the prestigious Metropolitan Opera National Council Auditions. At OSJ, Eichelberger sang many of opera's signature bass roles, including Leporello (*Don Giovanni*), Daland (*The Flying Dutchman*), Don Pasquale (*Don Pasquale*), Ferrando (*Il Trovatore*), Reverend Hale (*The Crucible*), and Mephistopheles (*Faust*). Eichelberger says of Opera San José, "It was extremely important in the development of my artistry. The great contribution was constant stage time, working with different directors and styles. OSJ gave me as a gift my first outing in the two biggest roles of my career—Mephistopheles and *Trovatore*'s Ferrando." Eichelberger has appeared in leading roles at companies throughout the U.S. and has an impressive 51 roles in his repertoire, plus an active recital career. Recalling his working relationship with Irene, Eichelberger adds, "Miss Dalis really believes in her singers. She told me, 'I'm the president of your fan club. If anyone can do this, you can.' She believed in me."

Scott Bearden and Kirk Eichelberger in *The Barber of Seville*, 2006

Yet there is the occasional rare discovery outside these regular opera channels. You've heard the expression "A star is born" to signify the struggling unknown performer who becomes an overnight sensation. But have you heard "A star is discovered at his daughter's music lesson"? That was the origin of bass **Silas Elash**'s opera career. He had been a proper Silicon Valley electrical engineer for many years when his young daughter tried out for the role of Dorothy in her middle school production of *The Wizard of Oz*. To help her chances, Elash took her to a local voice teacher, where the girl boasted, "My dad really has a pretty good voice. You ought to hear him." The 46-year-old Elash duly sang a few scales and impressed the Juilliard-trained soprano. At her encouragement, he began taking lessons and eventually singing for fun in restaurants and amateur productions. (P.S. His daughter got the role).

The next step is told by reporter Richard Scheinin: "Laid off by Sun Microsystems in 2004, Silas Elash did what any self-respecting chip designer would do. He became an opera singer." And an unusual one—beginning to sing professionally in one's 50s is almost unheard of. He didn't even know how to read music. But he did have an unusual advantage: His voice was admirably rich and mature, yet it was fresh, not worn from years of rehearsing and performing.

To continue the theme of luck that runs throughout this book: One evening Elash was performing at a concert in Palm Springs, belting out Verdi arias and pop standards like "Brother, Can You Spare a Dime?" In the audience was retired Metropolitan Opera baritone Norman Mittelmann. Back in 1961, when Mittelmann made his San Francisco Opera debut in *Lohengrin*, who was on the stage singing the villainess Ortrud for the first time but ... Irene Dalis. Mittelmann's career at the Met overlapped hers for years, and they stayed in touch. So after hearing Elash at this concert, he called her with the news: He had discovered a voice she just had to hear. So it was arranged.

"Where are you from?" Dalis asked in amazement when she first heard him sing. "San José? How come I've never heard of you?" Elash responded, "I've spent the last five years in the vocal studio." He added, "One of my dreams is to some day sing with an orchestra." He got the gratifying reply, "We might be able to help with that."

After making this memorable first impression, Elash was welcomed into the OSJ family. Irene continues, "Silas joined the chorus. When I heard the voice, I was totally impressed. I realized that he could not read music, so we arranged for special tutoring. He had to learn how to count and how to follow a conductor. That took two years before we offered him a residency. His progress has been remarkable." It has been well-earned progress. Bruce Olstad, who was OSJ's chorusmaster when Elash arrived, said, "Most people go through a lifetime of learning how to do this, and Silas has kind of shrunk the whole process down." Olstad was also one of Elash's vocal coaches for years and adds, "Silas probably works harder than any singer I've ever met. He eats, sleeps, and drinks this stuff." Irene emphasized how special he was.

> For him, I went to the board of trustees and asked that we eliminate one word from our mission statement. Where it said we would help "young emerging artists," we eliminated the word "young." This makes sense, for dramatic voices develop later than light, lyric voices.

After becoming a member of the resident company in 2008, Elash successfully tackled famous bass roles such as Scarpia, Don Magnifico, Dr. Bartolo, Prince Gremin, and Mephistopheles. Mentioning the coaching, the housing, and all the other resources that go along with being a resident artist, Elash says emphatically, "I would not be an opera singer without Opera San José. Opera San José was my university." Unlike many aspiring singers, Elash had no bachelor's or master's degree in music. "Miss Dalis had faith in me when no one else did."

Silas Elash in *The Elixir of Love*, 2008

Finding the most promising singers involves attending other companies' productions, tapping one's painstakingly built network of colleagues, listening to recommendations from current resident artists, and holding auditions. Irene once told a reporter, "We have our spies all over America—outstanding colleagues of mine—and they won't recommend a singer to me who just gets up and sings all these wonderful tones all the time but has nothing to express and doesn't have the ability to interpret." Such singers would not make the cut, because expressing and interpreting the character are the heart of OSJ.

As the next chapter will show, these searches turned up many talented singers who would go on to seed the opera world all over America and abroad.

SIX

We Don't Import Stars— We Export Them!

BRILLIANTLY TALENTED SINGERS ARRIVED EVEN BEFORE BOSJ was created. Back in the workshop days, Bill Erlendson, whose father had been Irene's piano teacher many years before, was teaching music at San José High School. He discovered a wonderful young talent and urged her to sing for Irene. The appointment was made. **Eilana Lappalainen** (the name is of Finnish origin) was originally a violinist. Not having had much vocal training, Eilana sang an aria she had memorized from a recording. Irene recalls, "There on my doorstep was this gorgeous girl. She sang for me and I said, 'You need to have a voice teacher.'" Remember, for Irene this was not a criticism but a sign that she had just heard raw talent worth developing. She sent Eilana to David Rohrbaugh to begin her vocal education. She enrolled in the SJSU opera workshop and became a very important member.

How important was she? Eilana was a stalwart leading soprano, singing principal roles during four years in the opera workshop, making such an impression with her talent and work

We Don't Import Stars—We Export Them!

Eilana Lappalainen and Anooshah Golesorkhi
in *The Barber of Seville*, 1988

ethic that she was selected as the first resident artist hired by Opera San Jose. As was made evident by her subsequent international career, OSJ had struck gold in its very first choice.

Irene directed her in *La Traviata*, and Lappalainen was a bit nervous. "I never thought I could memorize so many words." Irene was patient and sympathetic about this, but finally said,

"Okay, you have ten minutes in the back of the room to learn today's lines." She did it. At 22, she was cast as Butterfly. By this time, there were two casts for every production, and all the other singers were older. But Lappalainen was the perfect trouper. When the other sopranos, including the covers, got sick, she asked if she could do all the shows. Irene agreed, "as long as you live downtown." So Lappalainen moved into Barbara Barrett's informal Opera Boarding House and sang all five performances in the run. Including outreach programs, Lappalainen performed about 30 leading roles in her time at the workshop and OSJ, and says, "She gave me a foundation to start my life. Miss Dalis guided but did not control me. She let me spread my wings. You can't really have a career without a community. OSJ was a complete family for me."

Along the way, Lappalainen also tried musical theatre, but realized it wasn't enough. Toward the end of this phase, she was singing musical comedy songs at an outdoor event at the Santa Clara County fairgrounds. She was mortified when she ran into Irene afterwards. They were standing under a tree. Irene fixed her with a firm glare and said, "How much are they paying you? How much can I pay you to stop this? You're very good at this, but today you have to choose." Petrified but certain of her path, Lappalainen cried, "I choose opera."

Now the resident artist program doesn't allow the singers to have other jobs, except when they are formally released to accept outside opportunities. Lappalainen did want to explore the rest of the opera world, and she paid her own way to go to New York once a month and to Europe in the summer. In an echo of Irene's silent promise to herself in 1951 as her ship sailed to Europe, Lappalainen recalls, "I vowed I wouldn't leave OSJ until I had an international career." And sure enough, the year she left OSJ, she made her international debut in Mexico City and sang in five other countries. Then for fourteen years, she had Fest contracts in Germany. (Remember that such Fest contracts were the original model for OSJ). Lappalainen has sung leading roles at Carnegie Hall, Seattle Opera, New York City Opera, La Scala, San Francisco Opera, and many other opera companies around the world.

> What I had from Irene was the best. Every step was important—I can't imagine what I would have done without her foundation. She was definitely my support. She even interviewed my boyfriend. I trusted everything she said. I'm honored to know a star of the golden age of opera.

For her part, Irene remembers: "Eilana showed up at my door at age 17, sent by Bill Erlendson of San José Unified School District. In the workshop, Eilana sang everything. She never said no. Even though she doesn't play the piano, she can learn a role in less than a week. She is a musical genius." After four years in the opera workshop, she was one of the first two resident artists to be hired by OSJ. She stayed four more years and immediately began an international career. OSJ had exported its first star.

Creating an Opera Singer

So how does the resident company turn promising emerging talents into exportable stars? By honoring all aspects of the art form, and polishing the performers' skills in each one. Opera singers need many talents. The most basic element, the anatomy of the vocal cords, is part of the package they got at birth. Then they must have passion for the drama inherent in operatic music and the willingness to endure the grueling training in the things that can be taught: correct breathing, foreign languages, how to move onstage.

Work Ethic. Truly great artists never quit learning and aspiring. Irene says, "The wonderful thing about being a performer is that you can always improve. And you're only as good as your

Michael Dailey in *The Elixir of Love*, 2008

last performance." This sentiment is shared by artists in related fields. Legend has it that one day pianist Artur Schnabel was discovered practicing, even though he was already world-famous and in great demand on the concert stage. Asked why on earth he was practicing at this stage of his career, he responded simply, "I think I'm making progress."

Opera is the complete art form, so its performers must be versatile and hardworking. Training the voice, memorizing the roles, learning the blocking (movements), practicing extra skills like fencing, and then auditioning, rehearsing, going to costume fittings, fulfilling publicity requirements—it's endless. For the dedicated singer, that's part of the joy. But no matter how much one may yearn to be a professional opera singer, one may not always be feeling his or her best when the performance date arrives. That's when an ingrained work ethic takes effect. Tenor Michael Dailey credits OSJ with teaching him to perform successfully when he doesn't feel at the top of his form. This is the kind of professionalism that stands an artist in good stead throughout his or her career.

The Gypsy Lifestyle's Costly Glamour. It may sound glamourous, traveling around the country or around the world, being put up in a hotel and driven here and there, singing to great applause, and receiving a handsome check at the end of each engagement. The reality is not all glamour. Even in the best of circumstances, living in hotels, a month or two here and then there, means being away from home, away from loved ones—or hampered in the search to find a loved one or to start a family. The glamour comes with a cost. Irene said, "It may seem glamourous to have your own cook and housekeeper, as we did when I was at the Met, but it made Alida feel different from other kids. There were times I resented it too. I missed so many family weddings and even funerals."

Physical Stamina and Agility. Once upon a time, an opera singer could simply stand on stage and sing, a style fondly (or not so fondly) remembered as "park and bark." Nowadays, though, opera singers are expected to act, to move, to dance or wield a sword convincingly, to represent their characters in their full range of living actions. To the audience, this is a blessing. To the singers, it's an additional job requirement.

And for those operas and roles that are really long, such as Siegfried, a singer must have physical and vocal stamina. It's no accident that any man who can sing Wagner's major roles is called a heldentenor (heroic tenor). Bass Silas Elash declares frankly that a singer is an athlete. Daring production ideas that call for singers to run up and down ladders or tiptoe along the edge of the orchestra pit while reaching for high notes can veer dangerously close to an occupational hazard. So the singer must also take care of his or her body.

On top of all this, a singer fears falling ill. Imagine spending years building your skill, your network, your reputation, finally landing a coveted role in a major production—and then coming down with laryngitis during dress rehearsal and being replaced.

Healthy Ego. Ego strength is a group of traits, such as a sense of identity, the ability to accomplish goals, the right kind and amount of self-esteem, and the capacity to take criticism and bounce back from disappointments. In the opera profession, the top singers have an endless series of engagements with an ever-changing cast of colleagues, and those in the middle face an endless series of auditions. There is ample opportunity for disappointment.

Tenor Michael Mendelsohn, who has sung numerous supporting roles at OSJ, says his confidence fluctuates. "You're constantly opening yourself up to hurt and failure and disappointment over and over again. The career involves tons of rejection." How does one deal with that? Mendelsohn responds, "Love the music, the singing, the challenge of learning new difficult things. Also, you have to learn to shake the dust from your shoes. Go to an audition, then just put it out of your mind. If they call you, that's extra." He admits this is hard to do. "You can't take it personally, but you always take it personally."

This confidence must not be self-aggrandizing. Opera is a collaborative art. Hundreds of people are involved—the singers, orchestra members, set and costume crews, stagehands, administrators, and more. A diva (or divo) who puts on airs and makes life difficult for others may have a career for a while, but ultimately he or she gets a reputation, and the phone will stop ringing and the contract offers will stop coming. Irene comments, "Arrogance is usually a coverup for insecurity." One can be sympathetic to the insecure person, but the impresario must think of the production and the audience.

One trait that contributes to a healthy ego is the awareness that one's talent is a gift. A singer can't take credit for being born with the basic vocal equipment. There's also the luck factor, such as Irene's German language teacher pointing her to Otto Müller, or Norman Mittelmann discovering Silas Elash. An honest star will admit that there are many equally talented singers who remain undiscovered, through no fault of their own.

Yet it's not helpful to be too self-effacing. At the peak of her career, Irene struggled with the feeling that she did not really deserve all the applause and rave reviews she was getting. For people with this "impostor" issue, no amount of praise and reassurance eases the anguished self-doubt. Irene has known talented young artists who couldn't get past it and were not able to make opera their career. On the other hand, she sang many times with renowned tenor Franco Corelli, who was a nervous wreck, yet who somehow mastered his fears.

So how does one wisely balance proper confidence with proper humility? Irene comments, "Success is a very huge test. Some singers react and become superior (they believe the praise), and they become aloof, distant. But the true giants remain genuinely humble and have no ego problems." Perhaps C.S. Lewis said it best: "Humility is not thinking less of yourself; it's thinking of yourself less."

Quick Thinking. On March 7, 1964, *Don Carlo* was being broadcast from the Met. Irene, singing Eboli, was in the middle of the garden scene trio with Carlo and Rodrigo when the conductor gave the gesture indicating an upcoming cut. But where? What were they supposed to cut? Luckily, the prompter had been informed. He signaled Irene, giving her the pitch, for there was no orchestral accompaniment at that moment. She immediately picked up at the correct spot in the score and continued the scene. This all happened in a matter of seconds, but it seemed like an eternity. Later she learned that Corelli had sent a note to the conductor, telling him that this section of the trio was not done at La Scala and he didn't know it. The conductor told the orchestra but forgot to tell Irene. She was understandably furious at him.

So the performer must be able to handle onstage surprises and emergencies. Though such missteps have been rare in the history of OSJ, one night in 1987 during a run of *The Merry Widow* at the Montgomery Theater, the curtain was mistakenly opened too soon, revealing two singers who were innocently standing onstage waiting for the overture to end so the show could begin. Nick Lymberis, who was playing the embassy secretary Njegus, and Phil Olds, who was playing Baron Zeta, improvised on the spot. Olds pantomimed that he was busily giving instructions to his servant Lymberis, and Lymberis responded by nodding and bowing obsequiously. Whispering to each other, they agreed to exit to opposite sides of the stage. But the overture was still not over. As Olds stood in the wings looking across the stage at his co-conspirator in the opposite wing, he had another brainstorm and gestured his idea to Lymberis: the two of them would enter again, still during the overture, walking backwards as if lost in thought, and end up by bumping into each other in exaggerated surprise. This comic bit worked out perfectly, even concluding at the exact moment the overture ended. Reviewers loved it, and Irene told them afterwards, "I'm sure glad you two pros were there!" Laughing at the memory, she says, "Those two were fantastic actors."

Of course, Mother Nature might hand even the most well prepared company a surprise. In 2001 during a performance of *Rigoletto*, a short sharp shock startled everyone in the Montgomery Theater. An earthquake! Conductor Sara Jobin had never experienced an earthquake before. She thought, "Irene Dalis will know what to do. If she wants me to stop, she will tap me on the shoulder and I'll stop." There was no tap on the shoulder, so she proceeded and the performance went on, though there was a bit of nervous tension in the house. Jobin recalls, "Scott Bearden was the next singer with a line to sing, and as fate would have it, the line was 'Quel vecchio maledivami!' (That old man cursed me!). Bearden, in a moment of inspiration, delivered the line up

Sandra Rubalcava Bengochea in *Don Pasquale*, 2003

into the rafters that had just given a mighty shake. The whole audience dissolved into laughter, and the tension of the moment passed."

Making Difficult Decisions. Singers must sometimes decline a tempting offer. Remember that while Irene was still a student in Europe, Rudolf Bing, general director of the Met, expressed interest in her. But her teacher, Otto Müller, instantly responded to Bing by saying, "No. You will wait four years." Müller wanted her to be totally ready when she stepped onto that high-profile stage. Sure enough, four years later Irene was singing at the Met, and she was ready.

At least one former resident artist has declined an offer from the Met. Bass Kirk Eichelberger, who had sung minor roles at the Met, was offered a contract to be a regular cover (understudy). This would mean a steady salary, a chance to meet and rehearse with the world's top singers—and the off-chance that one day, when the scheduled bass is ill, Eichelberger might have his opportunity to make a life-changing breakthrough at the most important stage in America. But he turned it down. He wrote:

> Back in 2008, the Met offered me individual, pay-per-performance, covers for two roles: Fasolt in *Das Rheingold* and Monterone in *Rigoletto*. The issue was that I had outstanding offers to actually *sing* two roles at two different companies which conflicted with the offer.... My agents advised me at the time to take the jobs in which I was actually singing, over the covers at the Met. The difficulty here was that the Met offer came to $40,000 and the other two combined came to $24,000 or so. It was a financially difficult decision. The idea was that it looked better for me to be performing anywhere than covering, even at the Met... It was a calculated gamble and I did what my agents advised.

The Met did not hold a grudge and now Eichelberger, in addition to his performing schedule, is again regularly covering at the Met. But will his lucky day come, the star-making day when the scheduled bass calls in sick?

Patience and Perseverance: Restoring the California Theatre

The Fox movie theatre on First Street, a dilapidated ruin that had been the height of style in the 1920s and which Irene had attended as a child, had always been on Irene's mind. **Patrice Maginnis** recalls that in the late 1970s, as they walked past the shuttered movie palace, Irene said to her, "That theatre will be ours one day." Many obstacles had to be overcome before her vision became reality.

We Don't Import Stars—We Export Them!

Originally built as a 1927 movie palace, the California Theatre was everything the nation's budding film audience could desire: high ceilings with chandeliers, art deco furnishings, a glamourous proscenium, and seating for a thousand patrons. As a youngster, Irene went there many times. Classics like *Gone with the Wind*, *The Wizard of Oz*, *Destry Rides Again*, and (of course) *A Night at the Opera* were screened in the 1930s. Less memorable films from that decade were *Tarzan Finds a Son!*, *Quick Millions*, and *Revolt of the Zombies*.

If you entered the California Theatre during the 1940s, you could see *Casablanca*, *The Maltese Falcon*, *Spellbound*, and *They Died with Their Boots On* (plus the forgettable *Africa Screams*, *All This and Rabbit Stew*, and *Orchestra Wives*). In the 1950s, you could see *Ben-Hur*, *A Streetcar Named Desire*, and *The King and I* (plus *Rice with Milk*, *A Bucket of Blood*, and *Teenagers from Outer Space*). During the 1960s, the theatre was showing its age, but still managed to screen *Hello Dolly*, *Ship of Fools*, and *The Great Escape* (plus *The Beast of Yucca Flats* and *Santa Claus Conquers the Martians*).

But in 1973 the theatre was closed, and it remained shuttered for decades. The city changed around it, as San José became the third largest city in the state, the unofficial hub of Silicon Valley and the computer revolution. The city bought the property in 1985 intending to develop it, but for some reason, it remained vacant as more decades elapsed. The cavernous space stood in silence. Meanwhile, starting in March, 1980, just two blocks away, the San José State University Community Opera Theatre was producing fully staged operas and building a loyal audience in a friendly little space called the Montgomery Theater. Irene appreciated the place.

> I am eternally grateful for the years in the Montgomery Theater. Yes, the stage was smaller than some people's living rooms and the orchestra

pit only accommodated 26 players max, the few dressing rooms were antiquated, and there was not much backstage space, but it became a showcase for many talented singers.

Because of the need for a mid-sized theatre, in 1988 the City appointed an ad hoc committee, co-chaired by Blanca Alvarado and Nancy Wiener, to rehab the California Theatre. This committee, of which I was a member, met regularly for two years. Designs were created and approved. But in the end, the city funded the Mexican Heritage Foundation Center instead. I was called by the *San Jose Mercury News* for a statement after the vote by the City Council. What did I say? I was not original. I simply said, "I learned long ago to make lemonade when I receive a lemon."

Of course we were disappointed, but in retrospect, it was a blessing in disguise. Many years later, David W. Packard, professor of classics at UCLA and oh yes, of the Hewlett-Packard family, called me to say he was interested in renovating the California Theatre to accommodate the needs of Opera San José. What a thrill! But then reality set in. The feasibility study 20 years earlier had determined that it was "impossible" to deepen the stage to turn it into a working performance stage. But now we had a powerful ally. When a representative from the City Redevelopment Agency repeated that making the California into a live performance venue was "impossible," Packard responded, "'Impossible' is not a word in my vocabulary." He looked at the architects who were present and said, "It can be done. You must find a way to do it. Don't worry about the cost."

And they found a way. The stage was deepened and the orchestra pit was enlarged to more than twice the size of the Montgomery Theater's. Audience amenities such as the concession stands were improved. For the artists, backstage rehearsal rooms, ample dressing rooms, two conference rooms, and a comfortable green room were added.

Packard is known as a perfectionist and was involved in every aspect of the renovation, insisting on authenticity in the choice of colors for the interior. He would confer with me on issues that would involve the opera directly, but he is the one who worked daily with the Redevelopment Agency.

Packard met with San José Redevelopment Agency's Bob Ruff, architects, city planners, building historians, construction firms, and safety engineers. He ensured that the artistic restoration was genuine and beautiful, even bringing in artisans from New York to redo the entire interior. Here's one example of his drive for perfection: The colors used to paint the theatre's walls were very dated. Packard visited one day while the painting was going on and commented on them. "Oh, it will look fine," he was assured. When the job was finished and he came to see it, he stood there, looked around for a moment, and said tersely, "Do it over." Irene concludes, "The city should be eternally grateful to Packard, for without the gift from the Packard Humanities Institute, the beautiful California Theatre as it now stands would not exist."

Conductor David Rohrbaugh was consulted on the construction of the orchestra pit. Because he had experience in building sets and setting up orchestras, Rohrbaugh met with the architect, consultants, and acousticians to offer his input on the design. As a result, the pit is situated partway under the stage, a placement that helps the conductor balance the sound. Parts of the pit are on moveable platforms and can be moved up to extend the stage when that is desirable. Because the orchestra platforms were not readily available for the first production, Rohrbaugh designed and built a system of temporary platforms in order to figure out the best placement of orchestra members. Until the night of the grand opening, Rohrbaugh came to each rehearsal with his tool kit, ready to make on-the-spot adjustments. Subsequently he worked with Charlie Mitchell from the Packard Humanities Institute to refine and build a permanent system of risers and platforms.

When construction was almost completed and the orchestra began its first rehearsal, it was quickly apparent that the acoustics at the California Theatre would be superior, with excellent balance. That evening Rohrbaugh went home and said to his wife, "This is a true gem of a theatre. Everyone was giddy with excitement at how wonderful the sound was."

Associate conductor **Anthony Quartuccio** recalls the excitement of preparing for the grand opening of the new theatre. First, you must know that his earliest appearance for OSJ occurred when he was still a child, playing the accordion at Operathon. Now he was an adult, an experienced musician who had been conducting for OSJ for five years. Of the last exacting days before the grand opening, he recalls, "We staff members were at the new theatre day and night during the transition—combing through details, assembling the pit, and conducting exhaustive acoustic tests. It was thrilling for everyone to see a huge dream come true in establishing a real opera house in our hometown. Being in the middle of it all was the fulfillment of one of my life dreams."

If you're intrigued by the prospect of overhauling an abandoned theatre and finishing 85,000 square feet of old and new space, giving attention to every artistic detail, including backstage and operating mechanisms, visit shomler.com, the website of Bob

Shomler, one of OSJ's official photographers. Anyone who has ever built or remodeled a home will be awed at the magnitude of the job. With a handful of donors, this author toured the work-in-progress as the theatre was being renovated. Wearing hard hats and sturdy shoes, we admired the height of the entrance lobby, walked carefully through dusty passages to inspect the balcony, which at that time consisted simply of a bare raked floor, and marveled at the size of the stage, with its high ceilings and great depth.

The artists love this theatre, too. It has great acoustics, offering the singers a truly welcoming experience, plus backstage amenities and work spaces. The orchestra has its own lounge equipped with lockers for instruments. At the Montgomery, Virginia Smedberg had been squeezed so much that she had to put one foot up on the edge of the pit in order to attain the desired violinist's posture. She remarked that orchestra spaces are often so tight that musicians beg each other for a bit of room, asking plaintively, "Can you give me an inch?" The Montgomery took this cramping to extremes, and the orchestra members were thrilled to be entering a spacious new workplace.

An organ was installed in the lobby to treat patrons to old-fashioned popular songs from the last century as they arrive. The theatre even has a Mighty Wurlitzer, that amazingly complex invention that can produce the sound of every instrument in an orchestra. Ed Stout, who tended organs at San Francisco's Grace Cathedral and Fine Arts Museums for 42 years, remembers attending the California Theatre in the 1950s to see the movies of the day. The original Wurlitzer (intended for silent movies and special events) was removed in the 1950s, but the hydraulic lift still worked. When interest in renovating the California Theatre revived, the San José Symphony made plans to gut it, including the organ areas, and to put in spotlights and sound equipment there. Stout and Irene attended a meeting with city

California Theatre, stage right, after renovation

California Theatre lobby after renovation

officials, the Redevelopment Agency, and theatre historian Gary Parks to propose that the organ, instead of being removed, be restored. Packard generously offered to fund the restoration. Thanks to the Packard Humanities Institute, the California Theatre has a Mighty Wurlitzer. So when, at the end of Act I of *Tosca*, the score calls for a majestic Te Deum, the California can really deliver.

After so many years of dreaming, planning, and rebuilding, the grandly refurbished California Theatre re-opened in September, 2004. Irene was overjoyed about the new performing space, saying, "This is perhaps the highest moment I've had in my professional life. You're in for a treat. It's so beautiful, and it's been so lovingly restored." For the gala opening night, former resident artists flew in at their own expense—Lori Phillips, Mel Ulrich, and John Bellemer among them. At the three restaurants at which gala patrons were dining, singers appeared and treated them to a succession of their favorite arias.

Then came the performance, a production of Mozart's *The Marriage of Figaro*, directed by Lorna Haywood, with sets by Giulio Cesare Perrone, costumes by Julie Englebrecht, and lighting designed by Pamila Z. Gray. After the animated audience settled into their seats in the gorgeous hall, the orchestra played the sparkling overture. Let's enjoy the moment when the curtain rose.

> Miracle of miracles, the stage was filled with eye-popping sets worthy of a big-city opera company. Suddenly, we were transported to the Spanish estate, where this comedy, about mad midsummer love and mistaken identities, unfolds.
>
> Out stepped Figaro, sung by Joseph Wright, whose rich, booming baritone finally has a hall commodious enough to handle it. Then out stepped Susanna, Figaro's bride-to-be, sung by

> soprano Sandra Rubalcava, who conveyed all of her character's intelligence, sauciness, and spunk. These two are terrific comic actors with a frisky chemistry conveying the joy, anguish, and hormonal escalation of young lovers.

Acknowledging the special occasion, the reviewer concluded, "The audience gave a standing ovation to Irene Dalis, Opera San José's founder and general director, who joined the cast for a bow and deserved accolades. She has brought her company, and the local arts scene, to the threshold of a promising new era."

Another reviewer, who writes for the *San Francisco Classical Voice*, wrote of the finale,

> Under Rohrbaugh's baton, the orchestra played the accompaniment and the passage that follows as one musician, filling the hall with overwhelming beauty. In that moment, the company rose fully to the greatness of the music. The audience's appreciation was reflected in the ovation that greeted company founder-director Irene Dalis at the next-to-last curtain call; more than an expression of civic pride, it also acknowledged the exquisite finale.

The California Theatre has been Opera San José's performing home ever since. It is a jewel of a space, one of the most intimate yet fully equipped mid-sized professional opera houses in the country. Audiences love it. They enter a special world the minute they walk through the door into the Spanish Renaissance foyer with its painted ceilings, sculptured arches, and Art Deco trimmings. One reporter called it "a 1927 movie lover's fantasy. There's a merging of Florentine flourishes, Gothic arches, Islamic-flying-carpet and American Indian motifs. Look at it, and you could imagine you were anywhere in the world at any time in history."

Overall, Rohrbaugh concludes, "The opening of the California Theatre was a very exciting time. It was a dream come true to have such a beautiful venue in which to make music."

The Orchestra

From the beginning, OSJ has had a union orchestra, whose members have created their own little community. Some of them have been playing there for thirty years. David Rohrbaugh remembers when they all began.

> A very rewarding aspect of my job as music director has been the building of the orchestra. Many of the players have been with us since almost the beginning. The mutual trust and respect between a conductor and an orchestra develop only through many rehearsals and performances over many years of working together. I have been fortunate enough to have experienced this with our orchestra. The satisfaction of communicating through the music far exceeds the ability of words to describe feelings and emotions.
>
> There have been many times that I have felt that this process of communicating is magical. In performances, you never know when or where it's going to happen—it could be the way someone sings something, someone plays something, or conducts something, but when that happens, the moment becomes especially moving. The moment is ethereal, but it lives with you.

Patty Mitchell has been with OSJ since the beginning, when the orchestra rehearsed at the university. Then when they were rehearsing at the Children's Discovery Museum, their space had a window through which adults and kids visiting the museum could watch them rehearsing. Later, at the cramped Montgomery orchestra pit, she was the only oboist, and even played English horn or second oboe when needed. There were small platforms at the sides of the stage, and sometimes musicians were placed there. Mitchell recalls several "Tales from the Pit" (her phrase). One time, a singer slipped at rehearsal at the Montgomery and slid into the pit, hitting Bob Szabo's trombone. Luckily, no one was hurt, but the trombone needed repairs. On another occasion, the staging involved a game of billiards. Baritone Mel Ulrich played his part a bit too vigorously and a ball flew off the stage and hit the bassoonist. Mitchell adds with a smile, "But Mel was so good-looking we forgave him immediately." Looking back over thirty years, Mitchell says, "I have watched this group grow up. We had no kids, and now we have kids ages 24 to 31. We're quite a family, especially those who have been here from the start. We grouse about our teenagers, share our worries. I've never been tempted to leave and work full time elsewhere. Even after I retire from my other engagements, I will stay with OSJ forever."

Isabelle Chapuis, who trained at the Paris Conservatory, is proud to be part of the OSJ orchestra. She has been with it for 32 years, performing as principal flutist in every production except one, when a family health emergency took her back to her native France. She's so devoted that she insisted on playing for *La Bohème* when she was seven months pregnant. The baby kicked in its own rhythm, so Chapuis asked her orchestra neighbor to count and help her keep the correct tempo. She added with a smile, "Being a musician is not for wimps."

Chapuis stays because she loves playing the opera repertoire and she loves Irene, whom she calls "strong, vibrant, intelligent, talented, a 'grande dame' who inspires us to give our best." She appreciates that OSJ plays challenging works like *Falstaff* that most regional orchestras won't perform. After three decades in the pit, she says, "I recruit for my opera company, and I'm proud to be part of it. We all age and improve together. We are open to each other, ask advice from one another. We work well together because we're all proud of what we do. It's a remarkable professional orchestra. We celebrate birthdays, weddings, and births, and mourn the loss of parents. We have many close friends in the orchestra, and we meet at parties after each production." Her husband Mark Starr, a retired conductor, says, "OSJ is one of the most exciting companies on either side of the Atlantic."

The Real Estate Angel Smiles Again

After the move to the California Theatre, OSJ needed more space to build and store the larger sets that were now required, plus a larger staging area and costume shop. Fortunately, David W. Packard, who was so important in the renovation of the California Theatre, realized that it was pointless to move OSJ to the California without the proper support buildings. Irene saw an ad for a warehouse and called the listed realtor. It would be perfect, since it was only a few doors down from 2149 Paragon. The realtor was floored to hear her say that she would pay cash. This was made possible because the Packard Humanities Institute granted purchase money for the second operations building (now called The Scene Shop) on Paragon Drive.

We Don't Import Stars—We Export Them!

Many members of the Opera San José resident company have gone on to long and successful singing careers, engaged by important companies such as Boston Lyric Opera, Cleveland Opera, Dessau Opera (Germany), Hamburg State Opera (Germany), Hawaii Opera Theatre, Houston Grand Opera, Los Angeles Opera, Lyric Opera of Chicago, The Metropolitan Opera, New York City Opera, San Diego Opera, San Francisco Opera, Santa Fe Opera, Seattle Opera, Utah Opera, Vancouver

Mel Ulrich and Layna Chianakas in *The Marriage of Figaro*, 1996

Opera, Virginia Opera, Washington National Opera, and many others. To highlight just a few of these distinguished artists:

- Baritone *Mel Ulrich* has performed in Salzburg, Los Angeles Opera, San Francisco Opera, New York City Opera, Vienna Volksoper, and other companies through America and Europe.
- Mezzo-soprano *Layna Chianakas* has performed with Sacramento Opera, Sarasota Opera, Opera Santa Barbara, Cleveland Opera, and others, recently returning to Opera San José as a stage director. As

Irene once was, she is on the music faculty at San José State University and in charge of the opera workshop there.

- Tenor *John Bellemer* has performed leading roles at Opera Birmingham, Cleveland Opera, Opera Theatre of Saint Louis, Opera Omaha, Boston Lyric Opera, Arizona Opera, Buxton Festival, Opera de Rouen, Michigan Opera Theatre, Teatro Lirico di Cagliari, Opera National de Bordeaux, and many more.
- Soprano *Cynthia Clayton* has sung principal roles at Houston Grand Opera, New York City Opera, Utah Opera, Cleveland Opera, and many other American companies. While continuing to be in demand as a performer, she is also an Associate Professor of Voice at the University of Houston.
- Bass *Kirk Eichelberger* has appeared as Mephistopheles with Dayton Opera, Opera Grand Rapids, and Opera Birmingham. He has also appeared at Spoleto Festival USA, Festival Opera, Sacramento Opera, Monterey Opera, and others.
- Soprano *Lori Phillips* made her Met debut as Senta in *The Flying Dutchman*, a role she has also sung at the Washington National Opera. She has also performed the title role in *Turandot* at Seattle Opera and Atlanta. Other performances include the title roles in *Madama Butterfly* and *Turandot* at New York City Opera, *Tosca* in Boston, and Amelia in *Un Ballo in Maschera* at Seattle, Vancouver, and Memphis.

Many more OSJ resident artists have had solid opera careers. Some have become stage directors, artistic directors, or general directors of opera companies. Some have moved to teaching or administration, while others have created truly unusual careers.

Randy Cooper performed in Germany, where he was discovered by the director of a cruise line, and he has for years been a singer on German cruise ships. Jesse Merlin is now in Los Angeles, specializing in an intriguing genre—musical adaptations of classic horror films. Brian Staufenbiel, a workshop student from the early days, is now stage director at Opera Parallèle in San Francisco, producing modern chamber operas.

Some have even founded opera companies of their own. Baritone Constantinos Yiannoudes created Kyrenia Opera in New York, with the express purpose of fostering artistic and creative relationships with the island of Cyprus, his ancestral home. Tenor Dan Montez founded Taconic Opera, also in New York, now celebrating its 16th season.

Going for Gold

In keeping with her philosophy of encouraging emerging singers, Irene, with the support of an anonymous donor, established the Irene Dalis Vocal Competition in 2007, which is held in San José every spring. Ten finalists compete for $50,000 in cash prizes and the honors that go with them. The finals are open to the public, offering a rare glimpse into the career-building steps an aspiring singer faces. Each contestant prepares five arias, then chooses one to sing first. The judges, huddling together in the balcony, then select one of the other prepared arias for him or her to sing. By the end of the evening, the audience has heard ten talented singers perform 20 arias—some familiar, some rare. While judges are deciding on which singers will receive the top three prizes ($15,000, $10,000, and $5,000), the patrons vote on the Audience Favorite, who also gets a prize ($5,000). All of the finalists are awarded a $2,000 cash prize as well. Irene Dalis Vocal Competition finalists have continued or built significant careers; for instance, Audrey Luna

Awarding first prize to Rebecca Davis at the
Irene Dalis Vocal Competition, 2012

(2009) has since sung at the Met, Santa Fe, Tanglewood, Lyric Opera of Chicago, and the Spoleto Festival, among many other engagements.

Irene's dream of exporting stars, seeding the opera world with new generations of experienced singers, has come true.

SEVEN

The Impresaria

IN 1988, IRENE DECIDED SHE SHOULD reduce her visibility at OSJ because people were calling it "Irene Dalis's opera company." She didn't want people to think it was a whim. "I built it as an institution, not Irene Dalis's play toy. It's not my company, but San José's company." So she hired a professional administrator and named him executive director, while she remained as artistic director. However, he was not the fiscal and marketing wizard she was. Before long, the board begged Irene to take back the helm, for the company was facing its first deficit. She agreed, saying she would stay only long enough to get the company back to good financial health, which she accomplished in one season. That was more than twenty years ago.

So she plunged back into the demanding, joyful, artistic, and financial challenge of running an opera company. Fortunately for opera lovers, Irene had the grit and determination for the job—a very difficult job. The impresario is the one who pulls together the performers, the orchestra, the marketing department, and the box office to create a musical event, combining art and commerce, creating wonderful music while balancing the books so the company stays in business.

Eminent stage director and general director **Lotfi Mansouri** wrote, "Opera directing today is an immensely complicated art form. It requires a unique talent to integrate the musical, orchestral, vocal, theatrical and dramatic qualities of an opera. Contemporary opera directors must be aware of opera as a multi-dimensional art form and they must be able to affect their audience in many directions simultaneously. A successful opera production today affects an audience like no other performing art form." But with only dozens of performers, musicians, set changes, onstage murders, and irreplaceable props, what could possibly go wrong?

The audience rarely knows about glitches, emergencies, and the thousand natural shocks that an opera impresario is heir to. Rudolf Bing, Irene's advocate and ally, was perhaps the most celebrated impresario of the twentieth century. Reflecting on his experience running the Metropolitan Opera for 22 years, Bing wrote:

> There are two sighs of relief every night in the life of an opera manager. The first comes when the curtain goes up. The second sigh of relief comes when the final curtain goes down without any disaster, and one realizes, gratefully, that the miracle has happened again.

In his autobiography, Bing shared some of the little things he had to deal with: shushing the audience latecomers, providing a stool for the man who operated the elevator, enforcing the no-smoking rule backstage, chastising rude box office employees, ordering assistant conductors to stop congregating near the stage managers' desk and distracting them, and ensuring that the knife used onstage to kill Carmen was a rubber one whenever a certain overly enthusiastic tenor was in the cast. And all that was quite apart from his little day job of casting, approving contracts, raising huge amounts of money, managing the budget, supervising a wide range of departments, and handling the hysterics of the Met's more temperamental divas.

Irene admits she was unskilled in business dealings during her singing career. Once OSJ was born, she had to learn a lot of things quickly: budgeting, delegating, hiring, purchasing, marketing, and more. There were discouraging times—and there were moments that redeemed them. Said Irene in 1998, "I get all worked up about how we're going to meet the budget. Then I go to a performance and see the growth of these singers and this company, and I feel so blessed." That she has been successful is attested by 30 years of fine productions and the many resident artists who went on to have careers in the high-stakes world of opera. Eminent stage director and San Francisco Opera general director Lotfi Mansouri used the term *Impresaria* to describe her.

Nerves of Steel

Running an opera company has some similarities to a singing career. One must, of course, know the field and the repertoire. Yet in many ways it's very *unlike* a singing career. It consists less of Art than Administration. One's decisions affect hundreds of people. A general director must be a diplomat (to deal with unions), a human resources officer (to hire and fire), and have nerves of steel (to handle crises) plus excellent people skills (to soothe frazzled nerves and hurt feelings). Rudolf Bing certainly had nerves of steel and unparalleled ingenuity to solve emergencies. Remember the time Irene refused to climb a ladder and sing while standing at the top? Then there was the night Franco Corelli refused to come out of his dressing room—during a performance. Irene's good friend Jess Thomas tells the story. He was there, sitting in the audience.

> The show was great, the audience went wild. Then came the moment where the "auto-da-fé" scene was due. Being a tenor, you cannot keep from participating, even when you are a spectator. Awaiting the tenor's appearance, I nervously took hold of the

Professor at San José State University

armchair. In vain, because the tenor did not appear in spite of the fact that this was a live broadcast!

Apparently Corelli had said he was suddenly unwell. But as Irene had said earlier, "Management always knows who's in the audience." Sure enough, Jess was summoned backstage, where Bing was waiting for him.

> He handed me a costume and pushed me toward the wardrobe. I firmly protested, refusing to cover. Then we reached the tenor's dressing room. Bing opened the door without knocking and left it open long enough for the tenor to see me with the costume. Meanwhile he thanked me profusely, in a very loud voice. Then he closed the door and told me, "That should do the job." He had me wait there for a couple of minutes, until he returned with a

broad smile on his face, shaking my hand and thanking me once again. "You can return to your seat now and enjoy the performance. The tenor has decided that he has miraculously recovered!"

Besides handling such backstage theatrics, the general director makes decisions that will affect the company for the coming year. Irene described the process of designing a season at OSJ.

> Picking the repertoire is difficult because it's based on singers you have. We expect them to be flexible, but we do not ask the impossible. At the same time, we must think about what our San José audience will come to see, cycling through the warhorses about every five years, for we must offer our singers the opportunity to sing the roles that will be the bread-and-butter roles of their careers.
>
> When the repertoire is determined, then months are spent in budgeting. Each department head is responsible for preparing detailed backup reports to justify the costs—number of costumes per show, cost of each, number of sets, marketing, cost of guest artists per show, cost for orchestra, etc. Then we choose the creative team (director, designers, and so on). Sometimes I find it too expensive and may have to pick a different opera at that point.

Occasionally, as the managing director of a business, Irene has had to let people go for the good of the company.

> If a singer has persistent vocal problems, or can't hold the correct pitch, or can't move onstage, or can't stop looking at the conductor, I release them from their contracts. I've had to do this four or five times in 30 years. I work very closely with

David Rohrbaugh in making such a decision. Most times the problem can be solved. But sometimes it can't. This is hard for me to face, that I've made a mistake. It's a hard moment, and painful for the singer. But I want to build a public and can't disappoint them.

So, with all these competing demands and pressures, an impresario must be an incredibly strong and effective person. What do the people who work with her have to say about Irene the Impresaria?

The General Directors

A general director must solve a stream of problems during the rehearsal period (and even during performances) and withstand criticisms from unpleasable reviewers after opening night. At dinner one night, Lotfi Mansouri sighed, "As general director, everyone knows your job better than you do. You need a thick skin, and you need to know what you want." He admired Irene, saying, "Irene is a strong, warm person. She thinks not of herself, but of young singers. She took the experience of the world stage and brought it to San José. She even put on world premieres, and some well-regarded general directors attended."

Dan Montez, OSJ's first resident tenor, in addition to being a composer and performer, has created and run his own opera company. He wrote:

> Irene taught me everything about the business, not only how to have a career, but how to run a business. That knowledge was invaluable to me not only as a singer at a number of larger opera houses later, but especially in running my own opera company in New York. She always said, "If you don't got it, you don't spend it." I think that philosophy has been

one of the reasons my company has weathered the recession while almost every other company around us was folding in New York.

Doug Nagel, former resident artist, has gone on to teach and help run opera companies. Most notably, he served as artistic director of Rimrock Opera in Billings, Montana, for 13 seasons. While at OSJ, Doug had been impressed by Irene's attention to the budget, knowing she spent hours on it. He remembers that she had a keen eye for details and would make fixes to costumes and staging. "Irene is unique. She manages people with charm, which is rare in a businessperson. She knew when to praise and when to be tough. There was no monkey business at OSJ. That's a sign of a true leader."

The Right-Hand Man

Larry Hancock has been with Irene since the very earliest days of OSJ and has worked closely with her for over 30 years, filling so many roles that he's almost a one-man administration.

> She's the most intimidating person I've ever known. I don't find her predictable. After more than thirty years of working side by side, I am still sometimes surprised by her responses. After her absolutely direct honesty, perhaps Irene's greatest gift is her uncanny sense of the future. She quickly reads a room, makes fast first impressions of people, their motives and agendas, as if they're characters in a play and she's the stage director. Irene has always been practical with money and has understood when to save it and when to spend it, and on what. She has built a legacy that no other arts organization in San José can match.

The Impresaria

Larry Hancock at Los Gatos Music in the Park

The Stage Directors

José Maria Condemi has directed *La Traviata, La Rondine, The Barber of Seville, The Magic Flute, Don Pasquale, The Elixir of Love,* and *Falstaff* for OSJ. To Condemi, Irene is "the soul of the company, one of a kind, and a force of nature. She runs a tight ship, and managed her own career well, too. But her ego is small. It seems she doesn't realize how important she is." Condemi drew on an amazing memory to reach these conclusions—he remembers the interactions, exactly who worked with him, what they did and when. In the middle of the interview, this author started to share a few of the fascinating stories Irene had related about her career. Suddenly realizing I was talking instead of listening, I apologized. He smiled and said, "This is exactly what happens. You start to talk about Irene."

Timothy Near has directed *The Crucible, Lucia di Lammermoor,* and *La Bohème* for OSJ, and has been impressed that the two casts of performers were so well prepared and so supportive of each other. Clearly, OSJ has a hardworking but not cut-throat ethic. Near was gratified that Irene did not micromanage, allowing her to use her own method of letting the singers explore a role. Irene's faith was justified when the ultimate productions displayed fine artistic results. OSJ is, to her, very professional, with good technical support and enough rehearsal time scheduled so that the artists can build their roles.

Brad Dalton has directed *Faust, Il Trovatore, Anna Karenina, Idomeneo, Così Fan Tutte,* and *Madama Butterfly* (twice). He says of Irene, "She's an extraordinary diplomat, with amazing listening skills. You get 100 per cent of her attention. She never passes the buck and always fixes problems promptly. She asks for so few changes that when she does ask for a change, I immediately make it." Dalton adds that her custom of sending emails to the cast after dress rehearsals, congratulating them on their hard work and reminding them that she's proud and excited for them, is rare. Dalton once went to her with a problem he was having with a rude singer. Some other administrators would have cared only about their show, but Irene exhibited a level of personal concern that he's never forgotten: She said, "I don't like to see you unhappy," and addressed the problem at once. Perhaps referring to the luck which Irene is always willing to acknowledge, he concluded, "Serendipity happens around her projects."

Layna Chianakas was a resident artist in the mid-1990s and has become an associate professor and stage director at SJSU, while continuing her singing career. She has also directed two productions for OSJ, *La Voix Humaine* (which she had also performed in her time as a resident artist) and *Hansel and Gretel*. She comments that Irene cares about her singers and continues mentoring them after they leave: "I've been nurtured long beyond my stint at OSJ." Chianakas now teaches at SJSU and finds Irene "unbelievably generous" in loaning props or costumes. Furthermore, Irene is concerned about her as a person, urging her not to overwork. They have developed a lovely friendship, and Chianakas was touched to be invited to call her mentor by her first name.

Lorna Haywood has directed many productions for OSJ, starting with *La Traviata* in the Montgomery in 1999. This was followed by *La Bohème, Madama Butterfly, Il Trovatore,* and *Die Fledermaus*, which was the last production OSJ did in the Montgomery Theater. Because of the impending move to the California Theatre, the budget was extremely tight. Haywood managed to reconfigure an old set from a previous *Don Pasquale* production and made the party scene in Act II into a Grand Opera Ball, utilizing existing costumes in the wardrobe. The chorus had a wonderful time wearing glamourous principal singers' costumes from previous OSJ productions. In subsequent seasons, Haywood directed *Don Giovanni* and *Rigoletto*. She was particularly honored to be invited to direct the first two productions in the renovated California Theatre: *The Marriage of Figaro* and *Tosca*. As the much-anticipated opening performance in the California Theatre approached, Haywood worked closely with

Irene every day, coping with the numerous problems and unexpected issues that cropped up as they adjusted to the new venue. At the end of the workday, Haywood would drop into Irene's office with a progress report and find her working tirelessly on her computer, solving problems and studying the budget.

Some time later, Haywood faced a personal and professional crisis: Her vision deteriorated, and she was diagnosed with acute angle glaucoma. She was obliged to withdraw from her contract to direct *Carmen* for OSJ. She has since made a good recovery, but in the interim she lost several years of work and contacts with other companies. Instead of writing Haywood off, Irene called her throughout that dismal period, inviting her to return whenever she felt able to resume her directing career. The double bill of *Suor Angelica* and *Gianni Schicchi* in 2013 was her first directing job after her recovery. This actually was one of those last-minute crises that turned out spectacularly well. Irene called her on a Thursday because the scheduled director had suddenly withdrawn—and rehearsals were due to begin on the following Monday morning. Would Haywood accept the job? She agreed, boarded a plane in Detroit on Saturday morning, and went directly from the San José airport to a production meeting. Rehearsals began two days later. Lorna says, "I absolutely adore Irene. She's a pistol—courageous, passionate, incredibly enthusiastic, with active interest in every possible aspect of a production. I would do anything for that lady."

The Composers

Alva Henderson, whose *Medea* was created with Irene in mind, also composed a one-act opera, *The Last Leaf*. He sang it through for her, and it was first performed by OSJ at Villa Montalvo. Irene helped him continue his stint as artist-in-residence at SJSU so that he could write his next one-act opera. He describes her as "valiant," "charming," and "a force of nature," adding, "There is nothing small about Irene Dalis. The warmth of her personality can affect a whole roomful of people. Yet she is ruthless in criticism of her own performances, and she can be very stubborn if she does not see eye to eye with you on a point."

Dan Montez is a composer as well as singer, conductor, and general director, so he can offer a composer's eye view of Irene. In 2013 he emailed her,

> It's such a busy year. I have 6 productions I am staging or conducting in the next 8 months. We open *Norma* this weekend. Then I have *Lucia, Flute, Pirates, Italian Girl* and then the debut of my third oratorio, *Jonah*, in two cities. By the way, I can't believe how you sat through my first oratorio 23 years ago—I didn't even know how to compose—it was just awful!! But you were supportive anyway. I'm a much better composer now. I'm working on composing a second opera now as well. My company is in its 16th Season and I am 51 years old—how time flies! I've either sung or directed over 100 operas now.... I would never have had such an exciting life if it hadn't been for you.

Henry Mollicone was the composer for one of OSJ's world premieres, *Hotel Eden*. In one scene, the patriarch Abraham's son is born—onstage. At first, Irene was taken aback by this idea, but thought it over and approved it to be done (in a suitably restrained manner) for the production. To Mollicone, this illustrates both her traditional artistic roots and her adventurous willingness to try new things. He felt completely supported by Irene, who was always positive when she visited rehearsals and who arranged for critics from around the country and even from London to attend the premiere. Today he sees her as a dear friend, candid, friendly, and down to earth.

The Conductors

OSJ's Conductor David Rohrbaugh

David Rohrbaugh was OSJ's principal conductor from the days of the university workshop until he retired in 2014. Few people are in a better position to offer an informed impression of Irene. "We've worked very closely a long time under intense situations—money, venues, budgets, casts." He sees her as inspiring, direct, leaving no doubt about what she means, and not suffering fools gladly. Maybe he steadies her; they take turns being intense and they trust each other's rhythms and intuitions about which singers to hire. "Opera is a pressure cooker. There's never enough money or time. We have worked together all these years and never had an argument." Perhaps his own temperament helped. "It never occurred to me that I would have to have everything my own way." For her part, Irene says, "A better partner I never could have. I seem to get all the accolades about the company, but he was really my partner, and we worked together on building this company. It was always together."

Anthony Quartuccio, the one who started out by playing the accordion at Operathon, has in the last 15 years conducted almost 100 performances at OSJ. Here's his impression of Irene:

> She's tough and focused with the end goal always in mind. She's formidable yet warmly maternal. She's a lot of fun and remarkably witty. She can put people around her at ease with self-deprecating humor without pretense. But she can also be immediate and unfiltered if she is unhappy about something or someone. The most significant memories of Miss Dalis to me were her visits to my dressing room before each show. As she shared brief private moments, I always felt directly connected to her fascinating past life as a great singer—all this just moments before I was due to enter the spotlight. When she shared reassuring, personal thoughts and anecdotes (often with some humor attached) it evaporated any tension, and made me so eager to give everything for a great show.

Andrew Whitfield is OSJ's assistant conductor and chorus master. Like Irene, he has had luck on his side—several times, he stepped in at OSJ when a chorus master or assistant conductor left unexpectedly, and has become a respected part of the company. He says OSJ is unusual, in that assistant conductors may be assigned actual performances. Whitfield so impressed Irene and David Rohrbaugh in this role during *The Pearl Fishers* and *Il Trovatore* that they asked him to be principal conductor for the recent production of *Falstaff*. About Irene, he says, "I feel a deep affection and love for her. She's been unbelievably supportive of me. She's incredibly astute, especially about human nature. She's wonderful and I feel very blessed to know her."

Sara Jobin served as OSJ's assistant conductor for four years. She recalls the day she found her vocation. "The first dress rehearsal I conducted at Opera San José was Poulenc's *La Voix Humaine* with Layna Chianakas in the solo role. There was something so magical to me about the sound of the voice floating on a velvet cushion of orchestral sound. I knew from that moment that I was hooked on opera, for life." Irene called Jobin "a singer's conductor" and later attended San Francisco's *Flying Dutchman* when Jobin was making history as the first woman to conduct there. The courtesy of her presence meant a lot. Jobin has conducted at San Francisco Opera, Opera Santa Barbara, Opera Idaho, and other companies in the U.S. and Europe, as well as making several recordings. Having later worked with numerous former resident artists (sometimes several of them at once in the same production), she calls OSJ "my school, like my undergraduate degree in opera, the foundation of everything, a large extended family."

Robert Ashens met Irene at the West Coast auditions one year and was asked to be a judge in the 2012 Irene Dalis Vocal Competition. Maestro Ashens says, "I see 300-700 resumes a year. If a resume mentions OSJ, I know they've had rigorous training, and I pay extra attention to that one." He knows that, along with much experience, singers will learn things music schools don't teach (professionalism, decorum, backstage manners) and will get to know their colleagues well by living with them or riding together to outreach events. "San José's audience is lucky. Someone they're hearing could be great some day. And Irene maintains the grandeur of opera. Too many companies today are losing the special quality."

The Singers

Dan Montez, who a few pages ago commented on Irene with his composer hat on and before that as general director, was also a resident artist in the early years. He wrote,

> Miss Dalis is my hero. While I was there, I was scared to death of her. She would walk into any room and it would immediately fill with electricity. She was powerful. She always spoke her mind—not much of a filter between what she thought and what she said. For some, this was disconcerting, but I loved it! I always knew what she was thinking and where I stood with her. If I blew it, she let me know. If I nailed it, she heaped on the praise. When I needed support, she was always there with advice or even financial help. I knew that she also liked getting it straight from us as well. She always tested me, but that was exactly what I needed. I will forever be in her debt for my career.

Doug Nagel was one of the first two resident artists and has since focused his singing career in the northern states, performing with Cedar Rapids Opera, Helena Symphony, Intermountain Opera, Opera Idaho, and Eugene Opera, as well as companies in Virginia, Ohio, Pennsylvania, California, and more. He sang in the first Operathon and at the Sainte Claire hotel opera evenings. Soon Irene offered him a role in *The Merry Widow* and then invited him to join the company. At a *Widow* rehearsal when she felt he wasn't fulfilling his potential, she demanded, "Where are you? Where's the charm? Where is the person I hired?" Doug recalls, "That was like a bucket of water over me. I turned it up a notch and raised my level of interpreting the character of Danilo to her satisfaction." Doug's conversation about Irene was peppered with sports metaphors. "Irene is to Opera San José as Bill Walsh is to the San Francisco 49ers." "She told us how it was, point blank. Like a coach, she would bench you if necessary." "Coaches shape human lives. She never made me feel less than amazing. That was so confidence-building. Young people need that."

Daniel Cilli says Irene is a singer's biggest fan and genuinely cares about people. She can appear to be controlling, but she is also like a parent. "She may say, 'We own you' the day you sign your contract, but she actually will negotiate roles." She urged him to tackle roles he didn't think he could do, such as Enrico in *Lucia di Lammermoor*. "Enrico was a role that I didn't feel I was stylistically appropriate for, nor a character that I was particularly drawn towards, but Irene had a very persuasive argument: that it is worthwhile to explore a role I might not at first find appealing. Happily, she was right in that case, a case of OSJ as an arena for artistic experimentation."

Khori Dastoor was singing small roles while working on a doctoral degree in music at UCLA. She heard about OSJ from Daniel Cilli and auditioned. "Others weren't even looking for what Miss Dalis saw in me." Early on, Dastoor was nervous, but then at Operafest, Irene made an entrance dressed as Groucho Marx. That quickly put her at ease. Still, she says, Irene demands the best, and being in her presence is a real education. She is quite properly a stickler about taking seriously the job of covering. "I was having dinner with Scott Bearden when he was called in to finish a performance. That was a good lesson in professional integrity." Dastoor is now on staff at the Packard Humanities Institute and an advisor to OSJ. Referring to OSJ's principle of not forcing singers into vocal pigeonholes, she said, "At OSJ, we make our own rules. Other companies may think we're crazy because we take chances."

Daniel Cilli and Khori Dastoor in *Lucia di Lammermoor*, 2007

Michael Dailey recalls Irene as having a modest though strong personality. With a smile, he compared her to a godmother (the mafia kind), who can get things done and who values loyalty. "After my last show, she said she was proud of me. She's genuine and her compliments are real." **Silas Elash** says, "Nobody talks back to Miss Dalis. She's the strongest human being I've ever met." She loves the singers. Handing on a lesson she had learned, Irene told him, "You have to learn to be gracious in response to praise." **Cynthia Clayton** recalls that Irene can be intimidating, since she doesn't mince words. But as a result, praise from her really means something. She helps the singers build their careers, even bringing in agents to scout them.

Sandra Rubalcava Bengochea wrote, "I have many memories of Miss Dalis! I have always thought she was a terrific and captivating storyteller. I could listen to her stories all day."

Layna Chianakas sees Irene as strong, independent, "a formidable personality who made sure I was always at my best. I felt accountable. She's loyal, on your team." Chianakas also remembers Irene as charismatic and someone who would get emotionally swept away by their performances. At a rehearsal of *La Voix Humaine* in 1997, Irene said to her, "You were so good I cried my false eyelashes off!"

Patrice Maginnis, the vision-impaired singer for whom the illuminated baton was invented, became a music professor at University of California at Santa Cruz, where she taught for 27 years, and she has maintained an ongoing relationship with Irene. "When I need something for UCSC, such as orchestral score, Irene will fulfill my request, asking someone at the office to arrange it." Some years ago Irene came to talk to Maginnis's students, a visit they found inspiring. "You could say anything to her. She's brilliant, inspired, funny, and warm. She respected what you said if you had a point of view." Today, Maginnis says, "Irene is amazing, and she was a great stage director. She made me brilliant. She was a life changer. She had no sense of limitations. She'd give people a chance to see what they could do. This let me pursue my dream of teaching classical voice." Whenever Maginnis would try to thank her, saying, "You gave me my life, my career," Irene would brush off these thank yous as if it were the most natural thing in the world to let an almost-blind singer take the stage in leading roles.

Jesse Merlin says, "You always want to impress Miss Dalis, to go the extra mile and not let her down. She's supportive but can be tough." He emailed her in mid-2013:

> You are simply a wizard to have run that company so successfully for so long. Now that I've been able to travel and work at various different organizations, it brings into high relief how exceptional and unique Opera San José is in many ways. It makes me a little nostalgic to see two shows I remember so fondly—*Trovatore* and *Fledermaus*—back on the season this year. Doing Frank's melodrama

in *Fledermaus* is still one of my most favorite memories and experiences as a performer, and earned me some of the best notices of my life. I remember with delight having private rehearsals, off-the-clock, with Lorna back at Paragon as we developed that crazy scene. And it was a delight working with Doc Rohrbaugh so intimately in that scene, my old mentor, teacher, and friend.

Betany Coffland recalls Irene as being "so committed to us, always there for us in performances and final rehearsals. It was so comforting to have her rooting you on. She'd make constructive suggestions. What a wonderful strong presence, a mentor." Coffland appreciates critique, so Irene never scared her. On the contrary, she offered friendly advice about music, career, and relationships, for which "I'm forever grateful."

Betany Coffland in *La Voix Humaine*, 2011

Mary Elizabeth Enmann sees Irene as "very dramatic, sure about what she wants, and good at getting people to help her realize her vision. To some people, Miss Dalis can seem difficult to get along with, but that is only because they don't understand her passion for the company, and her desire to get the best for the performers. She is extremely loyal to the company singers and gives them as much support as she can." In 1979, Enmann was given the opportunity to sing the lead in *The Medium* (a joint production with SJSU Theatre Department), her first dramatic opera role. When the other soprano was incapacitated by illness, Enmann was called on to sing all the performances. To enable her to get as much rest as possible, Irene paid for Enmann's salary as a teacher's aide for two weeks. The performance was such a powerful experience and the applause she received at her entrance at the preview gala made her realize, "This is what I want to do the rest of my life."

Lettie Smith originally sang in the workshop and OSJ chorus in the 1980s, but when her kids came along, her schedule wouldn't allow it. She now works in OSJ administration, managing grants, outreach, and webmaster duties. She says,

> Irene can be an absolute tyrant to employees, but we always know she loves us. That inspires the loyalty we feel. Not many people could get away with a dictator style of leadership. She treats us like family. She's vocal and doesn't mince words, but we got used to it. She's strong. That's how she could navigate challenges in her career.

John Bellemer says, "Irene holds a very special place in my life. I have so much respect for her as an artist and for what she has done in San José. She really cares about young singers." For example, she recommended him for an important vocal competition, and she was there in New York when he auditioned. "This was above and beyond what one would ever expect. She was

The Impresaria

The gala celebrating 25 years as Opera San José, 2009

there for me and made sure I met the right people. She is such a powerful woman who could be so intimidating at times, but was also very kind and supportive, wanting only the best for her singers. She became like family to me."

The Orchestra

Flutist **Isabelle Chapuis** says simply, "I love Irene Dalis. She's my hero." How many general directors visit the orchestra before each performance to say she's proud of them and to wish them well tonight? Such attention is rare, says Isabelle; so often an orchestra is taken for granted. She pointed out that every member of the orchestra made a donation to help fund the 25th anniversary gala, and displayed a memento: a framed handwritten thank-you note from Irene. Irene sent one to each member of the orchestra. After a huge public event involving hundreds of people, somehow Irene found time to send individual thank-you notes, and her flutist framed hers.

Violinist **Virginia Smedberg** has been, like many other musicians, with the orchestra since before the Montgomery, and she says cheerfully, "We're going gray together." The whole OSJ organization feels positive to Smedberg, sharing the goal of making music, a mood she attributes to the leadership style at the top.

Oboist **Patty Mitchell** didn't speak to Irene much during her first 15 years, acknowledging that she is introverted. She calls herself a "pit sticker," not even going to the orchestra's lounge at intermissions. She was in awe of Irene, intimidated not by how she was but *who* she was—the boss. Finally Mitchell spoke to Irene at a reception and, finding such a friendly response, said to herself, "Why didn't I do this earlier?" Mitchell remembers that dreadful day, September 11, 2001. It was the first time OSJ had produced Verdi's *Falstaff*. Instead of canceling on September 11, OSJ went on with the show. Irene told her company, "You do not let the terrorists win. If one audience member arrives, we will perform." In fact, the theatre was packed. It was an emotional night. The entire company united backstage and sang the national anthem, along with the audience and orchestra. To acknowledge the horrible tragedy, OSJ canceled a planned pre-show event and instead played the national anthem (which is usually played only on opening night) every night for the rest of the run.

San Jose Repertory

James Reber co-founded San Jose Rep. Like director Timothy Near, he had extended contact with Irene in the Rep's early years.

> In 1980, I began the work of creating San Jose Repertory Theatre. As part of my efforts, I contacted Miss Dalis to meet with her.... I remember the absolute power of her presence when I introduced myself. She has a very stern look when she concentrates.

> I admit that I was a little intimidated by her, and I wasn't sure she was interested in what I was doing. I inquired about her opera workshop and she laid out her plans to have a professional company here in San José. Miss Dalis was able to convey both the grandeur of her vision and her appreciation for how difficult it would be to see it through. Despite a somewhat tense ambiance in that room, I couldn't help but feel enthused.... We have been friends ever since, and I am among her many unabashed admirers.

Timothy Near, who earlier described the first years of sharing the Montgomery Theater, adds, "She is a passionate, tough leader who knows how to be collaborative and supportive of her fellow leaders, knows how to keep the peace, and keeps moving towards the goals of a greater vision."

The Board

Frank Fiscalini was a founding board member at OSJ, and former president and chairman of the board. He says,

> I love Irene. She's one of the brightest people I've ever known. She's not only a star but also an exquisite businesswoman. It is so rewarding to see the singers develop and then go out on their own and perform on the opera stages of the world. The fact that many of our resident artists pursue professional careers is testimony to the effectiveness of our unique opera company. She never stops. She's probably working now on getting another warehouse.

Mort Levine, another founding board member, grew up in New York City and has been an opera lover since age 12. He heard Irene sing Kundry in *Parsifal* and Ulrica in *Un Ballo in Maschera*. "Irene takes no prisoners when she has her business manager hat on. This has enabled the company to stay healthy all these years." He remarked that she's good at getting people, including directors, singers, and conductors, to do things they didn't know they could do.

Richard Dorsay also grew up in New York City and has been an opera lover since his early teens. He prepared for each Met performance by listening to a long-playing record several times while following along in the libretto. "Opera touched me, came through to my heart." Referring to the strict expectations in the 1950s that males not have or (God forbid) *show* emotions, he adds, "I spent a lot of time being the persona that was rewarded by society. Opera transformed me for a moment, brought me to a place I didn't know how to reach by myself. I could access feelings I didn't know I had. It helped me realize I was human, not a robot." Dorsay is one of the lucky ones who heard Irene perform Azucena and Amneris. He gets chills just thinking about it.

> I've never seen a better Azucena or Amneris. She was awesome. She could really do wicked, and totally convinced me, this little woman with the enormous voice that filled the hall. Right now I'm getting tearful thinking about her on top of the tomb. She *was* that person who was spurned and angry. She gave me a glimpse into the fact that I did have feelings.

Dorsay joined the board and now knows Irene as a businesswoman. "Being in the black is always her message. She says the goal is to give singers a springboard, and OSJ must be alive to do so. Nobody puts anything over on her. She knows what she wants and is going to get it."

George Crow is another formerly unemotional and tightly controlled man who credits opera with opening his heart. "At opera, in the dark, I can let myself go and imagine myself in the show." George admires OSJ's traditional productions and is absolutely confident that nothing annoying or distracting will take away from singers and story. This artistic integrity has inspired him to subscribe for almost 20 years (so far) and serve on the board for eight of them.

Laurie Warner, longstanding member of the board of trustees and its current president, became a good friend of Irene's in the early 1980s, when they walked together for exercise every morning. Irene would tell her about her concerns and trials, related mostly to OSJ.

> Irene would thank me for helping her solve her problems. I really didn't offer much advice. I just listened to her think things through out loud. I still do that. I stay involved because I love Irene; I love our company, and I am passionate about our company's mission and keeping quality opera alive in our community. Opera encompasses all the arts: visual (sets and costumes), acting, drama, comedy, dance, orchestra, and most of all—glorious voices.

Arlene Okerlund was the dean at SJSU who defended Irene from faculty ire. She became such an admirer that she joined OSJ's board. "While I was on the board, there was never a deficit in the budget—because Irene supervised every detail. She was in complete mastery of the budget, a model of financial responsibility: she knew the cost of every production, the details of every line-item expenditure. But she also understood the need to spend money as needed to assure top-quality opera from the beginning." Okerlund emphasizes the absolutely unique quality that Irene has of combining artistic mastery with administrative talent, saying, "She built OSJ from *nothing!*"

Jeanne McCann became a part of OSJ in the early 1980s, its formative years, when Irene was at the SJSU producing opera workshops. When the workshop needed a supporting group or auxiliary, the Friends of Opera was formed, and she found herself in the middle of all the activities and leadership roles. One of its most famous activities was the Operathon. "At one of these events, Irene Dalis greeted the guests dressed right out of *Madama Butterfly*, complete with kimono, wig, and make-up. No one recognized her. Since those early years, Irene has been an inspiration and wonderful friend." McCann continues being a part of OSJ, serving as a Vice President on the Board of Trustees and financially supporting the resident artist program. She feels that Opera San José is her musical family and is proud to be a part of it.

Tricia Anderson calls Irene "one of the most focused people I've ever worked with. If she meets an obstacle, she goes around, over, or through it." In addition to creating the company, she always insists on high musical values, which make an intangible legacy. Tricia pointed out that OSJ has attracted a loyal and dedicated staff, who keep operations running so smoothly you hardly notice them. These are the non-singing and (heretofore) unsung heroes of OSJ.

Kitty Spaulding, former president and then chair of the board, now residing in Hawaii, comments, "She's so smart. She has such a grasp of both the business and artistic sides of the company, a trait that is not often found in other arts organizations. I've always felt she could successfully run any type of business." And yet this was not a hard-hearted kind of fiscal prudence. Kitty continues,

> Often Irene would make presentations to the board about the status of the budget, fundraising goals, etc., and there were a number of us that would get teary while she was speaking, she was so emotive and communicated in such a way to

The Impresaria

touch our hearts. We all wished we had been able to see her in one of her performances. She must have been incredible.

The Audience

Sarah Williams was entranced. She sat transfixed, watching the singers as they poured out a stream of heartfelt song. Wagner's music spoke to her, and she could watch the video of the Ring for hours. Finally she turned to her father and asked, "Why is the one-eyed daddy god so sad?"

Sarah was four years old. She adored the Ring and watched the video repeatedly, making up her own plot line as it went along. When her father **Scott Williams** mentioned that the nearby San Francisco Opera would be doing the Ring, she begged to be allowed to attend. Remembering how important supertitles are to understanding the complex plot, he said kindly, "Sarah, you may go see the Ring as soon as you're old enough to *read*."

Scott recounts these moments with paternal pride. He subscribed to OSJ from the day season tickets were offered, even though it meant driving 60 miles each way. Sarah had her own season ticket to OSJ performances from the age of five until she went to college. One year Scott took Sarah and her middle school classmates to see *Carmen* and recalls looking over at them during the final scene and seeing four girls crying their eyes out.

Let's revisit **Sharon Breden**, the high school sophomore taken by her piano teacher to a San Francisco Opera performance of *Lohengrin*. Breden was awestruck at Irene's rendition of Ortrud and wrote her a fan letter. Irene responded, and a lifelong friendship was launched. In 1962, Sharon arranged for her high school chorus to attend a performance of *Don Carlo* and invited "Miss Dalis" to visit her school. To her delight, Irene agreed. At the visit, she listened courteously to the choir's performance and then stayed afterwards, speaking to each individual student.

Even then, fifty years ago, Irene was involved in engaging and supporting young people.

A devout Catholic, Breden was about to enter the convent (unlike Manon, she actually did so). For her last wish before this solemn life change, she wanted to see Irene sing *Parsifal* in Bayreuth. In 1963, Breden and her piano teacher flew 6,000 miles to do just that. They were dismayed to learn that the performance was sold out. What to do? Sharon sat dolefully on the steps near the box office. Hour after hour passed, but no ticket-holder with a last-minute change of plans arrived to offer one. Finally, when Breden had given up hope, a kind woman from Scotland gave her a ticket. Victory! But what about her teacher? Then, miraculously, Irene got a second ticket. The newspapers took notice of this special event with headlines like, "American teenager gets last worldly wish." Many years later, Breden would come to the rescue just when Irene needed her the most.

After Breden entered the novitiate, Irene visited her there in 1964. In the late 1960s, when her father, Captain Breden, was stationed with the Air Force in Wiesbaden, he, his wife, and Sharon's sister **Mary Breden** would travel to Hamburg to hear Irene perform there and have breakfast or lunch with her. Once when Mary went to Hamburg to see Irene in *Il Trovatore*, the two of them stayed out so late afterwards celebrating that they had to wake up the night porter to get back into their hotel. Mary also became a lifelong friend. The Bredens recorded Irene's broadcasts and collected reviews, many of which are mentioned in this book.

Brad Wade has been a subscriber for over 25 years, ever since attending the 30-hour fundraiser Operathon in the late 1980s. He recalls, "I still remember the quartet from *Rigoletto*, and Eilana Lappalainen singing 'Sempre libre.'" Toward the end of the evening, the Friends of Opera had almost reached their fundraising goal. What could they do on the spur of the moment to raise the last few hundred dollars and reach the goal?

Someone had the idea to sell Irene's signature. "So there she was, running around the room signing people's programs for $2 each. Operathon was so much fun that I made it part of my opera schedule every year." Wade keeps coming back to OSJ for many reasons, mostly to hear great music in dependably good productions. He also loves to see the singers develop, to meet each new cadre of resident artists ("OSJ has a track record of finding good new singers") and, as a donor, to meet them in person. Wade is such a devotee that he attends two performances of each production, one of each cast. "Why miss our favorite singers? The tickets are so reasonably priced that that problem was easy to solve." He adds, "I also know I won't be assaulted by some ghastly directorial concept. OSJ is a community, a little jewel I enjoy being a part of. I have no official position, yet I feel a part of it."

Heidi Munzinger is a passionate opera lover who subscribes to half a dozen opera companies, from Seattle to San Diego, San Francisco to New York, including two series at OSJ so she can always see both casts. She has been known to fly across multiple time zones to see a special production. At San Francisco, she also serves as a supernumerary (non-singing member of the cast) and lightwalker (volunteer who stands or moves onstage, standing in for the principal singer while the technical crew sets up the lighting cues for upcoming productions). Munzinger compares OSJ to a cultural startup or incubator: an organization created to identify talented emerging singers, find the right roles for their voice types, give them performance experience, and launch their careers. She adds, "OSJ takes risks, doing unusual operas, not just the chestnuts. They've done *Idomeneo, The Pearl Fishers, Werther, Anna Karenina, The Crucible*. Who else has done that?"

Rita Elizabeth Horiguchi, who has spent over thirty years in software, management consulting, and non-profit volunteerism, credits OSJ with helping fill the void she felt upon leaving the cultural riches of New York to follow her then-husband to the West Coast. "I left New York with an aching heart to save my

Falstaff, 2013

marriage—and discovered this beautiful opera company. It really gave me back the art I missed so much." Horiguchi is so enthusiastic that she has played a major role in the revival of Friends of Opera San José. This volunteer organization is supporting OSJ in many ways: event planning and execution, promotion and audience development, patron outreach, education and hospitality, fund-raising, and facilities maintenance. You are warmly welcomed to contact this group if you'd like to participate.

Chris Mays, the friend to whom Irene wrote the long letter beginning on page 65, has known Irene for half a century. At first he was an enthralled listener at the Met. Irene could sing in a way that Mays calls verismo coloratura: "She could adapt her voice to so many styles and had a phenomenal range." In 1962, Mays was a call boy (the one who summons singers when it's time for their entrance) when the Met brought a touring production to his hometown of Memphis. He met Irene and began a long friendship that lasts to this day. Mays has a prodigious memory and knows the date of every performance of hers that he saw and can blithely allude to a high B-flat in such-and-such an aria. Mays says, "Every production I've seen at OSJ has her touch. What we see is a reflection of her. The calibre of the productions is so high, and the orchestra and conducting are always first-rate. OSJ's *Idomeneo* would have enhanced any opera house in the entire world. Everything about it was just stunning." Mays puts his admiration into action, driving more than three hundred miles from Southern California to attend every production.

Alma Taylor was a member of the original Friends of Opera group that helped get OSJ off the ground. As a child, she attended a one-room schoolhouse (the Purissima School), Palo Alto High School, and then San José State College three years ahead of Irene. She sang leading roles at West Bay Opera and has conducted choirs in churches of various denominations. She also invented Opera Bridge: since 1997, lovers of the card game gather for an afternoon or evening of bridge and make donations to their favorite opera company. Over the years, thousands of dollars for OSJ have been raised in this way.

In the audience one encounters people amazed by Irene's combination of art and administration. **Arlene Okerlund** was attending a performance at OSJ one night in 2011 and fell into conversation with the man in the next seat. She mentioned Irene, and he asked, "Who is Irene?" She explained, "'Irene Dalis, the founder of this company." He looked at her in amazement and said, "Do you mean Irene Dalis, the *singer?*" Thirty-four years after she retired from the stage, Irene's voice was still remembered.

How does one understand the woman with this mixture of traits—warm yet impatient, sternly disciplined yet a devoted mentor and supremely loyal? Alida Loinaz, Irene's daughter, gives an insightful portrait of this complex personality.

She's action-oriented, not receptive to whining or complaining. She really likes order and routine, loved to drive, liked being in control, a perfectionist—if it is worth doing, it is only worth doing well. She does not suffer fools, but had a way with people upon whom she had to depend—she befriended the costumers, dressers, hairstylists, make-up artists. If she had a special request, she had a knack of prefacing it with, "I don't see how you could possibly do this; this is simply too much to ask of you" or something similar, such that the other person would want to find a way to do the impossible.

Whatever may be the ultimate explanation for Irene's extraordinary combination of gifts, everyone who knows her agrees: It's rare.

EIGHT

Tragic Losses and Daunting Challenges

The Fire

ON FEBRUARY 10, 1990, AT 6 O'CLOCK in the morning, Irene's husband George woke her. "Honey," he said, "I smell smoke." The heat was turned up high that winter because George was in treatment for a recurrence of esophageal cancer. Irene opened the bedroom door and found the hall full of smoke. She tried to call 911, but the telephone was dead. The fire burned so rapidly that the attic was soon gone. "I was cool as a cucumber. I was focused, I got in the role," Irene recalls. George was hooked to an intravenous drip. Thinking quickly, she got him outside to safety. Suddenly she darted back inside the burning house. Her singing career helped—she knew to take a deep breath before she went back in. "I had to retrieve my robe," she explained. "I couldn't have people looking at me in a nightgown."

The fire department and other rescuers arrived and took charge. As soon as they were safe and resting at her brother's home, George looked at Irene and said, "How very fortunate we are. We are blessed." They had each other. Irene agreed. "It put

Irene and George, 1989

everything in perspective. Material things are of no value. Saturday night we said, 'We are blessed with the number of friends and the support they're giving.' People, family, and friends are the important things in life."

And the people around Irene proved that. The house next door happened to be vacant. OSJ resident artists and volunteers immediately leaped into action, moved into the empty house, and spent a week salvaging what remained in the burned building. University students joined in. Together, they retrieved what could be saved, polished silver, cleaned porcelain, and saved pieces of oriental carpets in case that would help with the insurance claim. It was opening night of *The Pearl Fishers*. Soprano Eilana Lappalainen, cast as Leila, arrived at the house to help. Irene told her to go back to work. "You've got to be on stage. Do this one for me." Lappalainen did so, then came back next day to join the band of salvage volunteers. Others who came to help included OSJ Board President Kitty Spaulding, baritone Anooshah

Golesorkhi, and the entire cast of the current production. Irene was deeply touched and says, "The only time that George ever cried was when he saw everyone pitch in to help."

San Francisco Chronicle reviewer Robert Commanday had been planning to ask Irene about donating her collection of memorabilia to the San Francisco Performing Arts Library and Museum. Alas, he was too late. Though she and George were safe, a lifetime of opera recordings and mementos went up in smoke. Lost were their library, paintings, opera scores with staging details written by Wieland Wagner, a score of *Der Rosenkavalier* with the composer's comments, a carved music stand given by her voice teacher Edyth Walker, piles of reviews and programs, the costly concert grand piano given by her family, and boxes of reel-to-reel tape recordings. Irene realized the house was really gone when chainsaws were used to cut apart her grand piano so the wreckage could be hauled away.

Once the immediate crisis was over, Irene had the fire investigated. The insurers found that it had been caused by a malfunctioning furnace and concluded that it had been damaged six months before by the Loma Prieta earthquake, whose epicenter was less than twenty miles away. Unbeknownst to Irene and George, the furnace had cracked and they had been at risk ever since.

With help from friends, Irene leased and furnished a home, but George never saw it, for his condition worsened. One month after the fire, on March 10, 1990, George died of cancer at age 76. During this painful time, Irene's solace was music. She spent hours daily at the piano playing Beethoven sonatas.

Irene recovered from these crushing losses, went back to work, and returned to the labor of love that was OSJ. She continued the resident artist program, put on four operas a year, and helped launch numerous singers' careers. Twenty years went by, and OSJ became an established and loved center of San José's cultural life.

The Car Crash and the Good Samaritan

On October 15, 2010, Irene's 85th birthday was celebrated at the San José Improv, a comedy club, with 240 guests in attendance. Along with friendly roasts by opera and civic leaders, attendees enjoyed a skit in which male singers dressed as women and vice versa, poking fun at the German system of classifying vocal types. Irene was even presented with a sculptured portrait of herself. Of course, it was a bobblehead doll, and everyone present received one. Ever the organizer, Irene said, "I brought a whistle and a timer for today, but I didn't use them. I was laughing too much." What a joyous occasion for this active, healthy person!

One week later while she was driving to work, a Chevy Tahoe lost control while entering the freeway from an on-ramp, skidded across three lanes, and smashed into her car. It was totaled. Yet somehow, Irene remained conscious and alert. When a good Samaritan stopped and pulled her out to safety, she knew who should be called in an emergency (Laurie Warner, president of the board) and even remembered Warner's phone number. Everyone who knows Irene well recognizes in this event the intrepid lady that can't be stopped, even by a speeding SUV. But it was a very serious accident, shattering her right ankle and breaking fifteen ribs.

Luis Quandt, the rescuer, is a field engineer for Pacific Gas & Electric, northern California's major utility company. A young man in his late 20s, he was driving to his nearby office in a company truck, well back in the middle lane behind her. He saw her car being struck by the SUV, spinning around, and coming to a stop facing the wrong way in the emergency lane next to the center divide. Quandt passed her, stopped his truck, parked in the emergency lane, and rushed back to see if she was okay. It was starting to rain. The front end of her car was crumpled. He opened her door and asked, "Are you okay?"

"I can feel my feet are wet."

"Does your neck hurt? Can you feel your hands and legs?"
"Yes."
"I'll get you out of here. Come on."
She said, "You can't. I'm too heavy."

Finally Quandt persuaded her to let him help. "Just put your arms around my neck." He picked her up, carried her to the back of his pickup, and placed her carefully on the lowered tailgate. He even went back to her car, brought her purse, and put it next to her. Though she was seriously injured, Irene was alert enough to follow what was going on, and said, "You're pretty strong." But she added, "My feet are wet."

Then Quandt saw that her right foot looked almost severed and was bleeding freely. Fortunately, she didn't look down to see the carnage. A man on the other side of the freeway yelled, "Are you okay?" He had already called 911. Quandt stayed with Irene. More than once he said, "Stop moving your neck."

"But I have a meeting. I can't be late."

Quandt said, in a patient understatement, "I don't think you're going to get to your meeting."

"You don't understand, I have to be at my meeting."

"Don't worry about it. Take it easy."

As you can probably tell by now, it's not a simple matter to get Irene Dalis to "take it easy." Quandt remembers that she was adamant about getting to her meeting. At the same time, she wasn't one to waste a moment, so during this enforced pause in her busy life, she asked him, "Do you go to the opera? I can get you tickets."

The paramedics arrived. Quandt told them what had happened and gave them his card. Irene also got his card, thanked him, and was whisked away. He went to work, rinsed the blood off his tailgate, and didn't mention the incident. The next day, a co-worker excitedly announced that an important OSJ woman had had a car accident the day before and had been helped by a good Samaritan. That's how Quandt found out who she was, and his co-workers found out about his good deed.

True to her word, Irene made sure he got an invitation to an OSJ production that he redeemed some months later. When he and his wife arrived, Irene enveloped him in a big hug (from her wheelchair), invited them to the Sainte Claire Hotel for the reception, and made them feel welcome. With pleased surprise, he said, "She acted like she had known me for years."

Asked what made him so strong, Quandt replied,

"My mom supported the family in many ways, but my dad and I were the ones who loved rebuilding cars in our back yard, especially Mustangs."

"Oh, you mean you did things like lift engines out and put them back?" That would certainly account for the hefty muscles visible from his short-sleeved shirt.

"Yes. I also worked out while I was in college. Still do. In fact, I just came from the gym."

So once again, luck was Irene's friend. Just when she needed him, this strong, compassionate, level-headed young man showed up and helped save her life.

But this was just the start of the road back. "At the beginning, I really thought I should depart," she later told a reporter. "'Let's find out what's on the other side of this world. Let's just do it.' That was my first wish, and I wasn't frightened or anything."

But she hadn't counted on her old friend Sharon Breden. Breden was actually due to volunteer at OSJ offices that very afternoon to organize the library, and she learned about the accident right away and rushed to the hospital. Irene said,

> I was glad to see her. Not only was she one of my dearest friends, she knew all about hospitals and surgery. Sharon had severe scoliosis and had undergone many surgeries herself. I was so injured and tired, and I confided to her, "Just let me go. I've had a good life." She held my hand and said fiercely, "No! You can't go. You have to write a book!"

This incongruous, impulsive exclamation was followed by many weeks of loving care, as Breden drove to San Francisco three times a week to visit Irene in the hospital. By this point, the immediate medical crisis was over.

"When I realized that I was not going to die, then I knew I had to do everything in my power to help this [body] heal." So she began the arduous regimens of rehabilitation. Even though she was in the hospital, Irene was "still feisty as ever," wrote the opera's director of development in a message to the community. "She's giving out directives and telling people not to send flowers or condolences, but to send donations to the opera instead."

Irene spent six and a half months in three different hospitals, undergoing numerous surgeries and grafts of skin and muscle. At the beginning, she recalls, "There was much talk that I might have to have the right leg amputated." Fortunately, that danger passed, and she began long-term convalescence. "Yes, there were moments of great difficulty, but somehow or other good sense came into my brain: 'Well, it's not going to help to be depressed.' So I just found a good thing to think about every day, something in my life—and I've had a wonderful life."

Did being in the hospital, facing one surgery after another, stop her from keeping an eye on Opera San José? Hardly. From her hospital room, she studied the company's marketing, development, and financial reports, and was kept informed by board president Laurie Warner and general manager Larry Hancock, for which she is eternally grateful. But she did miss many performances that her beloved company was offering that winter and spring. "Oh, I tell you, that was the biggest punishment. That was the hardest, knowing that my people were on stage, and where was I? I was in bed. Fifty miles away." But at least she could watch videotapes of the performances that were made and brought to her hospital room.

Over the years, Irene had built a strong, resilient team at OSJ. In fact, in a prescient moment some time earlier, she had told the board, "I could get hit by a bus, and the company would continue."

And it did. Irene is justifiably proud of this. Not a single performance was canceled or delayed. Still, the long months away from OSJ exacted a cost.

> This was six months doing nothing, and all I did was think and think and think. I'm not a religious person, but I spent a lot of time thinking about the Big One. And I think I relived my entire life, as well. I thought about my late husband, and about my childhood, and how I spent most of it at the piano. And I thought about college in the war years, and how, during World War II, people would hang stars in their living room windows [to represent sons or husbands in the armed services]. And the day my mother took down those three stars, and I knew my three brothers were well and coming home—they were all overseas in the military—I think that was the happiest day in my life.

While she was recuperating from the accident and the surgeries, friends and family rallied around: daughter Alida, grandsons Gregory and Scott, nephews, nieces, great-nephews, and great-nieces. Hundreds of people sent get-well cards.

Seven months later, a reporter asked about her future. "I'm moving forward," she said matter-of-factly. Was she planning to attend the fifth annual Irene Dalis Vocal Competition later that week? "Of course!" (As if there were any question). "It's an opportunity to show young talent that we do believe in them and we want to help them. That's what my whole life is about right now, to help them get going, to launch careers."

The Other Good Samaritan

The fire that destroyed her house cost Irene a lifetime's worth of mementoes. Most of these were irreplaceable—but what about the recordings? Could this collection be reconstituted? Unknown to Irene, a man who had sung in the workshop chorus years earlier quietly decided to do that very thing. Edwin Stafford, whom we met in chapter 4, had always been a record collector, and he knew that Irene regretted not having made more recordings. He regretted it as well, because that meant there were fewer recordings of her voice for students to hear and study. But at least the Met had broadcast and preserved many of her performances, and Stafford made a vow to collect them all. Over a period of six years, he gathered recordings of 58 of them. He even found an SJSU archival recording, so he and some friends huddled in the library's soundproof room, listening to this late 1950s record.

Stafford was helped by a network of opera lovers. An organization called Opera_sell is a global trading network, complete with daily emailed bulletins. Before long, he acquired a reputation as Irene's archive maven and found some recordings she didn't even know existed. It's no wonder she didn't know about them: they were contraband. Naturally the Met prohibited anyone from recording their performances, but an army of bootleggers was secretly doing just that, starting in 1950s. These illegal recordings were made by the fans for themselves to enjoy and to preserve history, not to sell for profit. A character known only as "Sam" even sneaked a reel-to-reel recorder into the hall. Since these are suitcase-sized devices, that was a real feat. Then there was "Mr. Tape," who led a group of bootleggers making these collections. One fan found, in a flea market in Germany, a rare recording of her doing selections from *Carmen*.

Stafford loves this collection because he can trace the history of the Met's performing traditions—cuts, additions, conducting styles—and the evolution of Irene's voice over time. Amazingly enough, he found a recording of the night that Franco Corelli and Leontyne Price debuted in *Il Trovatore* in 1961. He also found a recording of Placido Domingo's surprise debut at the Met in *Adriana Lecouvreur*, complete with the pre-curtain announcement about Domingo substituting for an indisposed Franco Corelli. "The gentleman I got it from had actually recorded it from the standing-room section at the back of the house in 1968 and stuffed it into a drawer."

Stafford got a recording engineer to transfer it to CD. He obtained several copies of each performance, then edited and spliced them to make the best possible reconstruction. He even bought a CD player on which one could change the musical pitch, to correct errors that had been caused by tired batteries. He wrote,

> Two of the fascinating aspects of building Miss Dalis's recording collection were: (1) Meeting so many people online around the world who were fans of Miss Dalis and all too willing to help me track down her recordings; and (2) Tracking recordings from the late 1950s to the mid-1970s chronologically, which allowed me to get an inside look at her career development.
>
> I met many people who recalled her in performance at the Met in the 1960s, some of whom sent me magazines and autographed pictures of her. One day, I got a call out of the blue from Martina Arroyo and her husband, who helped me track down cast information for a 1965 performance of *Il Trovatore* (Martina and Irene were in the same performance) at the Cincinnati Zoo (!!), where you could hear all sorts of birds and zoo animals in the background. Part of the challenge in building the collection is that full cast information has been difficult to trace, but

some people kept programs (after nearly 50 years) and were kind enough to share those with me. In short, Irene has fans still around and people were willing to share their stories.

And she has admirers in all sorts of places. In the section in this book called Awards is a long list of honors Irene has received. The latest was from the City of San José Arts Commission, the first annual "Cornerstone of the Arts" award. When she went to the podium to receive it, she remarked with characteristic wry humor, "I know why I'm getting this award. It's because I'm the oldest."

Oldest—and still growing and learning. To Alma Taylor, a friend and supporter who was, like herself, experiencing health problems, Irene wrote in 2013:

> We both have had marvelous lives, particularly blessed with the love of music and both talented as performers. Could it be that what we are now experiencing is a payback for so much joy? There have been many highs in my life and for every "high" there is a "low." Everything levels itself out eventually. You know that I spent six and a half months in the hospital, which gave me time (too much time, perhaps) to think. It is during those months that I realized that I may have been too independent during my life and that now I was put in a position where I could not do anything for myself. I had to depend on others for *everything!!*

But this dependence was not permanent, and Irene soon returned to her beloved opera company, wiser but as energetic as ever. In the same message, she added,

> Between the physical (3 times a week) and occupational (2 times a week) therapists and driving

lessons [for a specially adapted car] (3 times a week), I am kept rather busy. Add to that: working on budget, repertoire, and planning for the next three years for OSJ.

The fire, her husband's death, and the very serious accident slowed Irene somewhat, but they did not quench her spirit or her drive. Alida Loinaz, Irene's daughter, writes:

Opera San José is really a child of my mother. The OSJ family is her family. OSJ is the product of her vision, creativity, perseverance, and total commitment. We are all (the Dalises, myself, my sons) very proud of her. She is an incredible woman, with drive and passion and a can-do attitude that is very healthy but is also rare. I think that in that way her parents had a profound influence on her. She manifests the pioneering spirit that must have sparked the waves of immigrants who felt empowered to create the lives they envisioned when they came to the New World.

NINE

The Fine Art of the Opera Business

"No, you can't put that in the book," Irene said more than once. "Let's not get involved in making comparisons." But this author persuaded her to include the opinion, held by numerous people that had been interviewed and by the author herself, that sometimes Opera San José's productions are preferable to those staged by companies with ten or even twenty times OSJ's budget.

How does OSJ do this? In part because, after a lifetime in opera, Irene has strong artistic opinions and makes them the guiding values of her company.

Good Teaching

Good teaching is the foundation of an opera singer's art. Unfortunately, there are quite a few bad teachers, including some who were famous performers in their day. Lotfi Mansouri, never one to mince words, said that 90 percent of teachers are phony, flattering the students for a hefty fee. Bad teachers not only fail to improve the voice, they can get too close to students and make them dependent. Mansouri called them "criminals." He himself, a singer in his youth, had bad teaching and it took him two years to recover. Many retired stars made lots of money giving lessons. Opera humorist Anna Russell used to say, "My voice has been ruined by the best."

Luckily, Irene avoided that fate—partly because, as was seen in an earlier chapter, she did careful research before choosing her teachers. Then Edyth Walker made Irene do exercises for a full year before starting her on the repertoire and Otto Müller started each lesson with vocal exercises. So Irene was fully grounded in the basics.

Yet in the late 1960s, even though Irene had been doing starring roles for over a decade, eminent soprano Rosa Ponselle summoned her and offered some unsolicited advice. The diva told the younger woman to change her repertoire, dropping all but five roles, and to cancel all engagements for six months to study with her. Irene called George Schick, a conductor friend of Rudolf Bing's, to ask his opinion about this self-serving advice. Schick said firmly, "Irene, you are recognized as one of the top mezzos in the world. If Mr. Bing thought you needed extra work with Rosa Ponselle, he would release you to do it—and he would pay for it."

During thirty years of running OSJ, Irene has heard hundreds of auditions. When she hears a questionable voice, she often thinks, "There must have been a good instrument there at one time." She sticks to her decision not to do the teaching herself, but tells the singer, "You need a new teacher. Change teachers and come back in a year." Some of them take her advice and return greatly improved. Others are apparently too attached to their teachers, or don't want to hurt their feelings by leaving.

But good teachers and coaches can be hard to find, as Irene discovered in Milan while on her Fulbright scholarship. Teachers of the caliber of Walker and Müller are known only to the insiders in the opera world. If a singer is looking for a good voice teacher, Irene's advice is to find out who taught the good singers in his or her area.

One trend in the current crop of teachers is to make all singers sound alike. This irritates Irene. "I sometimes feel like a lone voice in the wilderness about not pigeonholing singers. My biggest peeve is vocal teachers and coaches who say to their students, 'You can't do that.'" Müller didn't believe in stereotyping, nor does David Rohrbaugh. But Irene assures us that OSJ is careful: "We don't ask them to force their voices."

And where did these bad teachers get these ideas? From *their* teachers. So there's an unfortunate lineage of well-meaning, opera-loving professionals who are not helping. Many of the people interviewed for this book agreed that there is a serious problem in the opera world with teachers who give poor advice and end up hurting people's voices. Several fumed, "There's no accreditation for teaching. Anyone can say they're a voice teacher."

Aspiring singers should know this: No matter how much praise you have received, even experts acknowledge that it's hard to predict who will succeed, especially when luck is taken into account. If you pursue an opera career, do it for love of the art. And find a good voice teacher.

Solid Preparation

Musicianship, the foundation of a musical career, means literally knowing the score, the music. Interpretation means knowing what the character is feeling, how one's aria fits into the scene. These are the genuine elements of opera that a singer must know—not the modern trend of "researching a role" by studying the composer's life, the original novel or play the libretto was based on, or the historical background. Because she had studied piano and other instruments for a decade before taking up singing, Irene was steeped in the language, notation, and art of music. She says,

> Conductors didn't have to worry about me. I could learn the roles myself without needing a coach. I

did not research roles. I just learned the words and notes. There's no correlation between researching a role and good singing. Think about not *how* you're singing, but *what*. It's all on the page. Just present what the geniuses, the composers, gave us.

Irene attributes her fearlessness onstage to her many years of piano training and practice. She was a master of notation and knew the scores intimately—"I was a total musician." Conductors could trust her, knowing she would sing exactly what was on the page. Even today she will correct people on musical points. Some of them don't believe she's right until they check the score.

But what if one has a sudden opportunity and can't spend weeks preparing a role? The habit of solid preparation can make quick study possible. This had happened to Irene, when Rudolf Bing asked her to do a scene from *Aida* in 1952. She rushed to her teacher's studio for study and had it ready by that afternoon. On another occasion she rose to an even greater challenge:

> In Oldenburg where I started, I was called Friday evening and told I had to be at a dress rehearsal for *Così fan Tutte* on Monday morning. Never having studied the role, I said, "I don't see how I can do it." And the manager said, "Well, if you can't do it, I'll have to tear up your contract." I worked with the main coach of the company all day Saturday and Sunday. On Monday I was in costume and makeup singing Dorabella at a time when I didn't even understand German. But I did it. It's not the ideal way to prepare a role, but it showed me that discipline is valuable.

Irene has heard many singers who can't sight read, don't know the entire role, or don't know how to prepare a role. So those who want a career like Irene's are urged to master the basics. Her motto is, "Success happens when preparation meets opportunity."

I'm often contacted by mothers whose children have shown an aptitude for singing. My best advice is this: have the child study an instrument, especially the piano. Then when his or her voice matures, start with voice lessons. True musicianship is the ability to read music, to count, to follow the line. You can't improvise in opera.

Irene warns her resident artists that there is no magic formula for making a career, and no guarantee. At least now it's no longer necessary to go to New York. "In my day," she says, "you had to sing at the Met to be considered successful. Now there are more companies, and you can have a perfectly good career without the Met."

Irene sums up the qualities a person needs in order to build an opera career: patience, professionalism, total commitment, fitness, dependability, total preparation, punctuality, discipline, and artistic temperament rather than temper. Then once the career takes off, one needs the ability to be alone, to cope with success, and to handle adulation, travel, and being away from one's family for long stretches. It's a daunting list, and makes one admire opera singers more than ever.

Good Staging

The standard opera repertoire goes back almost 230 years. Often, the classics are staged in a traditional manner that the composer and librettist would recognize. It is also possible to re-imagine the classic operas successfully, setting them in a different time or place: Laurent Pelly's *La Belle Hélène* set at the beach, Johannes Schaaf's *Barber of Seville* with Figaro arriving onstage on a Vespa, Marta Domingo's production of *La Traviata* set in the 1920s with Violetta making her first entrance in a glamourous Daimler. In OSJ's 2013 *Hansel and Gretel*, directed by Layna Chianakas, the witch zoomed around not on

Idomeneo, 2011

a broom but a Segway. The audience loved it. If the concept supports the opera, updating can work. Once the initial surprise wears off, the audience accepts the concept, enters the re-imagined world, and loses itself in the magic of music and drama.

However, today there are many ghastly stagings that are not genuine re-imaginings, but merely obvious attempts by stage directors to say, "Look at me! ME! ***ME!*** Aren't I clever?" Recent examples include the *Ring* that starred a hulking ferris wheel of disobedient planks; Bellini's *The Capulets and Montagues* in which several dozen saddles were suspended overhead from the ceiling and key scenes took place with supers clumping in high heels up and down a set of bleachers; and a *Macbeth* punctuated by stage bits using (among other things) a typewriter, hula hoops, nail polish, egg beaters, and a tape measure. Hearing about the saddles, Mansouri smiled knowingly and joked, "Maybe someone had the saddle concession."

Unfortunately, this has actually been going on for decades. Here's Mansouri, writing in 1982:

The Fine Art of the Opera Business

There was a recent production of *Aida* in Frankfurt, in which Aida and Radames, instead of being entombed at the end, are gassed to death in a concentration camp. There was a *Barber of Seville* in Munich in which the stage set consisted of a giant torso of a woman. When Almaviva serenaded Rosina, he had to climb up onto the pubic hair. I have seen a *Traviata* directed by Béjart in which Violetta arrives at the beginning of Act Three in a coffin, and a *Butterfly* performed inside a plastic tube.

The *Barber* that he refers to was staged in 1974; not only did the tenor have to climb up and position himself on the statue's groin, the Rosina was peering out from a hole cut in its left breast. Mansouri concluded, "There are too many directors who put their own ego gratification ahead of their duty to the work itself. They constantly call attention to their cleverness. Basically, they are pirates." Soprano Teresa Berganza said such directors should be put in jail. Irene says,

> I unabashedly stand for good productions. My number one desire is that singers should have a chance to perform the opera as the composer intended. Some directors now coming from the theatre world don't understand music. Too often the so-called concept is so far removed from the intent of the composer that I feel insulted and leave the theatre dejected. Supposedly, experimentation brings in new audiences.

But is there any evidence that edgy productions draw new audiences? Bass Kirk Eichelberger doesn't think so:

> Modernizing a production can work, if it's done well. Crazy modern productions do *not* attract young audiences. They do *not* sell out the house;

Christopher Bengochea in *Idomeneo*, 2011

the crazy productions backfire, keeping new people away. The director is the only one who benefits. By contrast, Miss Dalis wants to tell the story as intended by the composer.

Director Brad Dalton, who has done some wonderful productions for OSJ, including *Idomeneo,* has director friends who tease him about doing traditional productions there rather than setting an opera in, for instance, a trailer park. Dalton used to feel this way, thinking, "It should be set inside a cow's stomach or I'm not interested. Irene changed me. She gave me freedom, but I learned to respect traditional settings."

A director's goal may be to shock the bourgeois or get attention, even if it's negative attention. One director made no bones about insulting his audience to their faces. At Bayreuth, a German director recently put on a Ring so dreadful that at curtain calls he was booed for 10 minutes. Was he chagrined, or did he at least have the decency to scuttle away into the wings? No, he stood there defiantly and gestured to the audience, unmistakably conveying, "Go ahead, boo some more. Just what I wanted." Another director, when asked about audience reaction to his production in a major house, shrugged and said with heartless indifference, "Not my problem."

One explanation sometimes given for the aptly named "Eurotrash" is that there are so many opera companies in Europe (handsomely subsidized by the state, one might add), that to get attention, a director is desperate to appear unique. The irony is, these directors think they are being innovative, when in fact the whole trend of trying to shock people is now old and tired.

Rebecca Davis in *La Traviata*, 2012

Mansouri proposed a solution: To keep opera vital, companies should commission new works. "Rather than try to capture transitory headlines with yet another deconstruction of a masterpiece, let them challenge imaginative directors, conductors, singers, and musicians with new and interesting works that reflect the spirit of a given time and place." Santa Fe does this; San Francisco does; and OSJ has put on five world premieres: Alva Henderson's *West of Washington Square* and *The Last Leaf*, Henry Mollicone's *Hotel Eden*, George Roumanis's *Phaedra*, and Craig Bohmler's *The Tale of the Nutcracker*. The next world premiere will be *Where Angels Fear to Tread* by composer Mark Weiser and librettist Roger Brunyate. Based on the E.M. Forster novel of the same name, it premieres at the California Theatre in February, 2015.

In the overall arc of opera's history, there have been artistic cycles: singers were the stars in one era, conductors were celebrated the next. Now it's stage directors who get the attention. There's even a style named for them: Regietheater (German for "director's theatre"). But they should really be using their imaginations to serve the opera, not vice versa. Irene concludes, "I would have refused to do it. This fad will last until the public says no."

Fortunately, there are some hopeful signs. At the New York Met's Ring cycle, the one with the rotating planks, the audience did not flock to the production and management ended up giving tickets away. Likewise, the Los Angeles Ring of 2010 was so weird that in a virtually unprecedented move, leading singers actually went public with their disapproval and one principal artist left the production altogether. In 2013, David Gockley, general director of the San Francisco Opera, fired a stage director who had been engaged for *The Flying Dutchman* and gave the rest of the creative team the green light to revise the production. Judging by the production photographs of the intended version, the audience would have seen Senta in a cemetery, the Dutchman arriving in some kind of spaceship, weird extra-terrestrials on board Daland's ship, and Senta's friends dressed as tarts in a brothel. So Gockley wisely decided to make the change.

Scott Bearden and Zach Altman in *Falstaff*, 2013

With Irene's values firmly in place and Larry Hancock as the successor General Director, opera lovers can be assured that at OSJ, they will always see productions that celebrate what matters: the opera.

The Resident Company

Many people who know OSJ share Irene's conviction that the resident company model is a valuable one that should be expanded in the U.S. It's good for the singers. They get a stable home, guaranteed leading roles, a boost to their resumes, and the opportunity to stretch themselves. They make friends and contacts that can last a lifetime. And it can open doors the singers themselves might not have found otherwise. Soprano Sandra Rubalcava Bengochea found, "At OSJ, I had the opportunity to perform many major operatic roles with orchestra, perform in many outreach performances and stage direct various operatic scenes at San José State. That is what started my interest in directing and teaching. It gave me a chance to try things out and see what I was capable of doing." Conductor Anthony Quartuccio adds, "Working with young talented singers who are eagerly learning a role for the first time is incredibly stimulating to me personally. I feel enormous freshness combined with responsibility as a conductor to teach them a great opera with depth and understanding of what is between the notes so that their first experience performing a role reaches a very high level."

It's also good for the audience. In an era of typecasting and vocal pigeonholes, there's something special about seeing performers stretch their wings in a range of roles. In most houses, the audience may not even know that tonight's Mephistopheles can also do a hilarious comic turn, or that a languishing Violetta can also be utterly convincing as the fearless rowdy barkeep in *Girl of the Golden West*. At Opera San José, patrons have the chance to find this out. Tenor Alexander Boyer has sung the lovestruck, impetuous Alfredo in *La Traviata* and the comic socialite Eisenstein in *Die Fledermaus*. Cecilia Violetta Lopez has brought to life the somber nun in *Suor Angelica* and the flighty teenager Lauretta (*Gianni Schicchi*) in the same evening. Mezzo Layna Chianakas has sung the effervescent, lusty Cherubino (*The Marriage of Figaro*) and the tormented, heartbroken Elle (*La Voix Humaine*). The audience has the joy of watching emerging singers grow over the years and blossom into experienced opera artists.

So a resident company model is great for singers and audiences. But if it is such a good idea, why is it not adopted elsewhere in America? Short answer: It's hard on management. Many of the people interviewed for this book explained this. Director José Maria Condemi says that it's difficult to tailor a season to the abilities of the artists you already have, when it's so much

Opera San José's *Gianni Schicchi*, 2013

easier to fly in artists who can do the operas that your audience will surely want. Barbara Barrett called this task a "jigsaw puzzle" and adds that many companies are now being run by business administrators who may think they need to bring in a famous star in order to fill the house. Soprano Cynthia Clayton gave a multi-faceted response. A resident company needs a leader with personality, she says, who loves the surrounding community. It needs a sophisticated audience, but one that is located just a bit too far from a major opera company for frequent attendance there. Bass Jesse Merlin said that the resident company model "takes vision, long-term investment, and stewardship" (such as buying real estate). It's an incubator, and he wishes there were more like it. Former board member George Crow totally believes in the model, saying, "That's the way you grow wonderful opera singers." He thinks it's not common because others haven't had Irene's Oldenburg experience. Ernesto Alorda from Seattle Opera agrees that it's "the best thing for young singers" but rare because it requires incredible vision, money, and nerve. Director Lorna Haywood adds, "OSJ works because it is a unique concept—a company, custom built from scratch, nurturing a carefully selected group of promising young singers."

Should these difficulties prevent others from adopting the resident company model? Far from it—even as it challenges managers, it solves other problems. Tenor John Bellemer volunteered that adopting residency "would put opera in this country in a very different light. If the OSJ business model were more widely used in cities across the U.S., it could keep opera thriving for the next century." Mezzo-soprano Betany Coffland concludes: "It's mind-boggling that it doesn't exist more in America. It's where the art needs to go."

Dan Montez, the multi-talented singer, director, and composer, is doing his part to spread the concept (see Appendix).

> I believe every company in the U.S. should model itself on Opera San José. When singers get used to performing together, they create better art. Ensemble performances reach the audiences better than "diva" performances that feature a star. On top of that, singers that get to go home to their families at night are happier artists. My opera company (taconicopera.org) has a resident philosophy posted on our website for this reason. We wouldn't have done this if Opera San José hadn't made such a compelling case. Our singers are happy, and our orchestra and chorus are happy because of the atmosphere this creates.

Resident Company, 2013-2014

How to Build an Opera Company (and Sustain It)

Some of the same qualities go into building an opera company as into building a singing career—plus a few more.

Use Foresight. Early in OSJ's history, Irene realized that to give young singers the experience she had had in Oldenburg, they would need a place to live. Accordingly, OSJ bought an eight-unit apartment building. Then she bought another one, with six units, so OSJ can house the guest artists as well. Because she is adamant about staying out of debt, she bought them both for cash. In addition, Irene made sure to set aside money every year to create a cash reserve. Irene reiterates that her father was adamant about not buying anything unless you could pay cash for it. This lesson of frugality was never forgotten. This may be why Opera San José has survived when the economic downturn closed so many arts organizations. Shortfalls in income have occurred in recent years, but Irene had wisely built a substantial cash reserve.

Pay Attention to Finances. The idea of creating an opera company where none existed before is certainly a visionary one, but Irene was always attentive to money, never buying anything she couldn't afford and making up the difference by the sheer talent of the singers and the values of the productions. Her nickname among friends is Irene "Bottom Line" Dalis, or, according to late board member Rosa Cohn, Irene "It's Not in the Budget" Dalis. The watchdog organization Charity Navigator has six times given OSJ its top ranking of four stars. Said Irene, "We've shown that we know how to handle our resources. We simply don't spend what we don't have. Our sixth 4-star rating by Charity Navigator highlights this careful stewardship of funding. We're deeply committed to artistic integrity while appreciating the realities of the bottom line."

Managing money is a kind of art form in itself. When asked whether OSJ creates new sets and costumes for each production, Irene said that this was a complex matter with many variables. OSJ owns some sets which can be reused, but they may need to be repaired periodically. A new director for *Carmen* may have a different concept from the last one who directed it and want new costumes. Besides, singers come in many different sizes and this year's Faust may be six inches taller than the last tenor who sang the role. Sometimes it's less costly to rent costumes, but this has to be decided on a case-by-case basis. She concluded, "You can't predict. We don't sell widgets. You can't have a formula."

Get Advice from Experts. Grants were important in building the administrative skills that Irene, Hancock, and OSJ needed. In 1987, OSJ received the L.J. Skaggs and Mary C. Skaggs Foundation Institutional Stabilization Grant, and in 1992 the National Endowment for the Arts Advancement Grant. Hancock said, "Each gave us a year of advice and training by nationally recognized consultants, who worked with us in mission/artistic vision, long-range planning, marketing and more." This guidance was invaluable. The assistance of Dr. Robert Crawford was part

The Fine Art of the Opera Business

Larry Hancock, OSJ's second General Director

of the unsolicited grant from the Skaggs Foundation; he gave advice on business management, organization, and entrepreneurship for three years.

Attract the Right People. David Rohrbaugh, Larry Hancock, Barbara Barrett, and hosts of volunteers poured their time, energy, and talent into the idea of creating an opera company, which must have seemed crazy at first. Phil Livengood, who with his wife Judy managed the apartment buildings for 14 years, remembers when the surrounding region was farm country and says with a smile, "Miss Dalis must have been one bubble off plumb to start an opera company in the prune capital of the country." Phil and Judy were already long-term volunteers for various causes, yet they willingly joined the project. OSJ gave them the opportunity to exercise the skills their careers did not have room for: working with his hands for Phil (he is a retired airline pilot), and interior design for Judy (a psychotherapist). At a donor event in the mid-1990s, Phil asked the singers about their lodgings, deduced that there was no formal maintenance plan, and volunteered to do small jobs. This assignment expanded like yeast in bread. Meanwhile, Judy would scour thrift shops and sales for furniture so diligently that their staffs knew her by name. She and Phil even refinished second-hand furniture. One desk was badly damaged on one side, so they removed one stack of drawers and turned it into a printer stand and condensed the rest into a small one-stack desk. They furnished most apartments completely, down to the kitchen utensils. He speaks fondly of the residents as "our opera kids." Some were naughty, doing things like sneaking their pets into the building. His philosophy for dealing with this: "Help 'em when you can, and keep your mouth shut about the rest." Many other volunteers helped the Livengoods to maintain the apartments, a task that could in some months take 100 hours.

Persevere. Asked why she persisted in devoting her time to OSJ, Kitty Spaulding replied,

> I was impressed with the company and its mission, and with Irene. And the fact that despite initially meeting with so much negativity from the community, Irene forged ahead with her dream. It was not a whim, but a solid plan, and though at times fraught with difficulty, OSJ succeeded.

Attract Donations. Of the thousands of hours he and his wife have volunteered to manage the apartments, Phil Livengood says they do it because "Irene is so dear. We got to share her dream, to be part of it, to offer our humble gift. We've gotten as much as we've given." And would you expect an opera company to be offered a *house*? Jo Chisholm, the sister of Tony Piazza (founder of Raiders of the Lost Aria), advised the owner of that house to contact OSJ. The owner admitted it was situated near a landslide area. Livengood had majored in geology, so he and a geologist friend checked out the house and decided it was safe.

OSJ accepted the house, then later sold it and used the proceeds towards the purchase of the six-unit apartment building.

Sell the Art to the World. From Operathon and Operafest to free concerts in the Sainte Claire Hotel, from articles in the *San Jose Mercury News* and *Opera News* to outreach events, opera singers, patrons, employees and volunteers spread the word about this creative artistic venture in San José. Today, OSJ stages some of the most moving and delightful productions that new and experienced opera lovers have ever seen.

The Woman Who Cast a Shadow

Irene has created a legacy for singers, directors, conductors, and opera lovers that is unique. Standards of artistry, a powerful business sense, fearless decisiveness, and personal warmth have built an artistic community whose impact reaches far beyond the city she calls home. Irene's daughter Alida wrote:

> My mother's story is a good one. A smart American woman from a humble but fiercely supportive family found a way to carve a path for herself, always ready to face challenges and work hard to develop and use her God-given gifts. While her era was unique, the basic lesson is good for everyone and timeless: Do not accept limitations. Set your sights high and find a way to adapt to the changing situations along the way. Seek out and ceaselessly prepare for opportunity. Don't sit idly by and expect opportunity to land in your lap. When it does land, you'd better be prepared for it—or have the can-do attitude to meet it head on.

Irene Dalis's Parting Words

In 2013, OSJ founder Irene Dalis announced her farewell to the role of General Director, effective mid–2014. She faced this step with mixed feelings.

> After thirty years, I finally decided to retire as General Director of my beloved company. I am sad to leave a position I have relished and enjoyed (in spite of the almost-daily crises connected to a performing arts organization!), but I am also glad, because I know I am leaving this precious company in good hands.
>
> I am thankful that the Board of Trustees has chosen Larry Hancock as my successor. I cannot think of anyone more qualified for the position. His talents are numerous and he has honed them by holding almost every position possible in an opera company: singer, performer, pianist, chorus director, musicologist, set designer, marketing and development director, and finally production director. Since Larry was a leading tenor in the SJSU Opera Workshop and became my graduate assistant long before the founding of Opera San José, I have had the privilege of observing him in all of these capacities over the past thirty-eight years. He has been in charge of every department of Opera San José, other than finance and music, during its first thirty years of existence.
>
> One of his first duties as incoming general director was to select a new music director to succeed the retiring David Rohrbaugh. I am impressed by his choice. Joseph Marcheso is a protégé of Rohrbaugh, who brought him on board in 2007 as assistant conductor for *Lucia di Lammermoor*,

and he has conducted a total of eleven productions for OSJ. He trained at Dartmouth and the San Francisco Conservatory and served as conductor for the opera program there. Marcheso is also on the conducting staff of San Francisco Opera, where he was assigned the West Coast premiere of John Adams's *Nixon in China*, the San Francisco premiere of Jake Heggie's *Moby-Dick*, other world premieres, and a new production of Wagner's *The Flying Dutchman*.

Music Director Joseph Marcheso

I am leaving OSJ in the very capable hands of Larry Hancock, Joseph Marcheso, and a wonderful staff and board—but I'll always be nearby to offer advice (if asked), solve problems, and attend every single performance, as I have done since the beginning. I hope to see you around the California Theatre for years to come.

Celebrating Her Life and the Friends of Opera San José

In June, 2014, to celebrate Miss Dalis's life and work, we held a book launch party. A huge crowd assembled at OSJ's headquarters, filling the rehearsal hall with animated conversation. Luckily, a devoted OSJ fan had created a volunteer auxiliary, and this was its first event. I was rushing around making last-minute arrangements, and said to Miss Dalis, "Now I'd like you to sit here (at a table to the side of the audience) so after I give my presentation, people can ask you to autograph the book." In her inimitable way, she asked, "Why would they want me to sign it? *You're* the author." Vintage Miss Dalis!

Irene Signing Books at Launch Party

Friends of Opera San José has been a valued resource ever since, contributing thousands of hours every year to keep the musical engine humming. Light-walking at rehearsals, wrangling child choristers, staffing events, greeting patrons at the California Theatre, and more. Member Brad Wade presents highly praised previews before each production, with streamed presentations attracting up to 150 viewers. Friends of Opera San José welcomes new members. Visit operasj.org/friends-of-opera-san-jose/ or email us at friends@operasj.org

Farewell

Alas, her continued presence was not to be. Six months after the book launch party, Miss Dalis left us. The opera world took note, and a handsome tribute was published by the Metropolitan Opera.

> The Metropolitan Opera mourns the death of mezzo-soprano Irene Dalis, who sang 22 roles and 274 performances here from 1957 to 1976. She is remembered for a powerful dramatic voice that allowed her to take on a wide range of demanding parts from Amneris in *Aida*, her most frequent role, to Kundry in *Parsifal*, and the Nurse in the Met premiere of *Die Frau ohne Schatten*. A consummate professional, she was admired by audiences and colleagues alike.
>
> Peter Gelb, General Manager
> James Levine, Music Director
> *New York Times, Dec. 17, 2014*

Opera News, the flagship publication of the Met, sent monthly to thousands of subscribers around the country, wrote:

> At the Metropolitan Opera, Dalis's fiery interpretations of some of the meatiest German and Italian mezzo roles made her an audience and critics' favorite. She made her debut with the Met in March 1957, as [Princess] Eboli, and remained until 1976.... Her other home base in the U.S. was San Francisco Opera, where she debuted in 1958 (also as Eboli) and returned there frequently for fifteen seasons. After distinguishing herself in the U.S., Dalis was invited to Bayreuth in 1961, the first American artist ever to sing the role of Kundry.
>
> Brian Kellow, *Opera News*, 12/15/14

And here is a story this author shared with Friends of Opera San José:

> Shortly after Miss Dalis had agreed to collaborate on the book, and well before I was invited to address her by her first name, Brad and I dined with her, along with several important opera guests. A day or so previously, I had emailed her to share the news that two of my published books had just won prizes in a book competition, intending to reassure her that her newly acquired biographer was an experienced author and not just an enthusiastic flake. Well, during this dinner, she made a point of telling everyone about these prizes, and in fact repeated the news a little later to make sure everyone had heard. How considerate to remember my awards, which are surely small potatoes compared to her world-famous career and long list of honors, and to share the news with her guests.

> No wonder so many former resident artists fondly remember her as their greatest and most thoughtful cheerleader.
>
> *Friends of OSJ Newsletter,* January, 2015

For the memorial concert held several months later, her protégés came from all around America and the world, donating their time and talent to honor the woman who helped launch their careers. They have performed leading roles in too many cities around the country and the world to list here. They have also won vocal competitions, made recordings, and become stage directors, conductors, artistic directors, voice teachers, and professors. Some returned to OSJ to sing again or to direct productions. Several have started their own opera companies.

Another World-Famous Premiere

Opera San José has had a longstanding creative relationship with David Packard and the Packard Humanities Institute. You may recall that he helped design and fund the renovation of the California Theatre. More recently, he discovered a young musical prodigy, Alma Deutscher, who started playing the piano when she was two years old. A year later she was playing the violin. At six, she composed her first piano sonata, and at nine a concerto for violin and orchestra. She has performed as a concert pianist and violinist around the world. Conductor Zubin Mehta called her "one of the greatest musical talents today." Sir Simon Rattle agrees: "Alma is a force of nature. I don't know that I've come across anyone of that age with quite such an astonishing range of gifts."

Having discovered her, Dr. Packard decided that her opera *Cinderella* deserved a fully staged professional production. Opera San José was delighted to oblige, and in November, 2017, produced a sold-out run of the opera. One critic wrote,

A twelve-year-old British girl has written an opera of astounding wit, craft, and musical beauty … Deutscher has an effervescent sense of musical humor. The resulting complications from the [plot's] switched medical prescription are musically and dramatically hilarious… The sheer amount of orchestral and vocal invention is stunning. Deutscher's most impressive accomplishment is her mastery of the classical tradition's rich resources for expressing dramatic conflict.… A smart producer would mount *Cinderella* on Broadway.

Five years later, OSJ produced a revised version of the opera—and this time it was conducted by the composer, now 17 years old.

Alma Deutscher conducting *Cinderella* at Opera San Jose, 2022

OSJ Survives a Pandemic and Grows into the Future

Opera San José continues to seed the opera world with emerging talent. In the last ten years, thirty new Resident Artists have developed their artistry and gained valuable experience. World and American premieres of new operas have been presented. Resident Artist positions have recently included the roles of conductor, composer, and stage director, as OSJ broadens its mission to launch careers of other gifted opera professionals. Expanding its reach even further, OSJ launched its Heiman Digital Media Studio, housed at the company headquarters. This is a cutting-edge digital facility, with theatrical lighting and video and audio recording equipment, that allows OSJ to record and share high-quality productions worldwide. Emerging artists can also make professional quality audition videos here, preparing for their futures as they move into the broader opera world.

The timing of this studio's inauguration was perfect, allowing Opera San José to continue performing during the global pandemic. Five opera productions were created and broadcast during the lockdown, assuring continued livelihoods for our resident artists (whose singing friends were not so fortunate) and continued musical performances for patrons—and for people around the country and the world.

When audiences returned to live performances as the pandemic eased, Opera San José welcomed back faithful attendees and attracted new ones to the beautiful California Theatre for the traditional full four-production season. Shawna Lucey, our new General Director, enthusiastically embraced the founding mission and brings vast expertise and an international reputation to the company.

TEN

Juicy Tidbits and Opera Lore

Author's note: The present chapter was inspired by the opportunity I had to write an entry on Opera for the *Encyclopedia of Creativity* (3rd edition, 2020). It contains portions of that article, some of the outtakes I had to leave on the cutting room floor, and some new material. Enjoy!

Opera is the most enchanting, complete art form, with orchestra, singing, drama, and occasionally dance. Oscar Hammerstein asserted in 1910 that opera is "the most elevating influence upon modern society, after religion.... I sincerely believe that nothing will make better citizenship than familiarity with grand opera." Opera and film director Franco Zeffirelli proclaimed, "Opera is a planet where the muses work together, join hands and celebrate all the arts."

Justice for All

Opera also stands for social justice. Impresario Rudolf Bing deliberately established racial integration at the New York Met starting in the 1950s, paving the way for generations of brilliant

African American singers. He also refused to permit the Met to perform before segregated audiences and ensured that some tickets were affordable for poorer citizens.

Rudolf Bing signs Marian Anderson, 1954

Women now have opportunities once denied them. Trade organization Opera America sponsors women composers, one of whom recently had her work performed at the Met and broadcast worldwide. Even the conductor's podium is now open to women, who may become the permanent Music Director, such as Eun Sun Kim at San Francisco Opera. Grants, residencies, commissions, competitions, and positions in conservatories are now available for women composers and conductors. Aspiring opera administrators are supported by The Women's Opera Network.

Although 19th-century operas often had absurd plots, that doesn't mean serious matters were ignored -- though to mollify censors of the day, they were often veiled as stories about the past. Verdi's great chorale "Va pensiero," about the Hebrews in captivity longing for their homeland, became the informal anthem of living Italian revolutionaries hoping to unite fragmented Italy into one nation. His *Don Carlo* deplores the cruel oppression of

Flanders by the Spanish, and his *Un Ballo in Maschera* ends in assassination, while the plot of Moussorgsky's *Boris Godunov* turns on a regretted regicide. Wrote one commentator,

> Revolution is not an uncommon theme for opera, nor indeed are wars with victories and defeats, enslavement and liberation, peace treaties, state marriages, exiles and public executions, conspiracies, political assassinations, state visits, succession struggles, dictatorship, democracy, and many other political phenomena.

Opera *houses* themselves have played a role in history. Even people who were not operagoers felt that the opera house had deep meaning to their community:

> When the Vienna State Opera was bombed and burnt to a ruin during World War II, many Austrians who had never attended an opera there wept, and their weeping was not mere affectation. When it was reopened in 1955 with Beethoven's opera *Fidelio*, many people who could not get inside for the gala opening stood outside in the rain and heard the music over a loudspeaker system, though they could not see the stage. That is what possession of an opera house means.

Fame and Fortune.... at Oh, What a Price

The celebrity industry, often thought to be a scourge of recent vintage, actually dates back centuries, having its origins in "the eighteenth-century world of urban spectacle which produced the first stars. ... Those with the highest exposure became veritable public figures, even outside the theater hall: their names became known, their faces reproduced, their private lives the object of curiosity."

Perhaps the unlikeliest celebrities were the male singers who had been castrated as boys in order to preserve their high voices, at a time when women were not permitted to perform in public. Yet the castrato was not limited to female roles. In Handel's day, the roles of powerful emperors and soldiers were set in the higher registers; the castrato's voice was then "prized for its pure, mythological, static, disembodied and universal character." Far from being scorned, successful castrati enjoyed fame, enviable remuneration, and admiring acceptance in society. Adds Anthony Roth Costanzo, one of today's finest countertenors (see below), "These castrati became kind of the rock stars of their era, with women and men wearing little portraits of them on buckles and on belts and around their neck.... Music was written for them by not only Handel, but Gluck and Mozart and Monteverdi and Vivaldi."

The famous castrato Farinelli, 1750

Such fame and fortune came at a price that may have required some persuading. In 1685, a highly placed gentleman wrote to a certain young Monsieur Dery, who was contemplating having the operation:

> I would say to you, in an entirely discreet way, that you must sweeten yourself by means of a mild [!] operation that will assure the delicacy of your complexion for a long time and the beauty of your voice for your whole life. …. In three or four years, alas!, you will lose the quality of both if you do not have the wisdom to provide for this eventuality.…

One wonders if this gentleman, Monsieur de Saint Evremond, would ever consider taking this step himself. Depending on which form the castration took, the man lost only reproductive ability, not sexual capacity. This could have been an appealing feature in the days before reliable birth control. The persuasive society man continued to the young singer,

> But you fear, you say, to be less loved by the ladies. Be rid of your apprehension: we are no longer living in the age of idiots. The merit that follows the operation is well recognized today, and for every mistress that Monsieur Dery would have in his natural state, the sweetened Monsieur Dery will have a hundred.

The castratos' era faded, though some castrati were made during the 19th century and one lived into the 20th, leaving behind a few poignant recordings. In our era, the *countertenor* vocal type has risen. Normally endowed males with regular speaking voices learn to sing high, as in falsetto, and are making fine music and successful careers, mostly performing Handel and other Baroque operas.

The Music that Audiences Love to Hate

Twentieth-century music diverged drastically from the harmonious traditions of the previous three centuries. Called atonal, twelve-tone, or serialism, it featured dissonance, irregular rhythms, and jarring sounds, intentionally not lyrical or pleasant. It became fashionable among critics. Maybe it was a way of keeping their newspaper jobs and their stature as experts able to appreciate what the riff-raff couldn't begin to understand. Said one observer dryly as early as 1955, "Since both composer and critic are aware that the arrangement is not entirely honorable, they fight a sham battle now and then to keep up appearances. But for the most part they fight together against the public."

Riff-raff or not, American audiences didn't like atonal opera and stayed away in droves. Eventually, it stopped commanding the field, though clanking music is still being composed and performed. David Gockley, one of America's great impresarios, concluded:

> The atonal revolution of the early 20th Century, brought on by Schoenberg and his Second Viennese School, blew the musical world apart.... Finally, in the 1970s Philip Glass brought his signature minimalism to the Opera. It has helped to remove the stranglehold that serialism had exerted on the art form.

Luckily, composers like Jake Heggie and the wunderkind Alma Deutscher are creating approachable new opera music. The stranglehold may be over, but atonal opera is still being created and performed. Matthew Shilvock, General Director of San Francisco Opera, wrote, "European audiences don't necessarily have an aversion to contemporary forms of story-telling. There's still a very active and respected tradition of more atonal work, and more contemporary, non-lyrical works can sell out theaters in Europe."

Some Stage Directors Make It Worse (This Section Is a Guilty Pleasure)

The stage director decides how performers move around the stage and interact with each other, as well as creating the overall vision and working with costumers, lighting designers, and the conductor to create the whole. Talented directors make an opera come to life and give singers a platform worthy of their talents.

Some directors, on the other hand, determined to be thought "original," radically alter the opera. How bad can they be? Here's one example. The first scene of *Tosca* takes place in church, where the hero Cavaradossi is finishing his painting of Mary Magdalene. One director decided to place the artist's presumably still-wet painting flat on the floor, and instructed the performers to walk all over it, which they did.

Unfortunately, this was one of the milder directorial atrocities of recent decades. A scene in Verdi's *Masked Ball* was once set in a men's room, with the chorus singing while sitting on toilets. In a Canadian production of Handel's *Semele*, the betrothal ceremony was crashed by a two-person donkey, which reappeared during a love scene between Jupiter and Semele, flaunting a giant phallus. Chorus members engaged in nude onstage couplings as well. These are not accidents. One observer noted that two German directors' stagings are "regularly accompanied by scandals, furors, uproar and sensation." Not surprisingly, the style (officially Regietheater, or "director's theatre"), became known in places as "Eurotrash." Even Wagner's own opera house in Bayreuth has encouraged it.

> There were loud boos on each night of the opening week and when [German director] Frank Castorf showed his face after *Götterdämmerung*, the crowd

howled in anger. The director proceeded to milk the outrage, lingering before the curtain for more than 10 minutes and inserting himself into other people's bows. To all appearances, this finely nuanced performance as Directorial Narcissist was the only characterization to which Castorf had given serious thought.

The great twentieth-century soprano Gwyneth Jones wrote in exasperation, "Many avid opera-goers have given up trying to show their disagreement by booing, and are simply not going to such performances any more."

You may be surprised to learn that an "edgy" director is merely imitating a decades-old trend. Impresario Lotfi Mansouri was deploring it forty years ago. So when you write irate letters to the general director, and the board of trustees, and the local critic, be sure to say you weren't shocked by the latest bizarre directorial conceit. You were bored.

But there is hope. In 2013, David Gockley, the general director of San Francisco Opera, horrified by what the hired director had designed, fired him a few weeks before opening night and asked his staff to come up with a new staging. The quickly revamped show went on as scheduled.

Director-impresario Lotfi Mansouri, who brought the innovation of supertitles to American opera houses, said it best: "The most important principle for a stage director to follow is that he or she must remain faithful to the spirit of the work."

Critics with Their Wits About Them (Usually)

Opera can inspire torrents of vivid prose from critics, both in praise and condemnation. At Wagner's venue in Germany, audiences are forbidden to interrupt the opera with applause and must wait until the very end to show their appreciation. This rule is scrupulously obeyed, even if unwillingly. One critic shared her frustration—and admiration.

> What applause otherwise would express, this time was certainly proven by the several minutes of reverent silence in which the public remained when the final curtain fell. Any different reaction to such a deeply moving performance of the art of Wagner would be unthinkable. But, after the second act, *it took every ounce of self-control not to applaud* to hail an artist whose interpretation sent chill after chill up and down one's spine. She stood on the stage of Bayreuth for the first time. She sang Kundry, and her name is Irene Dalis.
>
> Her voice commands overall phenomenal possibilities of expression. She has the profound depth of a contralto and reaches heights of glittering, alluring splendor. Freely and easily, she deftly succeeds in attaining a smooth transition as she moves from a brilliant forte to a pianissimo of silver clarity.... From the sweetest-sounding melody into the hollow groan of anguished torture, from the hellish laughter and from the shattering depths in a siren song of unbelievable beauty.

Another night this same Irene Dalis *did* inspire the Bayreuth audience to applaud mid-performance, to the grave displeasure of management but to the glee of journalists in America, to whom news of the scandalous disobedience had been leaked.

Critics can also be uninhibited about issuing caustic takedowns. Wrote another reviewer:

> Silly and inconsequential incidents and dialogues. … are daubed over with splotches of instrumental color without reason and without effect, except

the creation of a sense of boisterous excitement and confusion.... the expression is superficial and depends upon strident phrases pounded out by hitting each note a blow on the head as it escapes from the mouths of singers or the accompanying instruments.

Puccini—superficial and strident? So thought H.E. Krehbiel in 1900, referring to *La Bohème*.

Predicting an opera's future success is risky business, but some critics are fearless in doing so. Wagner's third opera elicited this spicy judgment in 1869: "*Rienzi* tastes like a mixture of Verdi and Meyerbeer pounded in a mortar until it begins to ferment." Critics' prophecies can be mortifyingly inaccurate, like this confident judgment: "*Rigoletto* is the weakest work of Verdi. It lacks melody [!]. This opera has hardly any chance to be kept in the repertoire."

How to Make Musical Friends

Some people's whole social world revolves around opera. Even standing in line becomes a communal experience.

> Opera fanatics, since they spend much time waiting in queues, and because they arrive early to seek good places in the house, tend to converse with each other a lot.... In addition to talking about the music, they also give narrations that show their commitment, heroic tales of how long they stood in line for notable performances, the sacrifices they have made to attend.
>
> Novices have an interest in knowing more about the listening experience, while older members have an audience to tell their war stories to. These topics are extraneous to pure immersion in the music itself, but they show off the moral career

of the opera enthusiast, exhibiting the industrious self-discipline and sacrifice that it takes to acquire the refined abilities of the trained listener.

Now, don't be scared by all this heroism. It is not *required* for you to become an opera nut, just optional. But I do find it gratifying to be praised for moral discipline and sacrifice.

The Opera and the Ecstasy

Opera buffs are hard-core fans who subscribe to several opera companies, own opera books and recordings, and seek what one observer called "collective effervescence." The most ardent buffs have had experiences that "resemble religious mysticism… and [even] virtuoso religiosity." They seek "a response to the singer's voice that sets the hearer not exactly singing himself or herself but resonating with the singer's voice. At the peak moment, the sound goes right through you, it makes you weak in the knees, it makes you feel you are melting."

The trouble with becoming an opera habitué is that you discover that these magic moments do not occur every time. Still, you return, production after production, grateful for the customary excellence but secretly hoping to experience once again a mesmerizing moment you will remember the rest of your life. And sometimes you do.

ELEVEN

Onstage Surprises and Operatic Bloopers

As a performing art, an opera is never the same twice. Even if you have seen *La Traviata* or *Carmen* a dozen times, live opera never loses its potential for spontaneity. Even within the same production, there can be nuances of interactions between singers, last-minute cast changes that enliven the performance, and the rare mistake that may horrify everyone present—or inspire spontaneous improvisation from those onstage. At a performance in Manchester in 1956, the soprano's tooth fell out and was hastily stuck back in with chewing gum. Or the time the stagehand forgot to put the knife on Scarpia's dinner table, and the soprano singing Tosca had no choice but to stab him with the nearest pointed object—a banana. Scarpia dutifully died anyway.

Breaking news: This tale is a garbled version of an actual onstage disaster witnessed in Florida by Opera San José's Larry Hancock. He told me, "The director staged the scene such that Tosca was to back away from Scarpia, brace herself on the table, and happen upon the knife. Actually, her hand landed on a banana in the fruit bowl, but she stabbed him with it anyway."

Larry added, "The rest of the performance was rather spoiled by the fragrant aroma of banana that pervaded the house."

Once when Irene was singing *Tristan und Isolde* alongside Birgit Nilsson, the great soprano noticed that there was no one in the prompter's box. As the curtain slowly rose, Nilsson edged across the stage and whispered this frightful news to her mezzo co-star. Adding to the tension, Irene Dalis whispered back, "We're broadcasting!" Somehow they got through the performance, but you can bet they were determined to find out what had happened.

Turns out a feud was going on between the prompter for German operas and the prompter for Italian operas. The latter sneaked into the below-stage prompter's box and stole the *Tristan* score that was at the desk, ready for the day's performance. There was no one in the prompter's box because as the curtain rose, the prompter of the day was running around downstairs trying to find the score.

The art of recovering from a blooper so skillfully that it seems like part of the show is called "playing it" (at least it was fifty years ago when I was a stagestruck theatre wannabe). Instead of pretending nothing is wrong, the performer acknowledges the glitch, improvises on the spot, and incorporates it into the scene. One night, soprano Maria Jeritza fell down while singing "Vissi d'arte" from *Tosca*. Did she shamefacedly scramble to her feet, awkwardly breaking the mood? No -- she sang the rest of the aria from a reclining position and made it represent the tragic tone that the opera demands.

If it were possible to improve on this story, here is another version: This fall occurred during a rehearsal, and who should be present but Puccini himself? The composer thought this rendition of "Vissi d'arte" was perfect—and asked Jeritza to use it during performances, setting a precedent followed by many succeeding sopranos.

I was hoping to pepper this book with such tales of onstage mishaps and ingenious saves. But alas, no one I interviewed could

Onstage Surprises and Operatic Bloopers

remember such a thing happening at Opera San José. Gratifying as that is for audience and artistic staff alike, it disappointed this author, who thinks that no book about the performing arts is complete without an onstage calamity or two. So I filled the gap with some tales of disasters that actually occurred elsewhere .... Or are supposed to have occurred.... Or might have occurred....

At a Covent Garden production of *Carmen*, the director tempted fate by including an animal in the scene -- always a risky venture in live theatre. When the worst occurred, conductor Sir Thomas Beecham rose to the occasion.

> Halfway through the third act, Sir Thomas became aware that a horse was present on stage, intended to add local color to the smugglers' cave scene... It suddenly turned its back on the proceedings with a decisive and dramatic gesture, and performed the ultimate indiscretion. The music stopped, silence fell through the theatre, and from the pit came the judgment of Sir Thomas: "A critic, by God."

Of course, a performer just might be ready for a surprise. At one performance of Opera San José's 2022 production of Alma Deutscher's *Cinderella*, a patron's cell phone began to ring. Worse, he was near the front row. Soprano Stacey Tappan was at the front of the stage singing the mean step-sister Griselda preparing a song for the prince's music competition. Stacey handled it with aplomb. Here's her account:

> During the previous performance when we were making a recording, someone's phone went off SEVERAL TIMES. I told my sister and Alma that if it happened again the next night, I was going to throw an in-character diva fit, and they loved the idea.

So when that phone rang right at the moment I was trying to "compose" my aria for the ball, I was ready for it, and the timing couldn't have been better. I was to sing *a cappella* so there was no orchestra under me and I could take all the time I wanted. And I had already broken the fourth wall by visibly asking composer/conductor Alma to play a chord (which was scripted). So the setup was perfect for me to be aware of the audience, plus, of course, it was totally in character for me to react in a petulant way. I believe the phone went off TWICE. The patron silenced it after I glared at him, but then the person CALLED BACK, so just when I was about to continue performing, I rolled my eyes and looked at an imaginary watch on my left wrist, pointing to it impatiently and tapping my foot.

Stacey Tappan (left) as Griselda in *Cinderella*, 2017

Onstage Surprises and Operatic Bloopers

Stacey "played it" perfectly, charming the audience. She added in an email to this author, "Cell phones going off in performance is such a regular occurrence that confronting the person feels a little tired at this point, but as far as Griselda is concerned, it is a SIN OF THE HIGHEST ORDER, AND *HOW VERY DARE YOU.*" I love this quirky final phrase, which is *not* a typo, and plan to use it myself when the occasion arises.

The opposite of "playing it" is called "breaking character"—looking befuddled, halting the action, or visibly looking to the prompter for a cue. This shatters the illusion and reminds the audience that they are in a theatre watching a performance. But even breaking character can be done to great effect. In a classic opera story, the mechanical swan boat in *Lohengrin* was pulled offstage too soon by an overeager stagehand. The stranded tenor Leo Slezak was unfazed and addressed the audience. "Does anyone know when the next swan leaves?" Since this tale has been told and retold for eighty years, one suspects that really good onstage bloopers are cherished almost more than flawless performances.

Another *Carmen* went awry thanks to a building manager who kept a pet on the premises. It was usually locked away during performances, but one night it got loose.

> In the middle of the smugglers' scene, a gigantic Pyrenean mountain dog wandered on to the stage. ... The dog eventually roamed downstage opposite the conductor, where it became hypnotized by the baton, which by then was being used partly to conduct the music and partly to try to shoo the beast away. Unfortunately, the dog was also used to having people throw sticks for it to fetch, and was convinced that the baton was about to be thrown. When it wasn't, the dog became cross and emitted a series of mournful barks.

Now if one of the smugglers had been skilled in the art of "playing it," she would have promptly seized the dog by its collar, scolded it with exaggerated gestures as if it were her own misbehaving mongrel, and guided it offstage.

Of course, one can also handle a problem by tossing it like a hot potato to someone else. One night in the legitimate theatre, an onstage telephone rang in the wrong scene. A quick-witted actor picked up the handset, pretended to listen for a moment, and handed it to his co-star, saying, "It's for you."

Not all onstage predicaments are accidental. I think we must agree that the most memorable operatic mischief occurred during the final act of *La Bohème*. Musetta has pawned her earrings so that the dying Mimi may have her dearest wish, a fur muff in which to warm her cold little hands. In this perhaps apocryphal performance, the soprano, while all eyes are wet with the tragedy of her impending death, gratefully puts her hands into the muff—to find that some backstage imp has thoughtfully inserted a warm sausage.

Let's return to Opera San José. Instead of experiencing bloopers (no matter how amusing they may be to opera lovers), OSJ continues to mount flawless performances. The only surprises known to this author (and anyone she interviewed) occurred due to last-minute substitutions caused by late illness. Well, Opera San José had *one* onstage mishap. The leading baritone was injured doing a scripted cartwheel. He bravely finished the scene, and after intermission the performance continued smoothly with an excellent cover.

It's challenging to send one's book to press when exciting news continues to arrive. The latest: Lori Decter Wright (Resident Artist soprano, 2001-2006) has just been named General Director of Tulsa Opera. There will undoubtedly be news of further successes by the artists that Opera San José sends out into the world of the most marvelous art form of all.

To the Reader

OPERA SAN JOSÉ BEGAN AS THE dream of a successful singer who wanted to give to others the same gift she had received early in her career—a trusted home base where one can learn and perform the collective art that is opera. Opera San José has survived three economic downturns, the 1989 Loma Prieta earthquake, its general director's near-fatal car accident, her death, and a pandemic. It has been the little engine that could, bringing magical toys to music lovers near and far.

You can help Opera San José continue to thrive. Besides attending performances, you can bring your friends, make a donation, become a subscriber, give people copies of this book, host an opera party, join Friends of Opera San José, and encourage the young people you know to develop their musical tastes and talents.

- Make a donation. https://secure.operasj.org/donate/q/donate-now
- Buy tickets to a performance. www.operasj.org/productions
- Become a subscriber www.operasj.org/subscribe
- Buy this book at Amazon or Barnesandnoble.com.
- Join Friends of Opera San José: Friends@operasj.org

If you're not in the San Francisco Bay Area near San Jose, California, you could honor Irene Dalis and Opera San José by supporting the opera company in your region—and encouraging the management to learn about the Resident Artist model. See the next page to learn how one former OSJ Resident Artist created one himself.

APPENDIX

The Resident Company Model

One of the things that makes Opera San José so special and so successful is its adoption of the resident company model. One of OSJ's earliest resident artists, tenor Dan Montez, has had a flourishing singing and conducting career and has also created Taconic Opera, in Westchester County, New York. He wholeheartedly endorses the resident company model. The following essay is printed here with his permission.

Our Philosophy of Opera by Dan Montez

In the United States, opera is produced primarily through the import of singers as private contractors on a short-term, single-contract basis. Singers, under this system, often engage in agreements with agents, who set up hundreds of auditions that often result in few contracts. These singers travel from opera house to opera house, hoping to make enough money to survive during a year. It is difficult to maintain full-time employment apart from the opera career, because each opera requires an average of one month of resident rehearsals.

In Europe (especially Germany), opera functions mostly with what are called "Fest" contracts. This system engages singers at single opera houses with yearly renewable contracts. The singer lives in the city and sings all of the leading roles in that opera house (or at least the roles in their particular "fach" or voice type).

Up to this point, only one opera company, Opera San José, has successfully created a full, year-round resident opera company in the United States. This company engages full-time residents that are paid a living wage year round, twice monthly, with benefits and even housing. Not only has OSJ succeeded, but it has received worldwide recognition for doing so. Most important of all, it has never operated with debt. The company, founded more than thirty years ago by retired Metropolitan Opera star Irene Dalis, has made the case that the resident system can work in the United States.

Taconic Opera believes that resident opera is preferable to import opera. Here are a few reasons why:

1. It creates a more integrated experience, because the performers become familiar with one another on the stage and can anticipate and blend with each other's acting styles. Traditional American opera often presents a story that is unbelievable because of a lack of commitment to ensemble. Resident opera eliminates the "diva" syndrome that focuses on performers as individuals, and replaces it with a committed group of the artists working together to tell the story.

2. It produces better art because it engages people that lead lives that help them understand their audiences. These artists live in and participate in communities. They can have relationships for which they make sacrifices. Imported artists often have no permanent relationships or have broken families. Many travel from one superficial relationship to the next, marrying, in essence, their profession. As a result, the life experience with which they generate their art may be superficial as well. The characters they portray are often one-dimensional. Taconic Opera believes that the art cannot be separated from the artist. Who the artist is as a person is evident in the work that the artist produces. Taconic Opera rejects the popular idea that depressed artists make better artists and attempts to create an environment where artists are not torn between home and work.

3. It salvages incredible amounts of lost American talent. Each year thousands of wonderful artists decide not to perform because they cannot or choose not to endure the rigors of travel required by import opera. Many want to live normal lives, with families and communities. The sacrifice is often too much for most artists, and their talent remains unshared with the public. If opera in the U.S. were mostly resident, more American artists would enter the field. This would introduce not only a different artist mentality to the public (an artist who cares more about family and community than career), but also higher artistic standards. Great voices would enter the arena.

—From www.taconicopera.org/philosophy/philosophy.html

Young Artists in 2024

There have long been young artist programs at some established opera companies, offering participants lots of coaching, networking, and the chance to sing small roles onstage. Opera San José was always special, offering, in addition to these benefits, valuable opportunities to sing leading roles in mainstage productions, free housing, and free healthcare. In recent years, other companies have begun to host Resident Artists, sometimes called Artists in Residence. But they do not appear to offer OSJ's full package. Opera San José is still a very special opera company, committed to doing everything in its power to launch emerging opera talent.

Another Voice on the Resident Artist Model

Mezzo-soprano Diane Mauch, after her singing career and then years directing the young artist program at Florida Grand Opera, created a distinguished third life as a professor of voice, lecturer, and consultant. She knows the vicissitudes of a young singer's life, and explained that contract singers who fly from one engagement to the next never get to know their singing colleagues. They also don't get to know important backstage people: the stage managers who keep the performance moving, stage hands who move sets around, and those important props handlers who ensure that key props, like Tosca's knife, are on set before the curtain goes up.

By contrast, at Opera San José, said Mauch, "Emerging singers get to learn their craft on mainstage productions, projecting their voices to fill the house, working regularly with full orchestras, and getting to know a conductor's style. They get to sing a variety of roles and lead normal lives, making friends and knowing where the best restaurants and parking lots are."

Stagehands and parking lots: who would have guessed how useful it is to know them!

Selected Discography and Videos

DURING HER SINGING CAREER, IRENE DALIS made only one official recording (with the exception of the Telefunken records made in Berlin before her Metropolitan Opera debut). This was *Parsifal*, with Jess Thomas in the title role, Hans Hotter as Gurnemanz, and Hans Knappertsbusch conducting. This recording won the Grand Prix du Disc in 1964.

Parsifal. George London, Martti Talvela, Hans Hotter, Jess Thomas, Gustave Neidlinger, Irene Dalis. Chor und Orchester der Bayreuther Festspiele / Hans Knappertsbusch. 4 CDs. Philips Classics.

Fortunately, recordings of many of her Metropolitan Opera broadcasts are available, either on the Met archives or from various vendors. A link to a list of everything Irene sang at the Met is at http://bit.ly/1hg3DfN. Her performances at San Francisco Opera are listed here:

http://archive.sfopera.com/qry3webcastlist.asp?psearch=Irene+Dalis

The online store Operadepot.com is maintained by Andrew Whitfield, OSJ's own chorus master and associate conductor, who remasters old recordings, including many with Irene Dalis, and offers them on the site. Another online store called The Bel Canto Society (belcantosociety.org, no relation to San Francisco Opera's Bel Canto Legacy Society) has at one time or another offered the following CDs:

Don Carlo, April 15, 1961
Franco Corelli, Mary Curtis-Verna, Irene Dalis
3 CDs #Foyer-4281

Cavalleria Rusticana, December 8, 1962
Irene Dalis, Barry Morell
2 CDs #Foyer-4289

Macbeth, April 4, 1964
Cornell MacNeil, Irene Dalis
2 CDs #Foyer-4304

Salome, March 13, 1965
Birgit Nilsson, Irene Dalis
2 CDs #Foyer-4311

Aida, February 12, 1966
Leontyne Price, Richard Tucker, Irene Dalis, Robert Merrill
2 CDs #Foyer-4317

Die Frau Ohne Schatten, December 17, 1966
Leonie Rysanek, Christa Ludwig, Irene Dalis
3 CDs #Foyer-4324

Aida, January 3, 1970
Leontyne Price, Jess Thomas, Irene Dalis, Robert Merrill
2 CDs #Foyer-4350

Die Frau Ohne Schatten, January 16, 1971
Leonie Rysanek, Christa Ludwig, Irene Dalis
3 CDs #Foyer-4364

Parsifal, April 3, 1971
Sándor Kónya, Irene Dalis, Thomas Stewart, Cesare Siepi
4 CDs #Foyer-4371

Tristan Und Isolde, December 18, 1971
Jess Thomas, Birgit Nilsson, Irene Dalis, Giorgio Tozzi, Erich Leinsdorf
3 CDs #Foyer-4375

Un Ballo In Maschera, February 3, 1973
Richard Tucker, Sherrill Milnes, Irene Dalis
2 CDs #Foyer-4388

Videos and Online Clips

In 2009, a video was made to celebrate the 25th anniversary of Opera San José.

It includes a tribute from Placido Domingo, recollections from important figures from OSJ's history, and stunning arias performed by current and former resident artists. Email friends@operasj.org to request a copy.

In recent years, numerous short videos about OSJ have been recorded and posted online. For instance, this 8-minute video provides a wonderful introduction to Irene Dalis and Opera San José. http://www.youtube.com/watch?v=gJ25n2GnGdg

Many other audio clips from her career can easily be found on youtube.com and other websites.

OSJ Productions, 1978 to 2024

2023–2024
- *Florencia en el Amazonas* (Catan)
- *Rigoletto* (Verdi)
- *The Barber of Seville* (Rossini)
- *Romeo and Juliet* (Gounod)

2022–23
- *The Marriage of Figaro* (Mozart)
- *Cinderella* (Deutscher)
- *Falstaff* (Verdi)
- *Tosca* (Puccini)

2021–22
- *Dido and Aeneas* (Purcell)
- *Carmen* (Bizet)
- *West Side Story* (Bernstein)
- *Mozart and Salieri* (Rimsky-Korsakov)
    - *Streamed due to the pandemic*

2020–21 *All productions were streamed due to the pandemic*
- *Dichterliebe* (R. Schumann)
- *Three Decembers* (Heggie)
- *The Parting Glass* (Stark)
- *Love and Secrets: A Domestic Trilogy*
    - *Il Segreto di Susanna* (Wolf-Ferrari)
    - *Four Dialogues* (Rorem)
    - *The Husbands* (Cipullo)

2019-2020
Magic Flute (Mozart) *Canceled due to the pandemic*
Die Fledermaus (J. Strauss)
Hansel and Gretel (Humperdinck)
Il Trovatore (Verdi)

2018–2019
The Abduction from the Seraglio (Mozart)
Pagliacci (Leoncavallo)
Moby-Dick (Heggie & Scheer)
Madama Butterfly (Puccini)

2017–2018
Così Fan Tutte (Mozart)
La Rondine (Puccini)
Cinderella (Alma Deutscher)   World premiere
The Flying Dutchman (Wagner)
La Traviata (Verdi)

2016–2017
Lucia di Lammermoor (Donizetti)
The Barber of Seville (Rossini)
Silent Night (Puts and Campbell)
LaBbohème (Puccini)

2015–2016
Tosca (Puccini)
The Marriage of Figaro (Mozart)
Carmen (Bizet)
A Streetcar Named Desire (Previn)

2014–2015
Rigoletto (Verdi)
The Italian Girl in Algiers (Rossini)
Where Angels Fear to Tread (Weiser)   World Premiere
The Magic Flute (Mozart)

2013–2014
    Falstaff (Verdi)
    Hansel and Gretel (Humperdinck)
    Madama Butterfly (Puccini)
    Don Giovanni (Mozart)

2012–2013
    The Pearl Fishers (Bizet)
    Die Fledermaus (J. Strauss)
    Il Trovatore (Verdi)
    Double bill: *Suor Angelica* (Puccini)
                  Gianni Schicchi (Puccini)

2011–2012
    Idomeneo (Mozart)
    Double Bill: *La Voix Humaine* (Poulenc) *Pagliacci* (Leoncavallo)
    La Traviata (Verdi)
    Faust (Gounod)

2010–2011
    Anna Karenina (David Carlson)
    Tosca (Puccini)
    The Barber of Seville (Rossini)
    La Bohème (Puccini)

2009–2010
    Manon (Massenet)
    La Cenerentola (Rossini)
    The Marriage of Figaro (Mozart)
    La Rondine (Puccini)

2008–2009
    Eugene Onegin (Tchaikovsky)
    The Elixir of Love (Donizetti)

Così fan Tutte (Mozart)
Carmen (Bizet)

2007–2008
Lucia di Lammermoor (Donizetti)
Werther (Massenet)
Rigoletto (Verdi)
Madama Butterfly (Puccini)

2006–2007
Roméo et Juliette (Gounod)
The Barber of Seville (Rossini)
La Traviata (Verdi)
Madama Butterfly (Puccini)

2005–2006
The Crucible (Ward)
The Masked Ball (Verdi)
La Bohème (Puccini)
Don Giovanni (Mozart)

2004–2005 (First season in the California Theatre)
The Marriage of Figaro (Mozart)
Tosca (Puccini)
Carmen (Bizet)
The Flying Dutchman (Wagner)

2003–2004
Don Pasquale (Donizetti)
Double Bill: *Cavalleria Rusticana* (Mascagni)
                    Pagliacci (Leoncavallo)
The Pearl Fishers (Bizet)
Die Fledermaus (J. Strauss)

2002–2003
    La Cenerentola (Rossini)
    Faust (Gounod)
    Il Trovatore (Verdi)
    The Magic Flute (Mozart)

2001–2002
    Falstaff (Verdi)
    Così fan Tutte (Mozart)
    Manon (Massenet)
    Madama Butterfly (Puccini)

2000–2001
    Eugene Onegin (Tchaikovsky)
    The Elixir of Love (Donizetti)
    Rigoletto (Verdi)
    La Bohème (Puccini)

1999–2000
    The Barber of Seville (Rossini)
    The Tale of the Nutcracker (Bohmler) World premiere
    Carmen (Bizet)
    La Traviata (Verdi)

1998–1999
    The Rake's Progress (Stravinsky)
    Roméo et Juliette (Gounod)
    Don Giovanni (Mozart)
    The Merry Widow (Lehar)

1997–1998
    Of Mice and Men (Floyd)
    Lucia di Lammermoor (Donizetti)
    Il Turco in Italia (Rossini)
    Die Zauberflöte (Mozart)

1996–1997
Xerxes (Handel)
Double Bill: *La Voix Humaine* (Poulenc)
Pagliacci (Leoncavallo)
Faust (Gounod)
La Bohème (Puccini)

1995–1996
Eugene Onegin (Tchaikovsky)
Die Fledermaus (J. Strauss)
Le Nozze di Figaro (Mozart)
Madama Butterfly (Puccini)

1994–1995
The Pearl Fishers (Bizet)
Carmen (Bizet)
Così fan Tutte (Mozart)
La Traviata (Verdi)

1993–1994
The Barber of Seville (Rossini)
Tartuffe (Mechem)
Rigoletto (Verdi)
Don Giovanni (Mozart)

1992–1993
Die Zauberflöte (Mozart)
Phaedra (Roumanis) World premiere
The Merry Widow (Lehar)
La Bohème (Puccini)

1991–1992
Popol Vuh (Strange)   World premiere
Lucia di Lammermoor (Donizetti)
The Turn of the Screw (Britten)

Double Bill: *Il Tabarro* (Puccini)
                Gianni Schicchi (Puccini)
Un ballo in maschera (Verdi)

1990–1991
The Magic Flute (Mozart)
Vanessa (Barber)
The Elixir of Love (Donizetti)
L'Ormindo (Cavalli)

1989–1990
La Traviata (Verdi)
Hotel Eden (Mollicone) World premiere
The Pearl Fishers (Bizet)
Così fan Tutte (Mozart)

1988–1989
La Bohème (Puccini)
West of Washington Square (Henderson) World premiere
The Barber of Seville (Rossini)
Die Fledermaus (J. Strauss)

1987–1988
Tosca (Puccini)
The Medium (Menotti)
Don Pasquale (Donizetti)
Amahl and the Night Visitors (Menotti)

1986–1987
Double Bill: *Suor Angelica* (Puccini)
                Gianni Schicchi (Puccini)
Le Nozze di Figaro (Mozart)
The Merry Widow (Lehar)
Amahl and the Night Visitors (Menotti)

1985–1986
Madama Butterfly (Puccini)
Tartuffe (Mechem)
The Elixir of Love (Donizetti)
Amahl and the Night Visitors (Menotti)
Hansel and Gretel (Humperdinck)

1984–1985 (First season as Opera San José)
Die Zauberflöte (Mozart)
Albert Herring (Britten)
La Traviata (Verdi)
Amahl and the Night Visitors (Menotti)

1983–1984 (as San José Opera Theatre)
La Bohème (Puccini)
Double Bill: *La Serva Padrona* (Pergolesi)
   The Old Maid and the Thief (Menotti)
Die Fledermaus (J. Strauss)
Amahl and the Night Visitors (Menotti)

1982–1983 (as San José Community Opera Theatre)
Double Bill: *Seven Joys of Christmas* (Mechem)
   Amahl and the Night Visitors (Menotti)
Double Bill: *The Scarf* (Hoiby)
   Harrison Loved His Umbrella (Hollingsworth)
Così fan Tutte (Mozart)

1981–1982
Double Bill: *Trouble in Tahiti* (Bernstein)
   The Old Maid and the Thief (Menotti)
Amahl and the Night Visitors (Menotti)
Double Bill: *Suor Angelica* (Puccini)
   Rita (Donizetti)
Triple Bill: *Hin und Zurück* (Hindemith)
   The Little Harlequinade (Salieri)
   La Cantarina (Haydn)

1980–1981
    The Secret Marriage (Cimarosa)
    Double Bill: *Many Moons* (Doughtery)
                  Rising Stars (Revue)
    Amahl and the Night Visitors (Menotti)

1979–1980
    Triple Bill: *The Impresario* (Mozart)
               Chanticleer (Barab)
               Signor Deluso (Pasatieri)
    Dido and Aeneas (Purcell)

1978–1979 (San José State University Opera Workshop)
    Double Bill: *The Mother* (Hollingsworth)
                    Gianni Schicchi (Puccini)
    The Last Leaf (Henderson) World premiere

OSJ Resident Artists, 1988 to 2024

Alphabetized by last name

CARLOS AGUILAR, BASS 2005–2008
Zachary Altman, Baritone 2012–2014
Ravil Atlas, Tenor 1991–1993
Zhengyi Bai, Tenor, 2022-2023
Rochelle Bard, Soprano 2006–2008
Scott Bearden, Baritone 2000–2002
Vanessa Becerra, Soprano, 2020-2021
John Bellemer, Tenor 1994–1997
Christopher Bengochea, Tenor 2005–2008
Deborah Berioli, Soprano 2004–2006
Nicole Birkland, Mezzo-Soprano 2012–2014
Jeanette Blakeney, Mezzo-Soprano 1995–1997
Michael Boley, Tenor, 2014-2016
Melissa Bonetti, Mezzo-soprano, 2023-2024
Torlef Borsting, Baritone 2010–2011
Alexander Boyer, Tenor 2008–2013
Eugene Brancoveanu, Baritone, 2019-2023
Tara Branham, Stage Director, 2020-2023
Evan Brummel, Baritone 2012–2014
James Callon, Tenor 2012–2014
Heather Calvete, Soprano 2000–2001
Brian Carter, Baritone 1997–1998
Teresa Castillo, Soprano, 2021-2022
Lisa Chavez, Mezzo-Soprano 2013–2015
Layna Chianakas, Mezzo-Soprano 1995–1997

Daniel Cilli, Baritone 2006–2010
Cynthia Clayton, Soprano 1992–1996
Betany Coffland, Mezzo-Soprano 2008–2012
David Cox, Baritone 1988–1992
Michelle Ainna Cuizon, Stage Director, 2023-2024
Michael Dailey, Tenor 2008–2012
Khori Dastoor, Soprano 2007–2010
Rebecca Davis, Soprano 2008–2009
Lori Decter, Soprano 2001–2006
Jason Detwiler, Baritone 2002–2006
Michele Detwiler, Mezzo-Soprano 2002–2007
Christopher Dickerson, Bass 1997–2000
Barbara Divis, Soprano 1996–2000
Ashley Dixon, Mezzo-Soprano, 2020-2021
Kirk Dougherty, Tenor, 2014-2017
Darren Drone, Baritone, 2022-2023
Kirk Eichelberger, Bass 2001–2003; 2005–2006
Andrew Eisenmann, Baritone 1993–1996
Silas Elash, Bass 2008–2016
Jared Esguerra, Tenor, 2021-2022
Adam Flowers, Tenor 2000–2006
Nmon Ford, Baritone 1996–1997
Jennifer Forni, Soprano, 2013–2014
Vartan Gabrielian, Bass-baritone, 2023-2024
Elena Galvan, Soprano, 2019-2020
Mason Gates, Tenor, 2019-2020
Roberto Gomez, Baritone 1999–2000
Cybele Gouverneur, Mezzo-Soprano 2007–2009
Tori Grayum, Mezzo-soprano, 2012-2013
Megan Esther Grey, Contralto, 2022-2023
Stephen Guggenheim, Tenor 1990–1991
Katharine Gunnink, Soprano, 2017-2019
Susan Gundunas, Soprano 1988–1992
Jasmina Halimic, Soprano 2010–2012
Matthew Hanscom, Baritone, 2014-2017

Jonathan Hodel, Tenor 1999–2003
Isaac Hurtado, Tenor 2006–2008
Isabella Ivy, Soprano, 2014-2016
Jouvanca Jean-Baptiste, Soprano 2010–2012
Krassen Karagiozov, Baritone 2008–2012
Maya Kherani, Soprano, 2020-2022
Julia Kierstine, Soprano 1992–1993
Melody King, Soprano 2012–2013
Amanda Kingston, Soprano, 2017-2018
Matt Kirchner, Tenor 1995–1997
Eilana Lappalainen, Soprano 1988–1992
Sylvia Lee, Soprano, 2016-2017
Brian Leerhuber, Baritone 1997–1999
Johannes LÖhner, Conductor, 2023-2024
Cecilia Violetta Lopez, Soprano 2012–2014
Maureen Magill, Soprano 1997–1998
Christina Major, Soprano 1997–2000; 2003–2004
Julie Makerov, Soprano 2001–2003
Kenneth Mattice, Baritone 2006–2008
Robert McPherson, Tenor 1997–1999
Jesse Merlin, Baritone 2002–2006
Courtney Miller, Mezzo-soprano, 2023-2024
Dan Montez, Tenor 1989–1993
Joseph Muir, Tenor 2003–2004
Isaiah Musik-Ayala, Bass-baritone 2009–2012
Brian James Myer, Baritone, 2016-2017
Douglas Nagel, Baritone 1988–1992
Maria Natale, Soprano, 2018-2019, 2022-2023
Trevor Neal, Baritone, 2017-2019
Donna Olson, Mezzo-Soprano 2001–2003
Rene Orth, Composer, 2022-2023
Lori Phillips, Soprano 1995–1996
Ksenia Popova, Soprano, 2016-2017
Nikola Printz, Mezzo-soprano, 2021-2022
Colin Ramsey, Bass-baritone, 2016-2017

Christopher James Ray, Conductor, 2019-2022
Clifton Romig, Bass-baritone 1993–1997
Sandra Rubalcava-Bengochea, Soprano 2001–2004
Stephanie Sanchez, Mezzo-soprano, 2019-2020
Joshua Sanders, Tenor, 2023-2024
Natalia Santaliz, Soprano, 2022-2023
Carlos Enrique Santelli, Tenor, 2020-2021
Rebecca Schuessler, Soprano 2009–2010
Marc Schreiner, Tenor 2013–2014
Carlo Scibelli, Tenor 1992–1994
Etsel Skelton, Tenor 2004–2005
Chloe Smart, Soprano, 2014-2015
Efrain Solis, Tenor, 2020-2022
Melissa Sondhi, Soprano, 2023-2024
Nathan Stark, Bass-baritone, 2020-2022
Noah Stewart, Tenor, 2021-2022
Dane Suarez, Tenor, 2017-2019
Talise Trevigne, Soprano 2006–2008
Thomas Rolf Truhitte, Tenor 1997–2001
Tamara Tsoutsouris, Soprano 2002–2003
Mel Ulrich, Baritone 1993–1996
Maris Vipulis, Bass 1997–1999
Kerry Walsh, Soprano 1994–1995
Joseph Wright, Baritone 2000–2006
Constantinos Yiannoudes, Baritone 1999–2000

Irene Dalis's Awards and Honors

Principal Artist at the Metropolitan Opera, San Francisco Opera, Covent Garden, Bayreuth Festival, Chicago Lyric Opera, Staatischer Oper (later known as Deutsche Oper Berlin), Teatro dell'Opera di Roma, Teatro San Carlo, Naples.

Fulbright Award, 1951

Richard Wagner Medallion, Bayreuth, West Germany, 1963

Tower Award, San José State University, 1974

Honored by the Board of Directors of the Metropolitan Opera Association on the Occasion of Her Twentieth Anniversary Season, 1977

Woman of Achievement Award from the *San Jose Mercury News* and the League of Friends of Santa Clara County Commission on the Status of Women, 1983

Commendation from the Honorable John Vasconcellos, 23rd Assembly District, 1983

California Public Educators Hall of Fame, 1985

Award of Merit from the People of the City of San Francisco, 1985

Honored Citizen of the City of San José, 1986

Honorary Doctorate, Santa Clara University, 1987

Irene Dalis Day in San José, proclaimed by Mayor Tom McEnery, 9/24/1988.

The San Francisco Opera Medal, 1998. *

Honorary Doctorate, California State University, 1999

Italian American Foundation Annual Achievement Award, 2002

Lifetime Achievement Award from the Arts Council Silicon Valley, 2008

Beautiful Minds Award, 2010

Women of Impact from Notre Dame High School, San José, 2012

Career Award from the National Opera America Center, 2013

Cornerstone of the Arts, City of San José Arts Commission, 2013

Joined Advisory Board of Jussi Björling Societies of the U.S. and U.K., by invitation, May 2014

Opera America Career Award, 2014

* This honor has also been awarded to Placido Domingo, James Morris, Birgit Nilsson, Leontyne Price, Samuel Ramey, Leonie Rysanek, Joan Sutherland, and Frederica von Stade, among others..

Acknowledgments

THIS BOOK IS LARGELY AN ORAL history. Its primary sources are the people who generously shared with me their memories and reflections about Irene Dalis and Opera San José. They are singers, directors, conductors, audience members, trustees, volunteers, administrators, and of course Irene herself. The more people I met, the more impressed I was by the way Irene's vision and determination attracted people of talent and generosity.

In addition to spending many hours with Irene, I interviewed the following people: Tricia Anderson, Mary Breden, Robert Ashens, Barbara Barrett, John Bellemer, Petie Cassilly, Isabelle Chapuis, Layna Chianakas, Daniel Cilli, Cynthia Clayton, Betany Coffland, José Maria Condemi, George Crow, Michael Dailey, Brad Dalton, Khori Dastoor, Richard Dorsay, Silas Elash, Mary Elizabeth Enmann, Frank Fiscalini, Larry Hancock, Lorna Haywood, Alva Henderson, Sara Jobin, Eilana Lappalainen, Phil Livengood, Lotfi Mansouri, Jeanne McCann, Michael Mendelsohn, Patrice Maginnis, Patty Mitchell, Henry Mollicone, Heidi Munzinger, Doug Nagel, Nick Lymberis, Barbara Swartz Lymberis, Lori Phillips, Luis Quandt, David Rohrbaugh, Virginia Smedberg, Lettie Smith, Ed Stout, Alma Taylor, Brad Wade, Laurie Warner, Andrew Whitfield. and Scott Williams.

Those who provided written narratives and reflections were Ernesto Alorda, Kirk Eichelberger, Alida Loinaz, Chris Mays, Jesse Merlin, Dan Montez, Timothy Near, Arlene Okerlund, Anthony Quartuccio, Sandra Rubalcava Bengochea, Kitty Spaulding, and Edwin Stafford. Many of these also granted interviews. Alida Loinaz spent countless hours searching the family photo collection and scanning irreplaceable images.

I would also like to thank Lois Rew, who edited the book, and Jill Ronsley, who designed it. Bob Shomler generously shared his photographs and advice, and Laurie Warner prepared for printing the photographs that came from other sources.

People who reviewed a late draft of the book were Barbara Barrett, Larry Hancock, Randy and Carle Hylkema, Lois Rew, Joan Shomler, Brad Wade, and Laurie Warner.

Photo Credits

All photos are from the Dalis-Loinaz family collection unless otherwise noted

Front cover

Main image, Sara Rubinstein.
Inset, Irene Dalis as Princess de Bouillon, The Metropolitan Opera Archives.

Back cover

California Theatre. Bob Shomler.

Introduction

General Director Shawna Lucey. Ken Howard.

Chapter 1

California Theatre April 16, 1927. Gary Parks, courtesy of History San José.
Poster for concert by Yvonne Dalis, 1947.
Irene Dalis studio portrait.
Backstage with Carl Ebert.
As Kostelnicka in *Jenůfa*.
As Princess Eboli in *Don Carlo*. Photo by Louis Melancon. Courtesy of The Metropolitan Opera Archives.

Chapter 2

George Loinaz.
George and Irene backstage.
With conductor Wolfgang Sawallisch at Bayreuth.
Practicing makeup with daughter Alida.
Rehearsing with Jess Thomas. Photo by Margaret Norton. Courtesy of San Francisco Opera.
With Birgit Nilsson in *Tristan and Isolde*. Photo by Louis Melancon. Courtesy of The Metropolitan Opera Archives.
With Birgit Nilsson in a candid moment.
Backstage with daughter Alida.

Chapter 3

With Leontyne Price in *Aida*. Courtesy of The Metropolitan Opera Archives.
With Jess Thomas in *Tristan and Isolde*. Photo by Margaret Norton. Courtesy of San Francisco Opera.
With Jess Thomas in *Tristan and Isolde*.
With Renata Tebaldi in *Adriana Lecouvreur*. Photo by Louis Melancon. Courtesy of The Metropolitan Opera Archives.
As Lady Macbeth.
With Richard Tucker in *Il Trovatore*. Courtesy of The Metropolitan Opera Archives.
With Rudolf Bing.

Chapter 4

With George and Jon Vickers.
At her desk.
Young David Rohrbaugh. Courtesy of Opera San José.
Gianni Schicchi at the Center for Performing Arts. Courtesy of Opera San Jose.

Irene Dalis and Larry Hancock in the workshop's *Dido and Aeneas*. Courtesy of Opera San José.
Old van. Courtesy of Opera San José.
Irene Dalis at a fundraising event. Bob Shomler.

Chapter 5

Dan Montez in *The Elixir of Love*. Courtesy of Opera San Jose.
Mel Ulrich and John Bellemer in *Eugene Onegin*. Courtesy of Opera San Jose.
Cynthia Clayton in *The Marriage of Figaro*. Bob Shomler.
Lori Phillips in *Madama Butterfly*. Courtesy of Opera San Jose.
Scott Bearden and Kirk Eichelberger in *The Barber of Seville*. Bob Shomler.
Silas Elash in *The Elixir of Love*. Bob Shomler.

Chapter 6

Eilana Lappalainen and Anooshah Golesorkhi in *The Barber of Seville*. Courtesy of Opera San Jose.
Michael Dailey in *The Elixir of Love*. Bob Shomler.
Sandra Rubalcava Bengochea in *Don Pasquale*. Bob Shomler.
California Theatre. Bob Shomler.
California Theatre. Bob Shomler.
Mel Ulrich and Layna Chianakas in *The Marriage of Figaro*. Courtesy of Opera San Jose.
Awarding first prize to Rebecca Davis at the Irene Dalis Vocal Competition, 2012. Bob Shomler.

Chapter 7

Irene as professor at San José State University.
Larry Hancock at Los Gatos Music in the Park. Bob Shomler.
David Rohrbaugh. Bob Shomler.

Daniel Cilli and Khori Dastoor in *Lucia di Lammermoor*. Bob Shomler.
Betany Coffland in *La Voix Humaine*. Bob Shomler.
25th anniversary gala. Bob Shomler.
Falstaff, 2013. Bob Shomler.

Chapter 8

Irene Dalis and George Loinaz.

Chapter 9

Idomeneo. Bob Shomler.
Christopher Bengochea in *Idomendo*. Bob Shomler.
Rebecca Davis in *La Traviata*. Bob Shomler.
Scott Bearden and Zach Altman in *Falstaff*. Bob Shomler.
Gianni Schicchi, 2013. Bob Shomler.
Resident Company, 2013–2014. Eric Wolfinger, courtesy of Opera San José.
Larry Hancock. Chris Ayers, courtesy of Opera San José.
Irene Dalis in the California Theatre. Photo by Sara Rubinstein, courtesy of Martek and Beautiful Minds.
Music Director Joseph Marcheso, courtesy of Opera San José.
Alma conducts. Almadeutscher.com

Chapter 10

Rudolf Bing signs Marian Anderson. Metropolitan Opera.
Farinelli. Wikipedia.

Chapter 11

Stacey Tappan. Courtesy of Opera San José.

Sources

IF NO SOURCE IS GIVEN FOR verbatim quotations, this means they came from interviews I held or from narratives written and sent to me by the persons mentioned. See Acknowledgments for a list of all the people who contributed to the book in this way.

I also consulted books, newspapers, performance reviews, production programs, and other materials. The publication data are not complete on every entry. For instance, a few newspaper reviews found as clippings in the large Breden collection were incomplete.

For those interested in further information, the Irene Dalis-Loinaz Special Collection at the King Library* holds her papers, historical music scores, books, family and press photographs, audio-visual materials, ephemera, and art. Portions of the collection can be found at https://digitalcollections.sjsu.edu/islandora/object/islandora%3A83_93

*A partnership of San Jose State University and San Jose City Library, 150 E. San Fernando Street, San Jose, CA

Praise for Irene Dalis … and Opera San José

Lotfi Mansouri. Richard Scheinin, "Opera San José Founder/General Director Irene Dalis Will Step Down in July 2014." *San Jose Mercury News,* January 25, 2013.

Paul Jackson. (2006). *Start-up at the New Met: The Metropolitan Opera Broadcasts, 1966-1976.* Pompton Plains, NJ: Amadeus Press. Pages 199-200.

Placido Domingo, in a video interview on the occasion of Opera San José's 25th anniversary gala.

Andrew Bales. Richard Scheinin, "Opera San José Founder/General Director Irene Dalis Will Step Down in July 2014." *San Jose Mercury News,* January 25, 2013.

Paul Lorton (2010). *Mission Conceived versus Mission Achieved.* San Francisco: University of San Francisco Scholarship Repository. Analytics and Technology Paper 7, page 9. http://repository.usfca.edu/at/7

Arlene Okerlund. Interview conducted for this book.

Prologue

Page xi   "Miss Dalis met …" Raymond A. Erickson, *Musical America,* reviewing her debut at the Metropolitan Opera in New York, March 16, 1957.

Chapter 1: Roots

Page 2   "Sister Marge would play …" Richard Scheinin, "Irene Dalis's Career Didn't Really Start Until She Stopped Singing." *San Jose Mercury News,* September 7, 2008.

Page 2   "When I was a child …" Richard Scheinin, "The California Comes Full Circle," *San Jose Mercury News,* September 12, 2004. *San Jose Mercury News,* September 7, 2008.

Page 2   "She saw Clark Gable …" Richard Scheinin, "Irene Dalis's Career Didn't Really Start Until She Stopped Singing." *San Jose Mercury News,* September 7, 2008

Page 6   "My dad was just like …" Crystal Chow, "Irene Dalis Will Retire in July After 30 Seasons as General Director of Opera San José." *San Jose Mercury News,* August 28, 2013. ALSO in Joshua Kosman, "Diva Behind Success of Opera San José," San Francisco *Chronicle,* August 29, 2010.

Page 10   "By this time, I was mesmerized …" Richard Scheinin, "The Impresario." *San Jose Mercury News,* September 4, 2003.

Sources

Page 20   "All during my career ..." Robert Commanday, "Irene Dalis at Forty." San Francisco Opera program, 1998/1999 season. Performing Arts, pages 19-20, 44-45, 56-59.

Page 20   "A reviewer praised 'her enormous' ..." *Nordwest Zeitung,* quoted in "German audience hails contralto Irene Dalis" (no author), *San Jose Mercury*, September 1953.

Page 25   "I don't believe I took ..." From "Reflected Glory," *Opera News,* October, 1983, p. 70. Byline Irene Dalis..

Page 26   "Since she was technically a guest artist ..." Brad Kava, "Dalis' 'San Jose Idol' Contest Puts Spotlight on Opera." *San Jose Mercury News,* April 20, 2007..

Page 27   "The manager of a theatre ..." Wikipedia entry for "claque."

Page 28   "Am I really talking to Irene Dalis ..." Mr. Claque was referring to an article in *Time* Magazine, "Music: Europe's New Divas." July 22, 1957.

Page 30   "Irene Valis ..." Paul Henry Lang, New York *Herald Tribune,* "Don Carlo," March 18, 1957..

Page 31   "Miss Dalis has a warm ..." Winthrop Sargeant, *New Yorker*, March 23, 1957..

Page 31   "For the part of Eboli ..." Howard Taubman, New York *Times,* "Don Carlo Returns to Met Repertory." March 18, 1957.

Page 32   "Miss Dalis, young mezzo-soprano ..." Raymond A. Erickson, *Musical America*, reviewi ng her debut at the Metropolitan Opera in New York, March 16, 1957.

Chapter 2: Success

Page 33   "The opera world's foremost publication ..." *Opera News,* November 25, 1957.

Page 34   "There was no time ..." Richard Scheinin, "Thanks to Fan, San Jose Opera Star Regains Recorded Legacy." *San Jose Mercury News,* December 24, 2006.

Page 37	"The first year George and I were married …" Joshua Kosman, "Diva Behind Success of Opera San José." San Francisco *Chronicle*, August 29, 2010.
Page 38	"After the opening night performance, the chagrined composer …" Mosco Carner, *Puccini: A Critical Biography*, 3rd edition. 1992. New York: Holmes & Meier, page 150.
Page 38	"Singing honors went …" Raymond Kendall, Los Angeles *Mirror*, November 15, 1960.
Page 38	"Another first-rate performance …" *Opera News*, February, 1958. New York.
Page 38	"Irene Dalis sang her first Amneris …" John Gruen, New York *Herald Tribune*, 10/27/62, Aida at the Met.
Page 39	"From her compelling entrance …" Frances Robinson, "San Jose's Star of Opera Acclaimed in San Francisco." *San Jose Mercury News*. September 18, 1958.
Page 40	"'Irene Dalis, as the malevolent nurse …" Albert Goldberg, Los Angeles *Times*, November 11, 1959..
Page 40	"Irene Dalis as the Nurse received …" Charles Susskind, *Peninsula Living*, weekend of Sept 26-27, 1959.
Page 40	"Irene Dalis was the very embodiment …" Alfred Frankenstein, San Francisco *Chronicle*, September 20, 1959.
Page 41	"Miss Dalis's voice, for the most part …" Ross Parmenter, "Opera: Lady Macbeth. Irene Dalis Sings Role First Time at 'Met.'" *New York Times*, February 5, 1960.
Page 42	"'The opening-night ovation …" F. Paul Driscoll, "Leontyne Price." *Opera News*, March, 2013.
Page 42	"The Metropolitan can now boast …" Robert Sabin, "Irene Dalis Proves a Superb Kundry." *Musical America*, May, 1961..
Page 43	"What applause would otherwise …" Eric Rappl, "A Phenomenal Kundry." *Bayreuther Tageblatt*. July, 1961.
Page 44	"Young Irene Dalis was …" Heinrich Darius, "Irene Dalis: A New Kundry." *Die Presse*. July, 1961.

Sources

Page 45	"The American Irene ..." Erich Limmert, "'Parsifal' in Bayreuth." *Hannoverische Allgemeine Zeitung.* July, 1961.
Page 45	"He excitedly announced ..." Antonio Spadaro, "A Big Heart Open to God." In America, the *National Catholic Review*, September 30, 2013..
Page 46	"This rare case ..." Raymond Erickson, "World of Music," New York *Times,* September 2, 1962; Music News Notes, New York *Herald Tribune,* September 2, 1962; Jose *Mercury,* October 6, 1962; "Irene Dalis a German Sensation," San Jose *News,* August 16, 1962.
Page 47	"Cordell Shewell ..." Michael J. Vaughn, "Homegrown Diva: The Sensual Irene Dalis." *The Wave,* September 26, 2007.
Page 47	"Michael Barclay ..." Michael J. Vaughn, "Homegrown Diva: The Sensual Irene Dalis." *The Wave,* September 26, 2007.
Page 50	"One day when my daughter was ..." Jan Shaw, "Grandly, and With Fire." *The Business Journal*, week of December 3, 1984.
Page 52	"Connie (not her real name) ..." Linda Riebel and Jane Kaplan, *How People Recover from Eating Disorders*, 2004. Bloomington, IN: Xlibris, pages 32–33.
Page 55	"Irene retorted ..." Rene Seghers and Franco Corelli, *Franco Corelli: Prince of Tenors.* New York: Hal Leonard Corp., 2008, pages 293–294.
Page 56	Unless otherwise specified, passages in the section about Sharon Breden are found in an archive of articles, reviews, fan newsletters, and manuscripts that she collected; now in possession of her sister, Mary Breden in Redondo Beach, California.
Page 58	"Wagner's *Parsifal* was her favorite opera ..." *Bravo,* Volume 3, Number 2.

Page 58   "After traveling more than 6,500 miles …" Joan Sweeney, "Girl's Dream Wish Precedes Convent." Newport News (Virginia) *Daily Press,* October 11, 1963; "Dream Realized," *Daily Tribune,* September 26, 1963; *San Jose Mercury News,* October 11, 1963. no author. "Irene Dalis, Opera Star with Heart, Helps Young Girl's Dream Come True."

Page 63   "Irene Dalis was wonderful …" Birgit Nilsson (2007). *La Nilsson: My Life in Opera.* Lebanon, NH: Northeastern University Press, published by University Press of New England, page 7.

Chapter 3: The International Star

Page 74   "Kurt Herbert Adler I considered a genius …" Robert Commanday, "Irene Dalis at Forty." San Francisco Opera 1998/1999 season program. Performing Arts, pages 19–20, 44–45, 56–59.

Page 74   "With his charm …" Robert Commanday, "Irene Dalis at Forty." San Francisco Opera 1998/1999 season program. Performing Arts, pages 19–20, 44–45, 56–59.

Page 75   "Irene Dalis exhibited …" Reviews of the *Tristan and Isolde* in San Francisco, collected by Columbia Artists Management. Palo Alto *Times.*

Page 77   "'You decide' …" Robert Commanday, "Irene Dalis at Forty." San Francisco Opera 1998/1999 season program. Performing Arts, pages 19–20, 44–45, 56–59.

Page 82   "I was a female Boris Karloff." Crystal Chow, "Irene Dalis Will Retire in July After 30 Seasons as General Director of Opera San José." *San Jose Mercury News,* August 28, 2013.

Page 82   "I am destined …" Marta Morgan, "'Met' Star Dalis to Sing Monday; Native San Joséan." *San Jose Mercury News,* DATE ; Frederick Winship, "Dalis Finds Good in Being Evil—In Opera's 'Mean Female' Roles." *New York World-Telegram and Sun,* February 1, 1961.

Page 82	"I like characters …" John Ardoin, "Irene Dalis: Villainess with Charm." *Musical America*, March, 1963.
Page 82	"Maybe my true self …" A.M.L., "Roads to Stardom: Gentle Villainess." *Opera News*, March 18, 1961.
Page 82	"The great soprano Lucine Amara …" Eric Myers, "Reunion: Irene Dalis." *Opera News*, March, 2007.
Page 85	"When you talk to Miss D. …" Donald Dierks, San Diego *Union*, "Medea's Star' A Challenge Accepted."
Page 86	"The title role had been written …" Alva Henderson. "How My *Medea* Made it to the Stage." *Opera News*, March 24, 1973, pages 18–19.
Page 91	"Singing Santuzza for the first time …" A printed review preserved without attribution in the Breden archive.
Page 92	"After the first performance …" Marta Morgan, "Irene Dalis Returning for S.F. Opera Season." *San Jose Mercury News*, August 26, 1973.

Chapter 4: An End and a Beginning

Page 96	"I felt my career at the Met …" Barry Hyams. "The 'International Eboli' Began in San José.'" Published article preserved in the Breden collection without further identification. Hyams was a producer and publicist in New York and San Francisco.
Page 98	"In 1977 or 1978, I was asked …" Ludmilla Alexander, "The Destiny of Irene Dalis." *South Bay Accent*, August/September, 1995.
Page 124	"The reason I was allowed …" Ludmilla Alexander, "The Destiny of Irene Dalis." *South Bay Accent*, August/September, 1995. See also Richard Scheinin, "Irene Dalis's Career Didn't Really Start Until She Stopped Singing." *San Jose Mercury News*, September 7, 2008.

Chapter 5: The Little Opera Company That Could

Page 127   "To judge by this production ..." Paul Moor, "Opera San José: Puccini '*La Bohème*.'" *Musical America,* March 1989.

Page 127   "The Opera San José repertory is eclectic ..." *Opera News* article on Bay Area companies, date? 1988?

Page 128   "*Opern Welt*. 'The production of Floyd's' ..." March 1998. "Von Oldenburg ins Silicon Valley" ("From Oldenburg to Silicon Valley").

Page 129   "Tenor Tom Truhitte ..." Tessa de Carlo, "In a Week, Maybe Two, They'll Make You a Star." *Opera News,* March 28, 1998. pages 30–31, 53.

Page 139   "When Seattle Opera general director Speight Jenkins ..." Melinda Bargreen, Special to the *Seattle Times,* August 9, 2013.

Page 140   "The San Francisco *Chronicle*'s..." Joshua Kosman, "Gotterdammerung in Seattle." *On a Pacific Aisle,* August 19, 2013.

Page 141   "We had sets on Brokaw Road ..." Paul Hertelendy, " Space Voyage: Opera San José Has a Home, Now All It Needs is a House." *San Jose Mercury News,* August 7, 1994.

Page 142   "Irene said at the time ..." Paul Hertelendy, " Space Voyage: Opera San José Has a Home, Now All It Needs is a House." *San Jose Mercury News,* August 7, 1994.

Page 14   "Even the first one ..." Gizela O'Neil, "Dial O for Opera." *Metro Silicon Valley,* May 1–7, 1986.

Page 146   "All told, between 1979 and 2013 ..." Opera San José K-12 Outreach: Cumulative Report, 1979–2013.

Page 147   "The OSJ visit at our school ..." Opera San José website.

Page 149   "The next step is told ..." Richard Scheinin, "A Career Path from Chip Design to Center Stage." *San Jose Mercury News,* January 27, 2011.

Sources

Chapter 6: We Don't Import Stars—We Export Them!

Page 169   "'This is perhaps' ..." Nerissa Pacio, "Festive Crowd Welcomes California Theatre's Second Act." *San Jose Mercury News,* September 19, 2004.

Page 169   "Miracle of miracles ..." Richard Scheinin, "One Dazzling Debut." *San Jose Mercury News,* September 20, 2004.

Page 170   "Under Rohrbaugh's baton ..." Janos Gereben. Review of *The Marriage of Figaro.* In *San Francisco Classical Voice,* 2004. https://www.sfcv.org/arts_revs/operasanjose_9_21_04.php

Page 170   "One reporter called it ..." Richard Scheinin, "The California Comes Full Circle." *San Jose Mercury News,* September 12, 2004.

Chapter 7: The Impresaria

Page 178   "Lotfi Mansouri wrote ..." Lotfi Mansouri with Aviva Layton, *Lotfi Mansouri: An Operatic Life.* Oakville, Ontario. Mosaic Press, 1982. p. 53.

Page 179   "In his autobiography, Bing shared ..." Rudolf Bing, *5,000 Nights at the Opera,* Garden City, New York: Doubleday, 1972, pages 208–217.

Page 180   "I get all worked up ..." Tessa de Carlo. "In a Week, Maybe Two, They'll Make You a Star." *Opera News,* March 28, 1998. pages 30–31, 53.

Page 180   "The show was great, the audience went wild ..." Quoted in Rene Seghers and Franco Corelli, *Franco Corelli: Prince of Tenors.* 2008. NY: Hal Leonard Corp., pages 293–294.

Page 191   "'A better partner I never could have ..." Richard Scheinin, "Opera San José's David Rohrbaugh says goodbye." *San Jose Mercury News,* February 12, 2014.

Page 200 "In 1980, I began the work ..." James Reber, "Thank you, Miss Irene Dalis." www.sanjoseinside.com/news/entries/10_9_13_irene_dalis_opera_san_jose/

Chapter 8: Tragic Losses and Daunting Challenges

Page 211 "I had to retrieve my robe ..." Michelle Guido, "Opera Director Dalis' Home Damaged in Weekend Blaze." *San Jose Mercury News*, February 13, 1990.

Page 213 "The only time that George ..." Paul Hertelendy, "A Stage of Rebuilding." *San Jose Mercury News*, August 27, 1990.

Page 215 "'Do you go to the opera?'" Richard Scheinin, "After Accident, Dalis is Back for an Encore." *San Jose Mercury News*, May 15, 2011.

Chapter 9: The Fine Art of the Opera Business

Page 228 "Here's Mansouri ..." Lotfi Mansouri with Aviva Layton, *Lotfi Mansouri: An Operatic Life*. Oakville, Ontario. Mosaic Press, 1982, pages 53–54.

Page 229 "Soprano Teresa Berganza said ..." Alex Ross, "Mastersinger." *New Yorker*, October 7, 2013.

Page 231 "No, he stood there defiantly ..." Classicalite Newsdesk. "Wagner (at) Bayreuth: Frank Castorf's Gotterdammerung Booed out of Bayreuth." August 1, 2013.

Page 231 "Another director, when asked ..." David Ng, "A 'Ring' Divided." *Los Angeles Times*, May 13, 2010.

Page 232 "'Rather than try to capture' ..." Lotfi Mansouri with Donald Arthur, *Lotfi Mansouri: An Operatic Journey*. Boston: Northeastern University Press, 2010, pages 216–217.

Page 232	"Likewise, the Los Angeles *Ring* of 2010 …" David Ng, "A 'Ring' Divided." *Los Angeles Times,* May 13, 2010.
Page 232	"In 2013, David Gockley, general director …" In prepared remarks at a reception for volunteers of San Francisco Opera, October 19, 2013.
Page 238	"We've shown that we know …" "Opera San José Receives 4-Star Rating for Fiscal Management." September 17, 2013. www.operasj.org/wp-content/uploads/2013/10/4-star-rating-news-release.pdf
Page 238	"Hancock said …" Scott MacClelland. "Silver Memories." *Metro Silicon Valley,* September 17–23, 2008.
Page 248	"A twelve-year-old British girl …" Heather MacDonald, Review of *Cinderella, The New Criterion,* May, 2018.
Page 255	Matthew Shilvock, General Director of San Francisco Opera." Personal communication, March 6, 2019.

Chapter 10: Juicy Tidbits and Opera Lore

Page 250	"Oscar Hammerstein asserted …" Storey, J. (2005). The social life of opera. *European Journal of Cultural Studies, 6* (1), 5-35. Pages 10-11.
Page 250	"Impresario Rudolf Bing …" Wheeler, M.B. (2018). An unlikely champion: Rudolf Bing and the demise of Jim Crow at the Metropolitan Opera. *Notes,* 75 (2), 207-236.
Page 252	"Revolution is not an uncommon theme…" Gabriel, Y. (2017). Leadership in opera: Romance, betrayal, strife and sacrifice. *Leadership, 13* (1), 5–19. Page 6.
P.age 252	"When the Vienna State Opera was bombed …". Kotnik, V. (2013). The adaptability of opera: When different social agents come to common ground. *International Review of the Aesthetics and Sociology of Music, 44* (2), 303-342. Page 318.

Page 252	"The celebrity industry …" Lilti, 2017, quoted in S. Albinsson (2018). New bums on opera seats: The transition from feudalism to liberal society mirrored in European opera houses 1750–1824. Conference paper, 13th Sound Economic History Workshop, Gothenburg, page 21.
Page 253	The castratos's voice was then prized …" Davies, J.Q. (2005). Veluti in speculum: The twilight of the castrato. *Cambridge Opera Journal, 17* (3), 271–301. Page 272. See also Jenkins, J.S. (1998). The voice of the castrato. *The Lancet, 351,* 9119, 1877-1880, page 1877.
Page 253	"Adds Anthony Roth Costanzo …" Gross, T. (October 7, 2019). NPR interview, "After nearly losing his voice to cancer, Anthony Roth Costanzo takes on Akhnaten."
Page 254	"I would say to you …" Freitas, R. (2003). The eroticism of emasculation: Confronting the Baroque body of the castrato. *The Journal of Musicology,* 20 (2), 196-249. Pages 217-218.
Page 255	"Said one observer dryly …" Pleasants, H. (1955). *The agony of modern music.* New York: Simon & Schuster, page 59.
Page 255	"The atonal revolution …" David Gockley, Personal communication, January 6, 2019.
Page 255	"Matthew Shilvock, General Director of San Francisco Opera, wrote …" Personal communication, March 6, 2019.
Page 256	"Two German directors' stagings …" Kotnik, V. (2013). The adaptability of opera: When different social agents come to common ground. *International Review of the Aesthetics and Sociology of Music,* 44 (2), 303-342, page 306.
Page 256	"There were loud boos …" Ross, A. (2013). Wagner summer. *New Yorker,* August 26, 71.

Page 257   "Many avid opera-goers ..." Gwyneth Jones. Jones, G. (2014). *The perfect gift, the perfect possession.* Boston: The Boston Wagner Society, December 1. bostonwa.nextmp.net/reviews/wagner-experience-review-dame-gwyneth-jones/ Paragraph 11.

P.age 257   "The most important principle ..." Mansouri, L., & Layton, A. (1982). *Lotfi Mansouri: An Operatic Life.* Oakville, Ontario: Mosaic Press, page 53.

Page 258   "What applause otherwise would express ..." E. Rappl, A phenomenal Kundry. *Bayreuther Tageblatt,* July, 1961.

Page 258   "News of the scandalous disobedience ..." *The New York Times,* New York *Herald Tribune,* and the *San Jose Mercury.*

Page 258   "Silly and inconsequential ..." Slonimsky, N. (1953). *Lexicon of Musical Invective.* Seattle: University of Washington Press. Page 135, 232, 218, and 12.

Page 259   "Opera fanatics, since they spend ..." Benzecry, C.E., & Collins, R. (2014). The high of cultural experience: Toward a microsociology of cultural consumption. *Sociological Theory, 32* (4) 307–326, page 316.

Page 260   "Collective effervescence ..." Benzecry, C.E., & Collins, R. (2014). The high of cultural experience: Toward a microsociology of cultural consumption. *Sociological Theory, 32* (4) 307–326, page 313.

Chapter 11: Onstage Surprises and Operatic Bloopers

Note: Some of these stories can be found in two charming little books by Hugh Vickers. If you enjoy reading about onstage pratfalls and ingenious saves, these are the books for you.

Great Operatic Disasters. New York: St Martins Press, 1979.
Even Greater Operatic Disasters. New York: St Martins Press, 1982.

Page 261   "Breaking news: This tale ..." Personal communication, Larry Hancock.

P262   "Once when Irene was singing *Tristan* ..." Tim Anderson kindly sent me this story about the War Between the Prompters.

P262   "The fall occurred during a rehearsal ..." Mary-Lou Vetere, *The Last Verista: A Scream of Consciousness.* https://thelastverista.com/tag/tosca/

Page 263   "Halfway through the third act ..." Vickers, 1982, page 59.

Page 263   "During the previous performance when we were ..." Personal communication, Stacey Tappan.

Page 265   "In the middle of the smugglers' scene ..." Vickers, 1979, page 39.

Page 266   "Not all onstage predicaments ..." The sausage story may be a muddled version of a practical joke played on Nellie Melba by none other than Enrico Caruso. In Rodolfo's first meeting with Mimi, he takes her hand, saying it was so cold ("che gelida manina"). One night Caruso took this opportunity to slip a hot potato into her hand. History does not record whether she was able to keep a straight face. Vickers, 1982, page 20.

Apendix: The Resident Company Model

Page 372   "Emerging singers get to learn their craft ..." Diane Mauch, Personal communication, July 8, 2023.

Index

Bold indicates photograph.

Abduction from the Seraglio, The, 277
Abigaille, 77
Adalgisa, 19, 84
Adler, Kurt Herbert, v, 51, 74-76, 87
Adriana Lecouvreur, 63, 80, 220
Aida, iii, 8, 10, 19, 33-34, 37, 39, 60-61, 71-72, 81-82, 88-89, 92, 96, 99, 226, 229, 245, 274
Alorda, Ernesto, 45, 92-94, 235
Althouse, Paul, 10, 13, 14, 24
Amahl and the Night Visitors, 115
Amara, Lucine, 82-83
Amme (Nurse), 40, 66, 76
Amneris, iii, 33, 38, 61, 65, 66, 68, 71-72, 92, 202, 245
Ann and Gordon Getty Foundation, 129
Anna Karenina, 186, 207
Anderson, Judith, 86-87
Anderson, Tricia, 204
Armenat, Rosemarie, 50, 68
Arroyo, Martina, 96, 220
Artists in Residence, 271
Arts Education Week, 112
Ashens, Robert, 192-193
Azucena, 42, 47-48, 65, 82, **84**, 93, 202

Ballo in Maschera, Un, 202
Barber of Seville, The, 27, 38, **148, 153**, 186, 227, 229
Barclay, Michael, 47
Barrett, Barbara, 110, 117-118, 156, 235, 239
Bastianini, Ettore, 25-26
Bauer, Roberto, 15, 18-19, 25
Bayreuth, v, vii, 9, 15, 22, 24, 39, 43-48, 54, 57-59, 62, 73-74, 78-79, 81, 88, 101,
206, 230, 246, 256, 258
Bearden, Scott, **148**, 160, 194, **233**
Beecher, Wilford, 52
Belle Hélène, La, 227

Bellemer, John, 133-**134**, 137, 169, 175, 198-199, 236
Bengochea, Christopher, 139, **202**
Berganza, Teresa, 229
Bergonzi, Carlo, iii, 96
Berlin, vii, 21-24, 26, 32, 41, 47, 49-51, 64, 66, 68, 79
Billy Goats Gruff, 146
Bing, Rudolf, iv, 18, 19, 22, 25, 28, 33, 34, 37, 41, 48, 51, 52, 55, 61, 62, 63, 73, 74, 75, 77, 79-**91**, 96, 97, 161, 179-181, 224, 226, 250-251.
Bjorling, Jussi, xi, 25, 26, 47
Blaze, Sarah, 137
Bohème, La, 106, 127, 132, 172, 186-187, 259
Bohm, Karl, 77-78
Bohmler, Craig, 232
Bouillon, Princess of, 63, **80**, 93
Boyer, Alexander, 234
Brangane, iv, 19, 36, 63, **64**, 93
Brangane's warning, 21, 41
Breden, Mary, 206
Breden, Sharon, 56-60, 205-206, 216-216
Brunnhilde, 16, 139-140
Brunyate, Roger, 232
Bunzel, Jack, 98-100, 102, 107, 111, 114

Caballé, Montserrat, 84, 96
California Arts Council, 114-116
California Theatre, 2-3, 162-165, **170**, 170-173, 187, 232, 243, 245, 247, 249
Callas, Maria, 19, 71, 91
Capobianco, Tito, 126
Capulets and the Montagues, The, 228
Carmen, 77, 138, 179, 188, 205, 219, 238
Caruso, Enrico, 8, 310
Cassilly, Petie, 22, 37
Cassilly, Richard, 22
Cavalleria Rusticana, 90-91
Center for the Performing Arts, 111
Centner, Helen, 102, 113
Chanticleer, 109
Chapuis, Isabelle, 172-173, 199
Charity Navigator, 238
Chianakas, Layna, 132, 137, **174**, 187, 192, 196, 227, 234
Children's Discovery Museum, 141
Chisholm, Jo, 240
Cilli, Daniel, 133, 137, 194, **195**

Cinderella, vi, 247-**248**, 263-**264**,
City of San Jose Arts Commission, 221
Claque, 26-28, 37-38
Clayton, Cynthia, **135**, 175, 195, 235
Cleva, Fausto, 42, 89-90
Coffland, Betany, 138, **197**, 236
Cohn, Rosa, 238
Columbia Artists Management, 40
Columbia University Teachers College, 6, 113
Commanday, Robert, 213
Condemi, Jose Maria, 136, 186, 234
Cooper, Randy, 113, 176
Corelli, Franco, iii, 42, 55, 63, 66, 81, 96, 159, 180-181, 220
Cosi fan Tutte, 20-21, 138, 186, 226
Covent Garden, vii, 8, 27, 36, 39
Crawford, Robert, 238-239
Crow, George, 203, 235
Crucible, The, 148, 186, 207
Curtis-Verna, Mary, 34

Dailey, Michael, 133, 137, **156**, 157, 195
Dalila (Delilah), iv, 66, 70, 77, 93
Dalis, Chris. 2, 12, 94
Dalis, Irene (Yvonne), Childhood and family, 2-5; Education, 5-12; Fulbright, 12-14, 25, 94, 101; 224; Years in Europe 14-25; Name change, 19-20; Met debut 25-32; Marriage and family, 35-37, 48-50, 66-70; Principal Artist at the Met, 39-98; Bayreuth, 43-46, 73; colleagues, 51-56, 79-83; Fans, 56-63, 94-96; *Medea*, 84-88; San Jose State University, 98-113; Opinions of Irene, 178-210; Artistic values, 223-243; tributes, 244-247
Dalis, Louis, 2, 12
Dalis, Mamie Boitano, 1-4, 11, 13, 28, 77
Dalis, Marge, 2, 6-7, 9, 11-12, 25-26, 28, 30, 50-51, 54, 94, 108
Dalis, Nick, 2, 4-5, 12
Dalis, Peter, 1-2, 6, 50
Dallas, Tom, 6-7, 11-12, 26, 34
Dalton, Brad, 186-187, 230
Daphne, 20
Dastoor, Khori, 133-134, 194, **195**
Davis, Rebecca, **177, 231**
Decter, Lori, 137, 266
Delius, Frau, 14, 25
Dido and Aeneas, 117

Domingo, Placido, 63, 96, 220
Domingo, Marta, 227
Don Carlo, iii, xi, 16, 19-20, 25, **29**, 39, 57, **69**, 78-79, 83, 89, 159, 205, 251
Don Giovanni, 148, 187,
Don Pasquale, 148, **161**, 186-187
Dorabella, 20-21, 82, 226
Dorsay, Richard, 202
Drozdiak, Stephanie, 107

Ebert, Carl, 21-25
Eboli, Princess, iii, xi, 19-22, 26, **29**, 30-32, 39, 57, 65, 71, 79, 93-94, 97, 159, 246
Edgerton, Kathy, 113
Eichelberger, Kirk, 147-**148**, 161-162, 175, 229-230
Elash, Silas, 131-133, 149-**151**, **153**, 157, 159, 195
Elias, Rosalind, 60-62
Elektra, 8, 23, 51, 76, 92-93
Elizabeth II, Queen, 71-72
Englebrecht, Julie, 169
Enmann, Mary Elizabeth, 37, 113, 122, 198
Erlendson, Bill, 152, 155
Eugene Onegin, 134, 136
Eurotrash, 231, 256

Falstaff, 172, 186, 192, 200, **208**, **233**
Farrell, Eileen, 88
Faust, 136, 148, 186, 238
Fiscalini, Frank, 111, 141, 201
Fischer-Dieskau, Dietrich, 79
Flagstad, Kirsten, 74
Fledermaus, Die, 120, 138, 187, 196-197, 234
Flying Dutchman, The, 138, 175, 192, 232
Fonteyn, Margot, 72
Frau ohne Schatten, Die, iv, 40, 66, 73-74, 76-77, 79, 93, 245
Free, Lloyd, 62
Fricka, iv, 60-61, 66, 73, 93
Friends of Opera, 107, 110, 119, 123, 145, 204, 206, 209
Friends of Opera San Jose, vi, 146, 208, 244-246, 267
Fulbright scholarship, 12-14, 25, 94, 101, 224
Fullerton, Gail, 114

Gaea, 20
Garson, Jeanne, 116
George, Glen, 119
Gerard, Ron, 113
Ghaiurov, Nicolai, 94
Gianni Schicchi, 108, **112**, 118, 188, 234-**235**
Girl of the Golden West, The, 234
Giuseppe Verdi Conservatory, 14, 101
Glyndebourne Festival, 21
Gobbi, Tito, 96
Gockley, David, 232, 255, 257
Golesorkhi, Anooshah, **153**, 212-213
Götterdammerung, 20, 256
Grand Prix du Disc, 45
Gray, Pamila Z, 169

Hamburg Staatsoper, 23, 56, 74, 90, 92-94, 173, 206
Hancock, Larry, ix, 109, 113, 115-116, 141, 146, 184-**185**, 217, 233, 238-**239**, 242-243, 261
Hansel and Gretel, 146, 187, 227
Haywood, Lorna, 169, 187-188, 236
Helfgot, Daniel, 115, 121, 127
Henderson, Alva, 84-88, 188-189, 232
Herman, Robert, 77, 79-80, 128
Herodias, **23,** 66
Hoiby, Lee, 115, 128
Hollywood Bowl, 39
Horiguchi, Rita Elizabeth, 207
Hotel Eden, 189, 232
Hurok, Sol, 9
Hotter, Hans, 45

Idomeneo, 186, 207, 209, **228, 232**
Isolde, 9, 10, 63, 74-76, 77, 78
Italiana in Algeri, 189

Jacobson, Robert, 126
Jenkins, Speight, iii-v, 139-140
Jenufa, 20, 23-**24**, 84, 86
Jobin, Sara, 160-161, 192

Karajan, Herbert von, 83
Kelm, Linda, 94
Klose, Margareta, 23
Klytemnestra, 51, 76, 82, 92-93
Knappertsbusch, Hans, 43, 45
Kostelnicka, 20, 23-**24**, 86
Kundry, 9-10, 15, 25, 42-45, 66, 82, 93, 202

L. J. Skaggs and Mary C. Skaggs Foundation, 238-239
La Scala, 14-15, 27, 101, 155, 159
Lady Macbeth, 8-10, 20-21, 23, 41, 43, 66, **83**, 91, 93
Lang, Paul Henry, 30
Lappalainen, Eilana, 129, 152-**153**-155, 206, 212
Last Leaf, The, 188, 232
Let's Make an Opera, 146
Levine, Mort, 202
Lin, Steven, 123
Linduska, Mary, 113
Livengood, Phil, 239-240
Livengood, Judy, 239-240
Lohengrin, iv, 15, 19, 46, 56, 90, 103, 149, 205, 265
Loinaz, Alida, 48-**49**, 50, 55, 66, **69**, 70, 95, 157, 209, 218, 222, 241
Loinaz, George, 11, **35**, *36*-37, 59-60, 46, 48, 51-52, 55, 59-62, 72, 93, **97**, 107, 211-**212**, 213
London, George, 45
Lopez, Cecilia Violetta, 234
Los Angeles Opera, 232
Lorton, Madeline, 59-62, 128
Lucey, Shawna, ii, x, 249
Lucia di Lammermoor, ii, 186, 194-**195**, 242
Ludwig, Leopold, 74
Luna, Audrey, 176
Lymberis, Nick, 120-122, 137, 160

Macbeth, 8-10, 20-21, 41, 66, **83**, 88, 91, 93, 228
Madama Butterfly, 38, 106, 135, 138-**139**, 154, 186-187, 204, 229
Madeira, Jean, 61
Magic Flute, The, 186
Maginnis, Patrice, 113, 118-120, 162, 196
Mansouri, Lotfi, 178, 180, 183, 223-224, 228-229, 232, 257,
Marcheso, Joseph, 242-**243**
Mark, Peter, 126
Marriage of Figaro, The, 135, 138, 169, 174, 187, 234

Index

Mauch, Diane, 272
Mays, Chris, 208-209
McCann, Jeanne, 204
McGrath, Evelyn, 107, 119
Medea, 84-88, 188
Medium, The, 198
Mendelsohn, Michael, 135, 158
Merlin, Jesse, 138-139, 176, 196-197, 235
Merrill, Robert, iii, 42, 47, 56, 81, 94, 96
Merry Widow, The, 160, 193
Metropolitan Opera ("The Met"), iii-iv, vii, xi, 8-10, 13, 18-19, 22, 25-31, 33-34, 39, 41-43, 45, 47-48, 51, 60-63, 65, 66, 71, 75, 77-81, 89, 91-94, 98, 100-103, 114, 118, 125, 128-129, 139, 149, 157, 159, 161-162, 173, 177, 208, 219-220, 227, 245-246, 251
Milnes, Sherrill, 56, 96, 125
Mitchell, Patty, 171-172, 200
Mittelman, Norman, 149, 159
Mödl, Martha, 15-16, 24-26, 63, 73
Mollicone, Henry, 189
Montez, Dan, 130-**131**, 176, 183, 189, 193, 236, Appendix
Montgomery Theater, 9-10, 113, 117-118, 141-145, 160, 163-165, 167, 172, 187, 200-201
Morell, Barry, 89
Mother, The, 112
Müller, Otto, 14-17, 21, 27, 126, 159, 161, 224-225
Munzinger, Heidi, 140, 207
Musical America, 31, 127
Musicians' Union, 111

Nabucco, 77
Nagel, Douglas, 123, 128, 184, 193-194
National Endowment for the Arts, 238
Near, Timothy, 142-144, 186, 201
New York City Opera, 126, 155, 174-176
Nilsson, Birgit, 63-**65**, 66, 75, 81, 88, 91, 93, 96, 262
Norma, 19, 79, 81, 84, 189

"O don fatale," iii, xii, 16, 19, 21, 31, 32, 39-40, 78-79,
Oas, Judith, 94
Of Mice and Men, 128
Okerlund, Arlene, 100-101, 203, 209
Oldenburg, 17-18, 20-22, 24, 26, 70, 114, 226, 235, 237
Olds, Phil, 160

Olstad, Bruce, 150
Operafest, 122-124, 194, 241
Operathon, 122, 166, 191, 193, 204, 206-207, 241
Opera America, 251
Opera News, 33, 42, 116, 126-127, 241, 245-246
Opera San Jose, i-ix, 6, 70, 95; opera workshop, 102-113; as Opera San José, 122-210, 217, 222-249
Opernwelt, 128
Ortrud, iv, 15, 19, 21, 25, 45, 65, 76-77, 93, 149, 205

Paasch, Friedrich, 17
Packard, David Woodley, 164-166, 169, 173, 247
Packard Humanities Institute, 165-166, 169, 173, 175, 194, 247
Parnassus Club, 6
Parsifal, 9, 15, 25, 42, 45, 54, 58, 66, 74, 79, 88, 202, 206, 245
Pavarotti, Luciano, 96
Perrone, Giulio Cesare, 169
Philip, Prince, 71-72
Phillips, Lori, 138-**139**-140, 169, 175
Piazza, Tony, 145, 240
Plowman, Kim, 110
Ponselle, Rosa, 224
Price, Leontyne, 39, 42, 56, 63, **72,** 96

Quandt, Luis, 214-215
Quartuccio, Anthony, 166, 191, 234

Raiders of the Lost Aria, 145
Ratjen, Hans Georg, 17, 22, 25
Reber, James, 113, 122, 200-201
Regietheater, 232, 256
Resident Artists, 17, 123, 130-138, 144, 147, 150-151, 153-155, 161, 169, 173-175, 180, 183-184, 187, 192-193, 201, 204, 207, 212-213, 227, 233-237, 240, 247, 249, 267, 269-272
Resnik, Regina, 96
Rheingold, Das, 17, 73, 162
Rigal, Delia, 26
Rigoletto, 133, 160, 162, 187, 206, 259
Ritter, Joseph, 111
Ritter, Tony, 111
Rohrbaugh, David, 103-**104**, 105, 108, 115, 119, 126-127, 136, 138, 147, 152, 165-166, 171-173, 183, **102**, 192, 197, 225, 239, 242
Rondine, La, 186

Index

Roumanis, George, 232
Rubalcava Bengochea, Sandra, 137, **113**, 170, 195, 233-234
Russell, Anna, 224
Rysanek, Leonie, 55, 93

Salome, ii, **23**, 66
Samson and Dalila, iv, 70
San Francisco Opera, v, x, 39, 41, 47, 51, 56, 66, 73-77, 86, 89-93, 105, 115, 136, 138, 149, 155, 173-174, 180, 192, 194, 205, 207, 232, 243, 246, 250, 255, 257
San Jose Chamber Orchestra, 115
San Jose Repertory Theatre, 115, 142, 200-201
San Jose State College, 4-5
San Jose State University, 98-105, 113-114, 163, 175, **181**
Santuzza, iv, 66, 76, 89, 91, 93
Sargeant, Winthrop, 31
Sawallisch, Wolfgang, **46**
Scarf, The, 115
Schaaf, Johannes, 227
Scheinin, Richard, 149
Schick, George, 62, 224
Schippers, Thomas, 12, 94
Schnabel, Artur, 156
Seattle Opera, iii, v, 45, 92, 136, 139, 155, 173, 175, 207, 235
Secret Marriage, The, 119
Shewell, Cordell, 47
Shomler, Robert, 166-167
Siegfried, 16, 139-140, 157
Siepi, Cesare, xi, 25, 47, 96
Smedberg, Virginia, 106, 132, 167, 200
Smith, Lettie, 198
Solti, Georg, 64, 83, 93
Spaulding, Kitty, 204-205, 212, 240
Stafford, Edwin, 120, 219-220
Starr, Mark, 173
Staufenbiel, Brian, 113, 176
Steber, Eleanor, 10
Stein, Horst, 75
Stiedry, Fritz, 30
Stout, Ed, 167
Stratas, Teresa, 96
Suor Angelica, 117, 188, 234
Swartz Lymberis, Barbara, 120-122, 137
Sutherland, Joan, 79-81, 96

Taconic Opera, 130, 176, 236, 269-271
Tale of the Nutcracker, The, 232
Tannhauser, 92
Taubman, Howard, 31
Taylor, Alma, 209, 221
Tebaldi, Renata, 34, **80**, 96
Thebom, Blanche, 71
Thomas, Jess, 45, 54-**55**, 70, 73, **76**, 79, 93, 180-181
Thompson, Maurine, 5, 7, 10
Tosca, ii, 10, 77, 169, 175, 187, 256, 261-262, 272
Tozzi, Giorgio, 96, 125
Traviata, La, 106, 153, 186-187, 227, 229, 234
Trittico, Il, 94
Tristan und Isolde, 8, 19, 36, 41, 63-**64**, 71, 73-75, **76**, 93, 262
Trovatore, Il, 10, 42, 47, **84**, 148, 186-187, 192, 196, 206, 220
Troyanos, Tatiana, 55, 94, 125-126
Truhitte, Tom, 129
Tucci, Gabriella, 96
Tucker, Richard, **84**, 94, 96
Turner, Barbara Day, 115, 122, 127, 146
Turner, Claramae, 92

Ulrica, 202
Ulrich, Mel, **134**, 169, 172, **174**

Valkyrie, The. See *Walküre, Die*
Varnay, Astrid, 88
Venus, iv, 93
Vickers, Jon, 96-**97**
Vienna Staatsoper, 27, 52, 75, 252
Vienna Volksoper, 174
Vinke, Stefan, 140
Voix Humaine, La, 187, 192, 196-**197**, 234

Wade, Brad, vii, 206-207, 245
Wagner, Wieland, v, 16-17, 25, 46, 59, 73-74, 211
Walker, Edyth, 7-12, 14, 24-25, 27, 30, 41, 43, 213, 224
Walküre, Die, 16, 60-61
Walters, Gibson, 99-100
Waltraute, 20, 65, 93
Warner, Laurie, 122, 129, 203, 214, 217
Warner, Mike, 122

Weiser, Mark, 232
Werther, 207
West of Washington Square, 232
Where Angels Fear to Tread, 232
Whitfield, Andrew, 192
Williams, Sara, 205
Williams, Scott, 205
Wilson, Harry, 6, 11, 25
Windgassen, Wolfgang, 16
Women's Opera Network, 251
Wright, Joseph, 136-137, 169

Yettick, Keith and Carole, 138
Yiannoudes, Constantinos, 176

About the Author

LINDA RIEBEL, PH.D., retired psychologist and adjunct professor, has attended Opera San José for over 20 years, and in the volunteer auxiliary Friends of Opera San José has served as past president and longstanding chair of the Events Committee. Besides the present biography of Irene Dalis, she has published an encyclopedia entry on opera and offered opera lectures, including a video introducing the art form to newbies. Her other publications include books and journal articles on psychology, sustainability, and endangered species.

www.ingramcontent.com/pod-product-compliance
Lightning Source LLC
Chambersburg PA
CBHW062056290426
44110CB00022B/2608